Andri Gerber, Brent Patterson (eds.)
Metaphors in Architecture and Urbanism

Architecture | Volume 19

ANDRI GERBER, BRENT PATTERSON (EDS.)
Metaphors in Architecture and Urbanism
An Introduction

[transcript]

Published with the support of the Gerda Henkel Foundation, Duesseldorf

Co-edition Ecole Spéciale d'Architecture

Bibliographic information published by the Deutsche Nationalbibliothek
The Deutsche Nationalbibliothek lists this publication in the Deutsche Nationalbibliografie; detailed bibliographic data are available in the Internet at http://dnb.d-nb.de

© 2013 transcript Verlag, Bielefeld

All rights reserved. No part of this book may be reprinted or reproduced or utilized in any form or by any electronic, mechanical, or other means, now known or hereafter invented, including photocopying and recording, or in any information storage or retrieval system, without permission in writing from the publisher.

Cover layout: Kordula Röckenhaus, Bielefeld
Proofread and Typeset by Andri Gerber
Printed by Majuskel Medienproduktion GmbH, Wetzlar
ISBN 978-3-8376-2372-7

Contents

Préface
Odile Decq | 9

Introduction
Andri Gerber | 13

ARCHITECTURAL/URBAN METAPHOROLOGY

Johannes Binotto
My Home Is My Symptom: A Psychoanalytic Plea
for Flawed Architecture | 33

Gernot Böhme
Metaphors in Architecture – a Metaphor? | 47

Philippe Boudon
Référence métaphorique et référence métonymique | 59

Matteo Burioni
Naming Things. Terminology, Language Theory
and Metaphorology from Alberti to Vignola | 71

Rosario Caballero-Rodriguez
From Design Generator to Rhetorical Device:
Metaphor in Architectural Discourse | 89

Susanne Hauser
Skins in Architecture. On Sensitive Shells and Interfaces | 105

Bernardo Secchi
A new Urban Question 3: When, Why and How some
Fundamental Metaphors were used | 123

Caroline van Eck
Semper's Metaphor of the Living Building: its Origins in 18th
Century Fetishism Theories and its Function in his Architectural
Theory | 133

Benedikte Zitouni
Organic Metaphors and Urban Causalities | 147

METAPHORS AS MEDIUM

Elisabeth Bronfen
Remains of War: Battlefields, Ruins
and the Trick of Commemoration | 161

Richard Coyne
Calibrating Metaphors and Tuning Places | 175

Jelle Feringa
The Promotion of the Architectural Model | 185

Marcelyn Gow
Soft Monstrosities | 201

Stephan Günzel
Video Game Spaces as Architectural Metaphors | 217

Holger Schurk
Diagram, Plan and Metaphor | 227

Georges Teyssot
Crystals. The Entropic Landscape | 243

Chris Younès
Paradoxes et ambiguïtés de la métaphore en architecture | 265

THE METAPHOR PROJECT

Didier Faustino
The Hidden Pavilion | 275

François Roche
« Pour que la vérité soit vertigineuse, elle doit choisir d'avoir infiniment tort » | 281

Authors | 289

List of Figures/Copyrights | 299

Préface

ODILE DECQ

L'Ecole Spéciale d'Architecture est la première et la plus ancienne des écoles d'architecture en France, créée a l'initiative de Viollet-le-Duc pour réaliser une école qui soit différente.
Cette école s'est reconstituée et régénérée régulièrement tout au long de ses cent cinquante ans, et toujours aujourd'hui en utilisant son aspect « Spéciale ». Ce n'est pas une attitude d'opposition mais plutôt une vision positive de construction et d'imagination pour nous tourner vers l'avenir.

Aussi, lorsque Andri Gerber a proposé de monter un colloque sur le thème de métaphore, je me suis inquiétée du retour de la question de la métaphore. Je n'étais pas la seule car, et depuis que nous l'avons initié, j'ai reçu plusieurs e-mails m'enjoignant de ne pas relancer l'histoire de la métaphore alors que dans les années soixante-dix, c'est ce qui a créé le post modernisme. Ce serait donc terrible! A tel point que certains architectes revendiqueraient le refus de la métaphore tels que Diller&Scofidio, Bow-Wow ... Mais, pourquoi pas!
Et si, aujourd'hui, on pouvait reposer la question différemment ?

D'où vient cette crainte des architectes à propos de la métaphore ? Est ce la question de l'image, du symbolisme, de forme, de trivialité ou une peur de représentation et d'interprétation qui serait trop simple; une peur de faire comprendre au grand public des images trop faciles ?
Alors que, comme le dit Chris Younès dans son texte, la métaphore a l'avantage d'être suggestive, de ne pas tout dire et de laisser la part belle à l'imaginaire, à l'imagination, à la poésie, de laisser à celui qui l'énonce de ne pas tout dire et à celui qui l'entend d'en tirer sa propre interprétation. Dans ce cas, cela m'intéresse et je trouve cela passionnant.

Certains d'entre vous s'intéressent à la métaphore dans les jeux vidéo. Lorsque dans les jeux vidéos on représente la vie et/ou l'architecture, je n'ai pas l'impression qu'on soit dans la métaphore, mais qu'il s'agit plutôt d'une représentation très triviale de l'architecture et de l'urbanisme. Et cette représentation est une image un peu « Disneyland », une image un peu caricaturale de ce que serait la ville, de ce que serait l'urbain, de ce que serait l'architecture. C'est, en même temps, une image collective puisque c'est supposé être une représentation dans laquelle tout le monde peut se retrouver.

Image 1: Odile Decq

Alors, nous pouvons nous interroger encore une fois sur la peur de la métaphore chez les architectes. Pourquoi craindre l'utilisation d'un langage qui soit aussi facile d'accès pour le grand public que la métaphore ?

Il est vrai qu'il y a eu une grande lassitude de la post modernité et de l'utilisation souvent au premier degré de la métaphore lorsque l'image utilisée pour décrire le projet est devenue l'objet même du projet.

Qu'en est il à présent du fait que certains architectes utilisent aujourd'hui la représentation organique en reprenant de manière assez directe, on pourrait même dire au premier degré, des oranges, des fleurs et des fruits pour fabriquer la forme architecturale ? Sommes nous aussi directement dans la métaphore, et cette fois ci de manière très triviale ? Est ce grâce à l'architecture paramétrique que la métaphore va revenir, ou est déjà revenue ?

Alors, dites moi, où allons nous ?

Odile Decq
Directeur Général Ecole Spéciale d'Architecture (2007-2012)

Introduction

ANDRI GERBER

> "If you do not like metaphor, you do not throw it away, you dig into it to find out what it represses."
> Peter Eisenman[1]

This publication is the result of a three-day conference that took place in November 2009 at the Ecole Spéciale d'architecture and at the Centre de l'Histoire de l'Art Allemand in Paris on the subject of "Metaphors in/on Architecture and Urbanism." The interest in the subject – to start with a personal note – arose while writing my dissertation at the ETH in Zurich on the subject of the "city as text" of Peter Eisenman (actually explicitly only called "architecture as text") – as his work between 1978 and 1986 can be described. In the midst of my frustration at not being able to avoid the "theoretical swamps" of Eisenman's monstrous structure of references he erected around his work – to use several metaphors – and not producing any new insight on his work, I turned my attention to the term "city as text," realizing that this is a metaphor. After a search on existing literature on the theory of metaphors in architecture, I realized an almost total absence of such research, which, considering the enormous amount of metaphors used since antiquity in this context, appeared to me symptomatic and worthy of questioning. Paraphrasing Eisenman's initial quote, this was more than a reason enough, to ask what metaphors mean in this context but also to understand why such an investigation has never been conducted in the past.

---

1 | Eisenman, Peter, Nieto, Fuensanta, Sobejano, Enrique, "Interview Peter Eisenman," in *Arquitectura*, No. 270, 1988, p. 130

Image 2: Metaphors in/on Architecture and Urbanism, ESA Paris, 11.2009

I thus started my own investigation, which resulted in my PhD, a look onto Eisenman's "city as text" through the lenses of metaphors.[2] While I con-structed a theory of urban metaphors based on the one hand on existing metaphor-theories and on the other on Eisenman's "city as text" and his explicit references to metaphors, the desire arose to confront the issues with other people that had explicitly discussed the matter (such as Richard

---

2 | Gerber, Andri, *Theorie der Städtebaumetaphern. Peter Eisenman und Stadt als Text*, Zürich: Chronos, 2012

Coyne or Rosario Caballero-Rodriguez)[3] or who I imagined, could be interested in discussing it in the context of their own work. This was because I realized that my position in the PhD had covered only one of many aspects that this subject calls for. The conference could thus become a truly interdisciplinary forum to open up different aspects of metaphors in the context of architecture and urbanism.

The problem with metaphors, to start with, is twofold. On the one hand they are negatively connoted because they are associated with a "vilified" rhetoric, which has since antiquity been incorrectly reduced to the art of speaking craftfully, forgetting the richness it once had. On the other hand, while acknowledging how, in particular in the theory of science there has been a re-evaluation of metaphors as cognitive devices, as a medium of exchange and as creators of models, we are still confronted with a multitude of different theories on how metaphors work. Thus there is in fact no single metaphor theory.[4] Furthermore, metaphors depend on their context, as underlined also by Susanne Hauser in her essay, making their discussion context-dependent, architecture and urbanism being such contexts.[5]

In considering the first point it should just be mentioned how in the distinction made by Cicero in his *De optimo genere oratorum* (46 B.C.) metaphors would not only have to *delectare*, to delight, but also to *movere*, that is to impress, and *docere*, that is to teach. But the negative connotation of rhetoric and metaphors remained and can explain a general negative bias towards metaphors in general. Chris Younés in this regard quotes the critique of writer Le Clézio for whom metaphors divert from reality.[6]

As for the second observation, one can simply point to the fact, that the authors of the essays appearing in the following pages, almost never use the same reference to explain their position towards metaphors. Jakobsen, Ricoeur, Weinrich, Goodman, Blumenberg or Aristotle, to name just a few,

---

3 | Snodgrass, Adrien, Coyne, Richard, *Interpretation in architecture: design as a way of thinking*, London: Routledge, 2006; Caballero, Rosario, *Re-viewing space: figurative language in architects' assessment*, Berlin: Mouton de Gruyter, 2006
4 | Rolf Eckard counts 25 existing metaphor theories in total (Eckard, Rolf, *Metapherntheorien, Typologie, Darstellung, Bibliographie*, Berlin: Walter der Gruyter, 2005)
5 | See the contribution of Susanne Hauser, p. 105
6 | See the contribution of Chris Younés, p. 265

are all equally referred to, in order to explain how metaphors function and could be translated to architecture/urbanism.

We are thus faced on the one hand with the general and historically determined negative bias associated with metaphors and on the other with the absence of a theory of metaphors, which one could call a *metaphorology*, meaning that every discussion on metaphors – due to the very nature of metaphors – will remain on unstable ground.

Yet there have been some attempts to establish such a metaphorology, as was the case for German philosopher Hans Blumenberg and his *Paradigmen zu einer Metaphorologie* published in 1960. In Blumenberg's understanding, metaphors are something productive. They represent on the one hand what remains in the translation from *Mythos* to *Logos*, on the other they are also the indicator of something that cannot be translated to a literal, a proper condition. Something that cannot be translated in the realm of logic (yet architecture, to anticipate the following points, very likely, although not always, has a "literal," a built outcome). This is what he calls the "absolute metaphor." It implies that metaphors cannot be described through logic; that is they will never have a proper meaning. In his book, he discusses several key metaphors such as the light metaphor, the metaphors of truth, of power, of terra incognita, of the uncompleted universe, of the organic and of the mechanical, of the clockwork and of the book. Blumenberg developed the latter further in *Die Lesbarkeit der Welt* published in 1979, where he discusses the "world as a book"-metaphor: the world that can be read like a book.

Part of his theory of metaphors is thus based on the attempt to systematize metaphors, to establish a typology of the different kinds of existing metaphors. At the same time Blumenberg emphasizes how such a metaphorology could never be an independent discipline *per se*, but would always have to be part of a larger disciplinary frame. His project of a metaphorology is hence based on the shifting nature of metaphors which implies its very impossibility; a shifting between metaphor and concept, between metaphor and myth but also between the different disciplines that are necessary to get closer to an understanding of the nature of metaphors.

French philosopher Jacques Derrida, in his work on metaphors, discusses the need for and the possibility of such a metaphorology. And he too emphasized the impossibility of a proper meaning for metaphors. In his text of 1971, "La mythologie blanche" he explains how metaphor implies – in the logic of his critique of logocentrism – the impossibility of a proper, literal, ultimate meaning.[7] He calls for an analysis of metaphors in philosophy even though he admits that this would be the content of a life long work of research. Through the concept of *usure*, of consumption, he further explains how metaphors get corrupted, but he tellingly underscores, that in order to explain that, he needs another metaphor and this reveals how difficult it is to talk about metaphors without using other metaphors. To discuss metaphor thus implies always being inside metaphors, inside a process of skidding – as he calls it – that cannot be stopped. He came back on this position in a second text he wrote in 1978 – which was his presentation at a congress in Geneva on the subject of philosophy and metaphor and a reply to the attack by Paul Ricoeur (who himself had written a book called *la metaphore vive* in 1975 and who questioned some of Derridas assumptions). Derrida in reaction to the criticism of Ricoeur again underscored how metaphor means the impossibility of a proper meaning and that the relationship between this proper meaning and the metaphorical, cannot be stopped or held on; the only solution would be to completely suspend metaphors which is their annihilation. Interestingly in the same text Derrida uses an urban metaphor to describe this process.[8] Yet in philosophical discourse, references to urban or architectural metaphors are quite common.[9]

If we now refer to the investigations into metaphors by Blumenberg and Derrida, they appear to open up two main interrelated topics that are fundamental for an understanding of metaphors in the context of architecture and urbanism: on the one hand the shifting and elusive nature of

---

7 | Derrida, Jacques, "La mythologie blanche, la métaphore dans le texte philosophique" [1971], in Derrida, Jacques, *Marges de la philosophie*, Paris: Les éditions de minuit, 1972

8 | "Metaphora circulates in the city, it conveys us like its inhabitants, along all sort of passages, with intersections, red lights, one-way streets, crossroads or crossings, patrolled zones and speed limits. We are in a certain way – metaphorically of course, and as concerns the mode of habitation – the content and the tenor of this vehicle: passengers comprehended and displaced by metaphor." Derrida, Jacques, "The Retrait of Metaphor" [1978], in *Enclitic* Vol. II, no. 2, Fall 1978, p. 6

9 | For the urban metaphors in Descartes' thinking, for example, see the contribution of Johannes Binotto, p. 33

metaphors themselves and on the other, the consequent impossibility of a proper, literal meaning. In reference to the first point, Benedikte Zitouni tellingly calls metaphors – quoting Evelyn Fox Keller – "vague, unstable."[10]

The first point is essential in order to understand why metaphors are so often used in architecture and urbanism: by their very essence they mirror and express on the one hand the unstable disciplinary nature of architecture and urbanism and on the other the difficulty in describing the processes of these disciplines, that is, how these disciplines work. In fact, one has to emphasize that architecture is still struggling towards a "stable" disciplinary condition, oscillating between science and art, technology and artisan craft. Metaphors often served and continue to serve to underline the orientation architecture was aiming at: during the Renaissance, speaking of architecture as rhetoric or as music, served to support architecture's claim to be elevated to the status of *artes liberales*. In contrast, particularly in England at the turn of the 20th century, metaphors coming from sculpture and painting served to oppose the incoming professionalization of architecture and the losing of its "artistic" status.[11] The extensive use of biological metaphors in the context of the current computational turn in architecture, in contrast, again underscores a convergence towards science that excludes consideration of the artistic aspects of design (if not by the evident sculptural qualities of many installations). In the case of urbanism, the situation is even "worse." The discipline is not yet defined in its own terms and remains an "interdisciplinary discipline" with blurred boundaries towards urban planning, civic design and to those other disciplines – such as architecture but also engineering sciences, sociology and geography – that share its object, i.e. the city. Thus, the use of metaphors, which are themselves indefinite and shifting, mirrors the very indefinite and shifting nature of these disciplines. In detail, this means that metaphors also help us to understand the processes and instruments architecture and urbanism deploy in their very peculiar merging of theory and project, matter and idea, references and exterior discourses.

Yet this refers to another underlying problem: both architecture and urbanism have elusive and hard to grasp objects: space in the case of ar-

---

10 | See the contribution of Benedikte Zitouni, p.147

11 | "Architecture – a profession or an art? To the editor of The Times," in *The Times*, Tuesday, March 3, 1891 p. 9

chitecture;[12] the "post-urban" in the case of urbanism.[13] Metaphors appear thus in the discourse of architecture and urbanism not only when trying to establish the disciplinary boundaries, but also when attempting to grasp what is at the core of these disciplines, which can only partially be captured by language. In the case of space, one can refer to the extensive discussions at the beginning of the 20th century with German art historians introducing the understanding of architecture as space-production. Yet thus far, we lack, exactly because of its elusive nature, a theory of space for architects.[14] The same can be said of the post-urban. Metaphors appear thus, when architecture and urbanism are seeking a language to speak of their very basis. One has only to think about the fascination of architecture for some of the usual suspects from literature and philosophy (Georges Perec's *Espèces d'espaces* (1974), *La poétique de l'espace* by Gaston Bachelard (1957) or *Bauen, Wohnen, Denken* (1951/1952) by Martin Heidegger) and the exploding number of urban metaphors (city as network, body, bits etc...).

Therefore, architecture and urbanism are thus unstable, both as objects of investigation and as investigating/designing subjects (but this must not be considered simply in negative terms). The extensive use of metaphors both in the discourses concerned with architecture/urbanism and by architects and urbanists themselves, is a turnsole of this instability. In fact those who attempt to construct a theory of these disciplines are, as Manfredo Tafuri once described the architectural historian, permanently on the razor's edge or funambulists exposed to the changing winds trying to make him fall.[15] Again, metaphors are used to explain the metaphors of architecture and urbanism...

The second point opens a fundamental question: if architecture and urbanism in the end aim at realization into a spatial project, how literal can

---

12 | See: Brandl, Anne, Gerber, Andri, "A plea for spatial knowledge," in *SpecialeZ* No.4, Paris: Editions Ecole Spéciale, 2012, pp. 66-81

13 | See: Binotto, Johannes, Gerber, Andri, "Narration/Non-ville/Description," in: *SpecialeZ* No. 1, Paris: Editions Ecole Spéciale, 2010, pp. 32-39

14 | See the contribution of Gernot Böhme, p. 47

15 | "Il critico è colui che è costretto, per scelta personale, a mantener l'equilibrio su di un filo, mentre venti che mutano di continuo direzione fanno di tutto per provocarne la caduta." Tafuri, Manfredo, *Teorie e Storia dell'architettura*, 1968, p. 34. "La critica storica deve saper giocare sul filo del rasoio che fa da confine fra il distacco e la partecipazione. Tafuri, Manfredo, *La sfera e il labirinto*, 1980, p. 180

the metaphors that inspired these projects become? What is a text, a network, a body once they become built in space? They will obviously never really be a text, a network or a body, but are they still to be called metaphors? Has a metaphor always to be literal in the context of architectural and urban projects? And does literal mean figurative? This would mean an inversion towards the role of metaphor in language, where it can never be literal but only figurative. In language metaphors call for images, that are only possible in the realm of imagination, images that will never be true. But architecture and urbanism are forced this realm for reality. Roland Barthes gives an indirect confirmation of this necessary and problematic literality, when in a short text on the "city and the text" – which he unfortunately never developed further – he states that it is very easy to talk metaphorically of the language of the city, the true progress would be to speak literally of the language of the city.[16]

The models that metaphors create to understand the world, in architecture and urbanism, sooner or later will somehow become literal and "true" in their projects. And it is important to distinguish between metaphors as processes and metaphors as images.

This appears to be a fundamental implication for metaphors in/on architecture and urbanism. This problem is revealed in a commentary by Diller & Scofidio, who condemn any metaphorical interpretation of their "cloud" in Yverdon[17] thus referring to a possible figurative interpretation versus an intended "literalness." Furthermore, this commentary under-

---

16 | "La cité est un discours et ce discours est véritablement un langage: la ville parle à ses habitants, nous parlons notre ville, la ville où nous nous trouvons, simplement en l'habitant, en la parcourant, en la regardant. Cependant le problème est de faire surgir le stade purement métaphorique une expression comme 'langage de la ville'. Il est très facile métaphoriquement de parler du langage de la ville comme on parle du langage du cinéma ou du langage des fleurs. Le vrai saut scientifique sera réalisé lorsqu'on pourra parler du langage de la ville sans métaphore. Et l'on peut dire que c'est exactement ce qui est arrivé à Freud lorsqu'il a parlé le premier du langage des rêves, en vidant cette expression de son sens métaphorique pour lui donner un sens réel." Barthes, Roland, "Sémiologie et urbanisme," in L'architecture d'aujourd'hui, Nr. 153, Urbanisme, décembre 1970 – Janvier 1971, p. 12

17 | "The media project must be liberated from all immediate and obvious metaphoric associations such as clouds, god, angels, ascension, dreams, Greek my-

scores the general negative bias towards metaphors addressed above which exists also in the context of architecture and urbanism and which can be imputated in particular to a certain post-modern architecture concerned with façade-architecture.

But here the subject is not only a question of the traditional negative bias towards rhetoric; it must be brought back to a general association of metaphors in architecture with plane images, with the simplest mimesis. Atelier Bow Wow's protestation against any summarization of the city as metaphors can also be read in this way.[18] But it should also be brought back to the fact that here the term "metaphor" has been used in many different interpretations and, to some extent, also contrary interpretations. It is important to emphasize that few authors indeed made – even if only implicitly – the fundamental differentiation between metaphors and analogies, such as Peter Collins. In his book *Changing ideals in modern architecture, 1750-1950*, he identifies four analogies: the mechanical, the biological, the gastronomic and the linguistic.[19] Collins explains changes and contiguities in the history of architecture through the influence of certain analogies, ruling out the possibility that these could be metaphors. Or Spiro Kostof, who in his *The city shaped*, talking about organic city structures, emphasizes how the biologic references are nothing but analogies, thus leaving tenor and vehicle separated.[20]

A last point should be mentioned here, even though it is not possible to treat this point in detail in this book. Metaphors are also part of the very creative process of architectural design. In this sense, it is interesting to refer to the discussion between Cicero and his brother Quintus, on wheth-

---

thology, or any other kitsch relationship." Diller & Scofidio, *Blur: the making of nothing*, New York: Harry N. Abrams, Inc., Publishers, 2002, p. 325

18 | "In the 1980s there was a background of chaos affirming theory and Tokyology, and the spatial expression of architectural works displayed confusing urban landscape as a metaphor. We strongly wanted to get away from the attitude that the city can be summarised by metaphorical expression." Kajima, Momoyo, Kuroda, Junzo, Tsukamoto, Yoshiharu, *Made in Tokyo*, Tokyo: Kajima Institute Publishing, 2001, p. 10

19 | Collins, Peter, *Changing ideals in modern architecture, 1750-1950*, London: Faber & Faber, 1965

20 | Kostof, Spiro, *The city shaped*, Boston: Little, Brown and Company, 1991

er the capacity to create metaphors was innate or the result of a certain cultural context. It is undeniable, that architects invent metaphors in order to progress in design and to create particular unforeseen combinations.[21]

While the conference was divided into three distinct topics – metaphors as instruments of knowledge, metaphors in projects and metaphors in discourse – this tripartite structure seemed less useful for the organization of the texts in this book as most of them integrate all three aspects, often taking opposing standpoints on the matter. Furthermore, metaphors were discussed both in discourse and project, questioning the very possibility of separating these two aspects. Thus a new structure was chosen, dividing the texts into those which take a more general stance on the relationship of architecture/urbanism and metaphors aiming at a theory – an architectural or urbanistic metaphorology – and those which focus on the mediating nature of metaphors. But again, the differences are in most cases relative and minimal: all are contributions towards a better understanding of what metaphors in this particular context mean and what their use, both in project and text, implies. The impossibility of disentangling the different aspects was also announced in the title of the conference: "Metaphors in/on architecture and urbanism".

Architectural/urban metaphorology
Building upon the notion of the symptom in psychoanalysis, described by Jacques Lacan as a metaphor, **Johannes Binotto** polemically extends this juxtaposition to architecture and urbanism. He does this firstly by questioning the sanity of le Corbusier's urban plans, which he identifies as signs of a psychotic personality precisely because of the attempt to erase any symptoms of the city considered as a sick organism. Secondly, he proceeds by discussing the protagonist of Frank Capra's movie *It's a wonderful Life* (1946) who accepts the symptoms, revealed through the metaphor of the knob and is considered by Binotto as an example of a good architect. Metaphors are thus used here to identify the symptoms of architecture and its pathologies.

---

21 | For this aspect and the role of metaphors for design models see: Hnilica, Sonja, *Metaphern für die Stadt. Zur Bedeutung von Denkmodellen in der Architekturtheorie*, Bielefeld: Transcript Verlag, 2012

In the second essay, **Gernot Böhme** identifies in the many metaphors architecture uses to justify its own disciplinary boundaries, an emblematic absence of a discourse on its own terms. Instead of discussing and defining architecture in terms of its basic element, which is space, the history of architecture is full of references to external issues and other disciplines – Böhme makes particular reference to Charles Jencks and post-modern architecture. Based on this assumption, he distinguishes two different applications of metaphors in architecture, the first being unproblematic – the use of metaphors in the description of architecture. The second one is the use of metaphors in physical works of architecture in projects. The latter results in being extremely problematic, because it causes architecture to become a language and thus its elements to become signs, renouncing to build space. Metaphors reveal an ambiguous attitude in particular in post-modern architecture, to renounce to a spatial approach and to reduce projects to signs, which in the understanding of Böhme goes against the very nature of architecture.

Philippe Boudon took his participation in the conference as a chance to explore the meaning of metaphors within his general theory of "architecturology." He underscores that metaphors should always be considered in relationship to metonymy and never for themselves. His discussion on metaphors is furthermore based on the difference between metaphors in the perception and in the conception of architecture. While pointing out some inadequacies of the metaphor for the perception of architecture,referring to Roman Jakobson and De Saussure, he shows how the conception of architecture is always constructed around the duality *in absentia* – in absence – and *in praesentia* – in presence, which permits an understanding of the many relationships architecture builds to its context. This model thus should help us to understand the working of architecture and its relationship to the context.

In **Matteo Burioni**'s investigations on the use of language from antiquity to 18th century architecture, an interesting correspondence between language and architecture is revealed. The author highlights in particular those anamorphoses which appear between architecture and the human body and which are performed, consciously or not, by architects such as Alberti or Hugues Sambin.

In her investigation into the meaning of metaphors in architecture, with particular reference to architectural reviews and some exemplary case studies, **Rosario Caballero-Rodriguez** makes an important distinction between metaphors concerned with abstract knowledge and those concerned with visual knowledge, which reflects the twofold nature of architecture, between craft and art. Presenting an overview of the different kinds of metaphors appearing in architectural discourse, she furthermore emphasizes how metaphor is at the same time knowledge in all stages of the design for the architect, and also a necessary instrument for communicating the elusive nature of space, its core, and all the complexities related to its position inside society.

Susanne Hauser investigates the multiple meanings and implications of the skin-metaphor in architecture, in particular addressing the transformation this metaphor and its associated content have undergone – from transparency to ambiguity. With reference to the discussion about metaphors as models, which stressed their creative potential and which developed around 1960, Hauser discusses in particular the creative potential of the skin metaphor in the context of architecture: it tackles the relationship between skin, space and structure implying not least a transformation also of the perception of architecture. Hauser furthermore emphasizes how the skin metaphor in its contemporary application, indicates for architecture a transformation of the relationship between technology and biology.

Bernardo Secchi, speaking of metaphors in the context of urbanism, shows how these appear in urban discourse, when the urban condition is transformed and shifting; that is, when the urban condition changes. This calls for new ways of description and thus for metaphors. They are an index of the impossibility of describing the changing conditions inside urbanity with an old vocabulary. Secchi identifies two types of metaphor, both referencing fields other than urbanism to describe it, the first a more concrete – i.e. biological or mechanical metaphor – the other more abstract, which he calls "conceptual". But the most important aspect of Secchi's investigation, is that metaphors should always be interpreted as indices of those ideologies, which lie behind them and are driven by the different parties that are involved in the development and transformation of the urban.

Caroline van Eck makes an in-depth investigation of the metaphor of the living building in the work of Gottfried Semper and his *Der Stil*, her goal being to emphasize the differences between Semper's interpretation of this particular metaphor, which aimed at the animation of the inaminate, and previous as well as contemporary interpretations. Van Eck thus uncovers how Semper, using the metaphor of the living building, attempted to create a literal metaphor that would overcome the metaphor as a means of language and the constraints of language itself.

Benedikte Zitouni investigates the potential of organic metaphors for an understanding of the processes of causality in urbanism. She does this by making reference to different authors and the ongoing discussion about metaphors in the life sciences and also by reflecting on the investigations of causality brought forth by historical epistemology. These highlighted the complexity of such processes and the need to overcome deterministic and mechanical metaphors. This different view is then applied to the processes of urbanization and on all involved actors, particularly those usually neglected.

Image 3: Metaphors in/on Architecture and Urbanism, ESA Paris, 11.2009

Metaphors as medium
Elisabeth Bronfen shows in her essays how the architectural metaphors of the "home away from home" and of the "ruin" are staged and central for the construction of myths and narration, in movies such as *White Christmas* (1954) and *Holiday Inn* (1942). In the former, stage, set, and image are overlapping in a complex construction revealing the heterotopic condition the film addresses: the coincidence of war and peace and of home and front – a condition that joins different semantic paradigms and is constructed by a juxtaposition of sites and realities. The very actor of this overlapping is the metaphor of the remains of war. Bronfen thus reveals how cinema consciously uses such metaphors to create its own myths.

At the center of **Richard Coyne's** essay are two processes – tuning and calibration – that he reveals to be essential in order to understand both the nature of metaphors – which work by aligning, calibrating and tuning models, but also by calibrating two different things that metaphors bring together – and the nature of the design process which is based on the calibration and tuning of concept and reality. He illustrates this overlapping by discussing mobile, portable devices and how these calibrate the user with places but also with the acoustic environment they unveil.

Jelle Feringa addresses the contemporary architectural computational turn and the consequent transformation of the architectural model, from a metaphor to a literal definition of the project. The model is no longer a mediation between intention, concept and the reality of the project, but becomes part of this reality; it is its very definition. This transformation of the nature of the architectural model reveals a deep epistemological shift of the model itself but also of architecture in the context of new computer technology. Feringa furthermore emphasizes how the first biomorphic interpretations of the computational turn ignored this shift of the model, realizing figurative instead of literal transformations of the concepts behind the projects.

Marcelyn Gow refers to the blending of technological and organic metaphors in the context of Japanese architecture in the 1960s. For the specific blending of these two metaphors she coins the term of "soft monstrosities," underscoring the difficulty of negotiating between the implementation of the electronic and the biological paradigm, between image and performance, illustrating how her own work inside the collective *servo* should be seen as an attempt precisely to move on from images of technology and biology to projects that perform such metaphoric blendings.

Stephan Günzel investigates the nature of space in video games and emphasizes how the relationship between these and reality – understood not only as spatial but also as social reality – can be described as metaphorical and metonymical. Metaphor and metonymy are thus media which translate spaces and contents from reality to video game and from video game back to reality as is the case in the transformation of the movements between different levels from *Super Mario* to *Parkour* back to *Mirror's Edge*.

In his essay, **Holger Schurk** reveals the similarities between the processes of design and the metaphorical processes in language, both being complex, interdisciplinary and wicked. He performs this through an analysis of the particular role of the diagram in the design process of OMA and of the plan in the design process of SANAA. Both can be described as metaphors. The instruments and methods of design thus incorporate these metaphorical processes.

Georges Teyssot constructs a complex Möbius strip tied on to the theory of communication, cybernetics, and the philosophy of Gilles Deleuze in order to reveal the translating and thus metaphoric nature of art, in particular the art of landscape artist Robert Smithsons. Around the ambiguous nature of crystal and waste landscape, concepts such as entropy are translated into sensations and affects revealing the power of art and architecture to transcend language.

Chris Younès bases her discourse on the notion of the "living metaphor," by Paul Ricoeur, who described it as something that makes reference to reality and that transforms this reality in part also because of its innate ambiguity, between concept and image or between model and poetics. This ambiguity is revealed also in the very nature of architecture and is of the order of "and...and" rather than "either....or" as postulated by Gilles Deleuze. Younès illustrates this overlapping of metaphor and architecture by a discussion of the metaphor of the living, emphasizing its importance for the contemporary discourse of sustainability and architecture, because it forces us to think about coexistences and liaisons.

The metaphor project
Didier Faustino, in his own professional "ambiguity" – as both architect and artist – somehow metaphorical, was asked to produce a project for the conference that would illustrate metaphors. The result, the *Hidden Pavilion*, is a narration around the blending of three archetypes that reveal the overlapping of architecture, body, space and myth.

Metaphors are interpreted by **François Roche** as the possibility of delving exactly into the suspension between two poles opened up by these. It is in this ambiguous limbo, that Roche situates his work, illustrated by his recent projects.

Acknowledgements
Finally, this project would not have been possible without the help of many people. I thus would like to express my gratitude to the inspiring support of Odile Decq, Director of the Ecole Spéciale who made it possible for us to host this conference and to produce this book and who taught me a lot in my time in Paris. Many thanks also to Marie-Hélène Fabre, Director of Studies who supported us in this endeavor and in the preparation of

the conference. I am also indebted to Marie-Hélène Amiot, Amina Chady, Armelle Cochevelou and Magali Vannier of the administration of the ESA for their great support. This is also in memory of another ESA member, Guy Vacheret who took so many beautiful pictures of the school and of the conference, and who unfortunately has left us.

Image 4: Metaphors in/on Architecture and Urbanism, ESA Paris, 11.2009

It should be emphasized how this conference was only possible through a generous grant by the *Gerda Henkel Stiftung*, to which I would like once more to express my gratitude. The *Gerda Henkel Stiftung* also generously supported the publication of the present book.

I would also like to thank Andreas Beyer, director of the *Centre Allemand de l'Histoire de l'Art* in Paris who agreed to host the third conference day at his wonderful location on the *Place des Victoires* and who was an inspiring interlocutor for the final discussion.

I am obviously also deeply indebted to the conference speakers for their time and for their helpfulness in truly opening a space for discussion. I hope they will be pleased with the result. Also I must thank them for their patience with this book, which has taken some time to come out.

I am furthermore indebted to Alexandra Lacombe and Anne-Laure Chantepie who skilfully designed the poster and the conference documents even whilst deeply entangled in their diploma theses.

Many thanks also to the other students who helped us in the preparation and hosting of the conference: Erol Ugur Can, Maxime Cottard, Alexandre Goinard, Pauline Marie d'Avigneau, Yoan Ledoux, Elodie Doukhan, Valérie Philippe, Chloé de Smet, Achille Thorel, Sasha Cisar and Zuhal Kuzu.

Image 5: Drawing attributed to Bernini, Saint Peter's Square

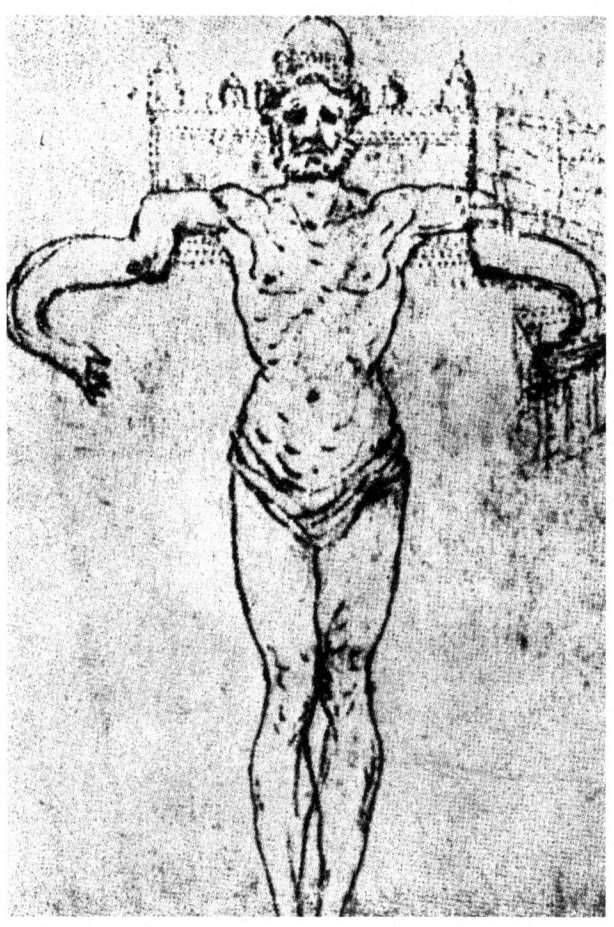

As for the publication I am indebted to Hasty Valipour Goudarzy for the transcripts of some of the conference papers and Pauline Marie d'Avigneau and Marie-Hélène Fabre for editing the French texts. We decided in fact to keep the bilingual experience of the conference also by keeping some texts in French, as they were presented.

Many thanks also to my parents for their help in the finishing of this book.

Last but not least, this book and the conference would not have been possible without the association with Brent Patterson, who took care of the editing of the texts and has since been an invaluable dialogue partner.

This book is for Poul and Constantin

Architectural/urban metaphorology

My Home Is My Symptom
A Psychoanalytic Plea for Flawed Architecture

JOHANNES BINOTTO

We suffer from metaphors. In his seminal paper *"Fonction et champ de la parole et du langage en psychanalyse"* from 1953 Jacques Lacan argues "metaphor [is] but a synonym for the symbolic displacement brought into play in the symptom."[1] And four years later in his essay *"L'instance de la lettre dans l'inconscient"* the psychoanalyst will state apodictically: "The symptom is a metaphor, whether one likes to admit it or not."[2]

The metaphor is a symptom
On first sight the equation of metaphor and neurotic symptom may seem rather far fetched. But in fact, the analyst did nothing else than take the classic definition of metaphor as proposed by Russian linguist Roman Jakobson seriously. In his essay "Two Aspects of Language and Two Types of Aphasic Disturbances," Jakobson defines metaphor as a paradigmatical *exchange* of signs (in contrast to metonymy, which is defined as a syntagmatical *combination* of signs).[3] In analogy with the metaphor where one sign stands for the other, the neurotic symptom functions as a stand-in for something else. Thus, the symptom is to be regarded as a metaphor for an unconscious psychic conflict.

However, what needs to be stressed here is the very unique meaning the term symptom has in psychoanalysis, one, which sets it apart from most of the other sciences, most notably medicine. In medicine a symptom

---

[1] | Lacan, Jacques, *Écrits*, Paris: Seuil 1966, p. 260
[2] | Ibid., p. 528
[3] | Jakobson, Roman, *Selected Writings II: Word and Language*, The Hague: Mouton 1971, pp. 239-59

is usually regarded as an indexical sign, which – according to the definition by semiotician Charles Sanders Peirce – is "physically connected with its object."[4] As in Peirce's famous example the "veering of a weathercock" is a direct result of and therefore an index for the blowing wind[5] so does the physician takes a medical symptom as a direct expression of certain medical conditions. As indexes their meanings can be learned in medical school and be looked up in the respective handbooks. However, in psychoanalysis – and this may be a reason for its bad reputation among medical scientists – the symptom is never as unequivocal as Pierce's weathercock but rather resembles a (Saussurian) signifier which is not naturally but only *arbitrarily* linked to the signified. The symptom in psychoanalysis is not an index, but always remains an ambiguous metaphor. And as the poet creates new metaphors whose meaning cannot be looked up in a dictionary, so too does the unconscious. Similar to the literary critic who has to decipher metaphors on the basis of the very text in which they appear, so too in psychoanalysis the symptoms need to be interpreted via the patient's discourse and nothing else. In contrast to medical science there is no manual, no standard key for deciphering the symptoms. Rather, the analyst faces the predicament that in the discourse of neurosis anything can be a symptom but isn't necessarily one. A signifier, which for one patient may be a crucial symptomatic metaphor for his suffering, most certainly will have no symptomatic value at all for any other patient. This is precisely why Freud insisted so much on the fact that the science of psychoanalysis cannot simply be taught but needs in fact to be re-invented by every analyst and for each and every patient anew.

Thus, from a psychoanalytic point of view speaking about metaphors also means speaking about symptoms. It follows that the discussion of the intersections between metaphor and architecture will also inevitably entail a discussion of the relation between symptom and architecture. Curiously enough, architectural theory is already more than familiar with such a discussion. Considering architecture symptomatically has in fact a well-known tradition which is probably as old as the earliest writings on

---

4 | Peirce, Charles Sanders, *The Essential Peirce: Selected Philosophical Writings*, Vol. 2: 1893-1913, Ed. The Peirce Edition Project. Bloomington: Indiana University Press 1998, p. 9

5 | Ibid., p. 274

architecture. It is Vitruvius who in his *De Architectura libri decem* compares dwellings with human bodies, thus implying that both are prone to similar harms and diseases. Alberti in the third book of his *On the Art of Building* further develops this comparison by proposing that the architect "with every type of vault, [...] should imitate nature throughout, that is, bind together the bones and interweave flesh with nerves running across every possible section."[6] By identifying buildings with human bodies, architecture thus becomes almost a matter of life and death which also becomes obvious when looking at way we still talk about buildings. Architectural critics will argue that walls 'need to breathe' or one talks about a building's 'healthy structure.' As architecture is supposed to be modelled after the image of the human body, conversely its aberrations are taken as forebodings of bodily harm. On a larger scale, the whole city was and still is widely believed to reveal symptomatically the malfunctions of society. Famous examples which spring to mind here may be Friedrich Engels "The Condition of the Working Class in England"[7] or Jane Jacobs influential study *The Death and Life of Great American Cities.*[8]

Probably the most notorious example of such a symptomatic reading of the city is of course to be found in Le Corbusier's *Urbanisme* from 1925 where the architect considers the development of urban architecture in general, and of Paris in particular, as indicating nothing less than the degeneration of mankind as a whole. "Man strides forward in a straight line because he has a goal; he knows where he is going [...] The donkey walks in zigzag line, takes a little nap, dumb from the heat and distracted [...] The donkey has left his mark in all the cities of the continent, in Paris too, sadly enough."[9] Such are the famous opening lines of the first chapter entitled "Le chemin des ânes. Le chemin des hommes" – "The path of the donkey. The path of man." In contrast to authors such as Franz Hessel or Walter Benjamin, Le Corbusier sees no advantage in an urban architecture that forces its inhabitants to wander around as "flaneurs." On the contrary:

---

6 | Alberti, Leon Battista, *On the Art of Building in Ten Books*, Transl. J. Rykwert, N. Leach & R. Tavernor, Massachusetts: MIT Press 1991, p. 86

7 | Engels, Friedrich, "Die Lage der arbeitenden Klasse in England," in *Karl Marx & Friedrich Engels*, Werke. Band 2, Berlin: Dietz 1957, pp. 225-506

8 | Jacobs, Janet, *Death and Life of Great American Cities*, New York: Vintage 1992

9 | Le Corbusier, *Urbanisme*, Paris: Arthaud 1980, pp. 5-6

to him the curved streets of the old Paris and its labyrinthine spaces are nothing but the traces of a brutish society. For Le Corbusier, Paris is not a city made by humans but by donkeys.

His notion of an *imbrutement* of architecture rather uncannily foreshadows the notion of "entartete Kunst" – "degenerate art" that the Nazis will deploy only few years later. The utter brutality of Le Corbusier's analysis becomes even clearer by looking at the illustrations in his book. Particularly the aerial shots of old Paris in the fifteenth chapter are revealing since in the captions Le Corbusier compares the sight of old Paris with a view of Dante's hell: the old parts of French capital are nothing than an abhorrent and revolting sight/site. However, what seems even more significant is the very position from which these pictures are taken, since it is the point of view a bomber pilot takes in military attack. The very perspective of the images reveal what the caption can only insinuate: It would be preferable to radically erase the existing architecture and its history, to give way to a homogeneous, uniformed urban space.

Le Corbusier is thus picking up on a thought that Descartes already proposes in his *Discours de la méthode* where he argues: "those ancient cities which, from being at first only villages, have become, in course of time, large towns, are usually but ill laid out compared with the regularly constructed towns which a professional architect has freely planned on an open plain [...] when one observes their indiscriminate juxtaposition, there a large one and here a small, and the consequent crookedness and irregularity of the streets, one is disposed to allege that chance rather than any human will guided by reason must have led to such an arrangement."[10]

Problematic as the Cartesian ideal may already seem, Le Corbusiers plan to turn the philosophers abstract and only textual utopia into an actual city becomes all the more frightening. Who would seriously want to live in a city cleansed of all its contradictions and devoid of all symptoms? The very lack of any symptomatic disturbance becomes the sign of an even more dangerous sickness.

---

10 | Descartes, René, *Discourse on the Method*, Transl. J. Veitch, New York: Cosimo 2008, p. 7

Image 6: Le Corbusier, Urbanisme, 1925

Est-ce une vue du septième cercle de l'Enfer de Dante? Non. Hélas, c'est le gîte effroyable de centaines de mille d'habitants. La Ville de Paris ne possède pas ces documents photographiques dénonciateurs. Cette vue d'ensemble est comme un coup de massue. Quand dans nos promenades, nous suivons le dédale des rues, nos yeux sont ravis par le pittoresque de ces paysages escarpés, les évocations du passé surgissent....., La tuberculose, la démoralisation, la misère, la honte triomphent sataniquement. La « Commission du Vieux Paris » collationne les fers forgés.

Le Corbusier wants to cut away the symptomatic excess of the city like a surgeon. However, from a psychoanalytic point of view it becomes clear how fatal such an operation would be, as for the analyst the symptom is not to be erased but rather to be preserved.

In his late teachings and most prominently in his 1975 seminar entitled *"Le sinthome"*[11] Lacan suggests a radical new reading and eventually a valorization of the symptom. On the one hand the symptom encapsulates

---

11 | Lacan, Jacques, *Le Séminaire. Livre XXIII: Le sinthome*, Paris: Seuil 2005

the patient's suffering. The symptom is – as was already pointed out – a metaphor for his pain, a representation for everything that does not function properly. However, without the symptom, things would become even more problematic. The symptom, as Lacan stresses continuously, is not the psychic dysfunction itself but rather a way to deal with this very dysfunction. Or to put it differently: The symptom is nothing else than a way to make things work.

This ambivalence of the symptom may best be seen in the hallucinations and delusions of psychosis. The delusion, being a symptom of psychosis must not be mistaken for the psychotic breakdown as such. Rather it is a way to make sense – although a strange and twisted one – of the psychotic breakdown itself. The conspiracy theories psychotic patients grow convinced of, or the instructions they believe to be given by hallucinated voices – all these symptoms are in fact protective shields against the frightening abyss of pure psychosis, an abyss of utter nothingness and nonsense. Thus the symptom has a double function: it is both a sign *for* but also a safeguard *against* psychic breakdown. It thus becomes all the more problematic if the analyst aims for a complete removal of all symptoms. In fact, erasing all symptoms will not result in mental health but destroy it. Perfection as such is ultimately psychotic. At least, that is how Lacan sees it when he characterizes the absence of any symptom as a characteristic of paranoia.[12] This would also explain why this striving for perfection and the removal of all symptomatic flaws in both Le Corbusier's *Plan voisin* for Paris from 1925 and Descartes' radical philosophy it is based on, seem so terrifying and paranoid to us. But how then should one deal with the symptom?

The symptom is a knot
In his seminar "*Le sinthome*" Lacan proposes to think of the symptom as a knot, which holds together what otherwise would fall apart. Although the analyst may be tempted to remove and untie all the symptoms of his patient it is crucial that certain symptomatic knots remain.[13] Similar to what Freud called "the navel of the dream" – the knotted detail in the dream text which resists interpretation, but which is also its kernel[14] – the mysterious knot of

---

12 | Ibid., p. 53
13 | Ibid., pp. 45-57
14 | Freud, Sigmund, "Die Traumdeutung," in *Gesammelte Werke*, Bd. II/III, London: Imago 1942, p. 530

the symptom haunts the subject. Nontheless, it is this very enigmatic detail that guarantees the sanity of the subject. By posing a kind of irresolvable problem it keeps the subject "on its toes" so to speak.

In order to fully understand the importance of the notion of the knot for Lacan, we have to be reminded that for psychoanalysis the psyche is never understood as one coherent whole but as consisting of different elements and registers which are at odds with each other. Freud described these contradictory aspects with his model of the psychic apparatus consisting of the consciousness, the preconscious and the unconscious. However, at a later stage he will replace this first model by a second model of the Ego, the Super-Ego and the Id. Lacan then will supplement the Freudian model with his famous triad of the Symbolic, the Imaginary and the the Real. While in Freud one could be tempted to understand the three registers of the psyche as separate areas, Lacan insists that Symbolic, Imaginary and Real are always implicated in one another. Not only because in the psyche these three registers are intertwined and interlinked but also because every act of the subject has at the same time a symbolic, an imaginary and real aspect to it.

Image 7: Borromean knot with four rings, representing the Lacanian subject

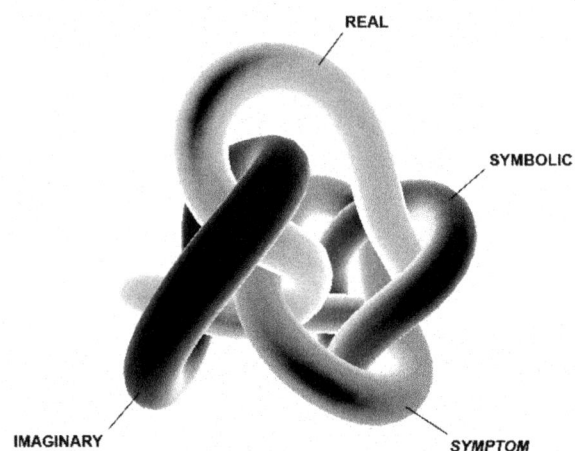

However, in the knotted subject of Lacanian psychoanalysis the interlinking of the three registers is never perfect. The knot of the subject is never a neat and tidy one but more or less unsafe. As the word trauma indicates, meaning literally "to open a wound" or "a hole," the knot of every subject is loosened and damaged to some extent by traumatic experiences. This is where the symptom as both result and remedy of trauma comes into play. The symptom functions as a fourth element which serves to bind and repair the faulty knot of Symbolic, Imaginary and Real.

Image 8: Borromean knot with four rings, cutting of the ring of the symptom

Image 9: Borromean knot with four rings, complete dissolution of the knot

Although the symptom renders the knot of the psyche all the more complex and convoluted it also guarantees its safety. In contrast to that, by cutting off the symptom, the three remaining registers would fall apart and the subject as a whole would disintegrate.

Complete cure thus becomes destruction. That is an insight already Freud hinted at in one of his last essays, "Analysis Terminable and Interminable" where he – rather pessimistically – argued that any analytical cure can never be completely finished but has to stop pre-ultimately. Final analysis on the other hand could only be disastrous.[15]

Considering the symptom as a knot makes the term all the more attractive for architecture. As the knot brings into play the question of stability, cohesion and enclosure it can be regarded itself as an allegory, a metaphor for architectural construction. Furthermore, one could read the three registers of the Symbolic, the Imaginary and the Real in analogy to the three axes of three-dimensional space. However, in contrast to the Euclidian space with its three dimension of length, width, and depth, the space of psychoanalysis is a topologically warped and folded one – a knotted space. The symptom then is built both within this warped psychic space but at the same time enwrapping it, giving it consistency.

This spatial aspect to the symptom is also consistent with the observation that dwellings so often function as shelter against neurotic anxiety, most prominently in the case of agoraphobia. This example shows once again the duplicity of the symptom: the enclosing space of the house or room in which the agoraphobic retreats is both prison and refuge. The symptomatic space of the shelter is at the same time constraining and enabling. As the psychoanalyst Patrick de Neuter has argued, the castles by Ludwig of Bavaria could be regarded as probably the most extravagant examples of such a symptomatically knotted architecture.[16] As we know, Ludwig of Bavaria obsessively built a whole series of castles of which Neuschwanenstein is only the most famous "castle-prothesis" as de Neuter puts it. Furthermore, when Ludwig died he left a huge collection of plans and designs for castles that were never erected. De Neuter then argues

---

15 | Freud, Sigmund, *Gesammelte Werke*, Bd. 16, London: Imago 1950, pp. 57-99
16 | Patrick de Neuter: "Die verrückten Leidenschaften Ludwigs II. von Bayern. Bauen, um zu überleben," in *RISS. Zeitschrift für Psychoanalyse*, Heft 50, 2001/I, pp. 51-74

quite convincingly that planning and constructing buildings was the king's strategy to hold a mental breakdown at bay. It seems safe to say that it is this very duplicity that makes the fantasy architecture of Ludwig's castles so haunting until today: as much as they seem to reveal the mental instability of its builder they obviously function as shelters against insanity. It does not come as a surprise that it was precisely when Ludwig was hindered to pursue his architectural obsession – not the least because he spent all the tax incomes on his castles –, that his illness became apparent.

The knot is a knob
A less obvious but certainly equally poignant example for such an architectural symptom can be found in Frank Capra's famous Christmas movie *It's a Wonderful Life* of 1946 – a movie which should be mandatory viewing for any young architect. It seems this classic has never ever been considered as being of much significance for architectural theory, which is all the more surprising since the protagonist of the film is actually an ambitious architect with high hopes. In an early scene of the film we see our protagonist, young George Bailey, standing in front of an old, derelict house, talking to his high school sweetheart Mary about his big plans which seem rather prototypical for a future architect. First, he claims, he will

Image 10: Frank Capra, *It's a Wonderful Life*, 1946

study the masters. "I'm gonna see the world. Italy, Greece, the Parthenon... the Coliseum." Then he wants to "build things" as he puts it. "I'm gonna build air fields. I'm gonna build skyscrapers a hundred stories high. I'm gonna build bridges a mile long." Knowingly or not George Bailey presents himself as a new Le Corbusier, who, as we know from his travel diaries was so much enthralled as an architect by the sight of the Parthenon.[17]

But, as the audience knows from the very beginning of the movie, all these dreams will never be achieved. Instead of skyscrapers for the big companies, George Bailey will construct one-family dwellings for the working poor and instead of building a new city à la Le Corbusier, he ends up staying in the crummy little town he was so eager to leave. Furthermore, the derelict house he used to mock and whose windows he used to smash in will eventually become his own home. As the movie progresses Capra shows us in a short montage sequence how the couple, after getting married, try to make a living. While Mary eagerly revamps the house, the exhausted George comes home from work and as he goes upstairs he holds on to a knob at the end of the banister, which then comes loose. Thoughtfully George stares at the piece of wood in his hand. Obviously enough, the loose knob is proof for how bad of shape the house is still in.

Image 11: Frank Capra, It's a Wonderful Life, 1946

---

17 | Zaknic, Ivan (ed.), *Le Corbusier. Journey to the East*, Cambridge: MIT Press, 1987

As the movie progresses, the derelict house will eventually turn into a happy and cozy home. However, the knob will never be fixed. Several years later on Christmas Eve 1946 a distressed and frustrated George, whose building and loan firm has just lost all the savings of their clients, comes home and takes his despair out on his family. Going up the stairs once again the knob at the end of the banister comes loose. Angrily and disgusted he slams it back to its place.

The loose knob becomes a symptom for all those dreams that didn't come true, a constant reminder of all those flaws that hinders the home and life of George Bailey from being perfect.

In the course of that same Christmas evening George's frustration about his situation becomes so unbearable that he grows convinced all would be better if he had never been born. However, when attempting to commit suicide, God sends an angel down to earth to show George how life would have been, if he hadn't been born. The crummy house George lived in would still be a ruin and his family wouldn't even exist. His brother Harry would be dead, since George was not around to save him from an accident when they were children. Consequently, all the soldiers Harry had saved in the Second World War would also have perished. His mother is shown to have become a lonely, embittered widow running a boarding house, and George's wife Mary would have become a spinster librarian. Shocked by this vision George calls upon God to let him live again. When his prayer is answered George storms home. He runs up the stairs to embrace his family and while hanging on to the banister one more time the knob falls off. But this time George is not so much irritated but elated. He actually kisses the knob in a moment of sheer relief because the lose knob is proof that everything has gone "back to normal."

The symptomatic knot/knob is ultimately acknowledged not as something to get rid of but as something to be cherished. As a symptom it still points to everything that is unhomely within one's own home, revealing all those flaws which render any kind of perfection impossible. However and as George has seen in his vision: without those flaws, things would be even worse. Thus the lesson Frank Capra teaches us is surprisingly akin to that which Lacanian psychoanalysis has in store for us: One can either have a flawed home or no home at all. To have something to live for entails that there are certain things you have (k)not. One either accepts the symptom or one will lose everything.

Image 12: Frank Capra, It's a Wonderful Life, 1946

Lacan would even go so far as to claim that once a patient has understood the symptom and no longer is simply subjected to it but can put it at a minimal distance, he or she ultimately has to identify with it:

"In what does [...] an analysis consist? Would it, or would it not be to identify with the symptom, albeit with every guarantee of a kind of distance? To know how to handle, to take care of, to manipulate ... to know what to do with the symptom, that is the end of analysis."[18]

And that is exactly what George Bailey does in the end: He "handles" in both a concrete and metaphorical sense the knot/knob of his symptom.

Having this in mind, Rem Koolhaas' essay "Toward the Contemporary City" from 1989 will take on a new poignancy. As Koolhaas argues there is a tendency in modernist architecture, which prefers the plan to the actual building.[19] This tendency has even increased since the time Koolhaas wrote his text. One only needs to consider the many architecture competitions in which not even the winning projects will ever be built. More than ever

---

18 | As quoted in Verhaeghe, Paul, Declerq, Frédéric, "Lacan's Analytic Goal: Le sinthome or the Feminine Way," in Thurston, Luke (ed.), *Re-Inventing the Symptom. Essays on the Final Lacan*, New York: Other Press 2002. p. 59-82; here: p. 65

19 | Koolhaas, Rem, "Toward the Contemporary City" [1989], in Nesbitt, Kate (ed.), *Theorizing a New Agenda for Architecture. An Anthology of Architectural Theory 1965-1995*, New York: Princeton Architectural Press 1996, p. 328

contemporary architecture happens mostly on paper and in computers, never turning into an actual building but remaining a plan. This tendency actually is in accordance with the idealist strive for flawless architecture as it is only in the state of planning that pure perfection is even possible. But – as Koolhaas insists – in contrast to the modernist's ideal and therefore paranoid utopias the true realm of architecture must still be the actual, geographical site. In the strategies Koolhaas outlines one should be able to "confront the buildings of this period and the different types of space – something that was impermissible in the pure doctrine of modernism. From them one can also learn to play with a substrata, mixing the built with the ideal project. This is a situation comparable to one or which the nineteenth century was much criticized, when in Milan, Paris, or Naples the strategy of remodelling without destroying the preexisting city was applied."[20]

Acknowledging the history, the limits and boundaries, even the ugliness of a given place and finding a way to deal with all these flaws that is according to Koolhaas the true task of contemporary architecture. Or to put it in Lacanian terms, the architect has to identify with the symptom, accepting it less as a weakness but rather as the very basis of every creation. In other words: We don't need more Le Corbusiers, we need more George Baileys!

---

20 | Ibid., p. 329

Metaphors in Architecture – a Metaphor?

Gernot Böhme

Architecture as language
It was the architectural theorist Charles Jencks, in his writing about postmodern architecture, who underscored the importance of metaphors for architecture. While recognizing in the architecture of his time a lack of the acknowledgement of the importance of metaphor, he thought that that would change, because "metaphor plays a predominant role in the public's acceptance or rejection of buildings."[1] Now it can be said, that Jencks himself was caught up in the fashionable theoretical trends of the time, looking at everything through the lenses of semiotics. His proclamation of a new epoch for architecture, that of Postmodernism, has to be seen in relation to its understanding of architecture as language. The understanding of architecture through the metaphors of another art/discipline – in this case literature – arises because of the quite strange, but at the same time classic embarrassment to state what architecture should be as discipline in its own terms.[2] A discussion about a work of architecture is often conducted through references, comparing it to a sculpture, a painting, a musical composition, for example a fugue, or a poem. This should be questioned given the common knowledge that architecture is mainly a spatial art. But one hesitates to state this quite simple truth and to use it in the description because space alone does not communicate what one associates with architectural space that is the aesthetic qualities and the emotional emanation of

---

1 | Jencks, Charles, *The Language of Post-Modern Architecture*, London: Academy Editions, 1977, p. 60
2 | See my article "Atmosphere as the Subject Matter of Architecture," in Ursprung Philipp (Ed.), *Herzog & de Meuron: Natural history*, Montreal: Canadian Center of Architecture; Lars Müller Publishers, 2002, pp. 398-406

its works. The reason lies in the fact that our conception of space is strongly influenced by geometry, by space *formale Anschauung*, as Kant would say, – i.e. space as formal intuition or as a medium of three-dimensional representation. While the architect indeed has a lot to do with this geometrical space – he has to arrange his works in the context of things and therefore to consider distances and volume, and even more, he has to use space as medium of representation for his designs, such as through drawings, models and simulations. Yet, what matters in the end is the space in which we live, the bodily space. Each work of architecture creates or constructs a space, in which we, the visitors, move and in which we feel something. Thus, the architect works with the geometrical space, but he uses it to design the space of our bodily presence,[3] he determines the premises of bodily space experience, in short, of our feeling inside the space. If one makes reference to this space, the space of bodily presence, the experience and the effect on visitors is always already implicit and there is no need for metaphors.

Although the discussion about metaphors in architecture stems from the – remediable – embarrassment to talk in general about architecture in its 'own' terms, it is necessary to question whether one can speak of a language of architecture, of architecture as language.

What are metaphors?

The term *metaphor* stems from linguistic theory, to be more precise, from the theory of literature. It has been introduced by Aristotle in his *poetics*. This happens in a paragraph were he discusses in particular words and their use. The Metaphor is not a class of words but rather a particular usage of words.

Its definition is: "A metaphor is the application of a noun which properly applies to something else. The transfer may be from the genus to the species, from the species to the genus or according the rules of analogy."[4]

---

3 | For this differentiation see my articles "Leibliche Anwesenheit im Raum," in *Ästhetik und Kommunikation* Nr. 108, March 2000, pp. 67-76, and "Der Raum leiblicher Anwesenheit und der Raum als Medium von Darstellung," in Krämer Sybille (ed.), *Performativität und Medialität*, München: Wilhelm Fink 2004, pp.129-140, engl: http://www.ifs.tu-darmstadt.de/fileadmin/gradkoll/Publikationen/space-folder/pdf/Boehme.pdf

4 | Aristotle, *Poetics*, transl. Macolm Heath, London: Penguin books, 1996, p. 37

The types of transfer are not interesting for us in this context; Aristotle introduces those types considering the question of how the transfer logically is arranged. It should be only mentioned that the modern use of metaphors is not reduced to the last type, which is analogy.[5]

What is crucial for us is that the transfer is always transferring to another object or discipline than the one which the word in question is originally related to. A classical example, used by Aristotle in his *rhetoric*,[6] comes from the *Iliad*[7]: there, Homer names Achilles a lion for the way he attacks Aeneas. Here the term *lion* is transferred to a man.

It is very important to underline that the transfer implies not only a dislocation on the level of the signifier, that Homer instead of saying *Man*, uses the term *Lion*. That would be simply false – because not a lion penetrates in Aeneas, but the man in Achilles. Homer on the contrary wants to say something extraordinary about Achilles, by calling him a lion, or better, to let him appear in a particular light. He wants to articulate his audacity, his recklessness.[8] Thus we arrive at the question of the cognitive function of metaphors.[9] It is namely insufficient to consider metaphors only as an adornment of speech, as Aristotle does, because he treats them mainly inside his *Rhetoric*.

The application of metaphors allows seeing the object, on which the word in question is transferred, in a particular light. They articulate aspects of this object that in simple denomination would not be cognizable. We can even demonstrate – to stick to the example: "Achilles the lion" – that the Greeks only became aware of the character and mood of somebody

---

5 | According to W. Weinreich. See his article "Metaphor," in Historisches Wörterbuch der Philosophie, Bd. 5, Stuttgart: Schabe, 1980, pp. 1179-1186
6 | Aristotle, *Rhetoric*, III.4, 1406b
7 | Homer, Iliad, XX, pp. 158-177
8 | Precisely speaking Homer does not call Achilles a lion but says the he attacks Aeneas like a lion, λεων ως. A metaphor is also called an abbreviated comparison.
9 | See Lakoff, George, Johnson, Mark, *Metaphors We Life by*, Chicago: UP, 1980. For an overview over modern theories of metaphor see Goschler, Juliana, *Metaphern für das Gehirn. Eine kognitiv-linguistischen Studie*, Berlin: Frank & Timme, 2008

through analogies with animals.¹⁰ Therefore: courage is what one sees in the lion, timorousness in the deer.

The cognitive function of metaphors would not be understandable or would even be unnecessary if objects were already given to us concisely articulated as to their properties and structures. This is not the case. Rather objects are normally opaque, or one could say, they are given in a compact way.

The metaphor, i.e. the word, which is transferred on this object from another field of reference, transports a scheme, which organizes the perception.¹¹ In the example: the movements and gestures of Achilles are brought to the focus by the scheme *Lion*. Thus the metaphor does not apply a signifier to an already completely definite object but rather the representation of the object is organized through the metaphor. The proximity of metaphors to models in science stems from here: they allow for an initially diffuse amount of data to be theorized. Therefore it is clear that the term *metaphor* – through the 2000 years-long history of the theory of metaphors – has experienced an expansion of its domain.

But it has to be said: metaphors always have their place on the level of the signifiers, that is, of language, but these signifiers are metaphors only in a particular relation to the signified, to the things. We can therefore hold onto the following: metaphors are a phenomenon of language that however only appears when a discourse is a discourse about something – or towards something or somebody, to include also the convivial address and the insult. This will become important for the discussion of metaphors in architecture: if architecture is a language, what then is it talking about?

If one wants to judge what role metaphors play in architecture, so one has to decide if the focus is on the discourse or on concrete works of architecture.

---

10 | See my article "Über die Physiognomie des Sokrates und Physiognomik überhaupt," in Böhme, Gernot, *Der Typ Sokrates*, Frankfurt: M. Suhrkamp, 3. extended edition, 2002, pp. 210-233

11 | Kant says in his *Critique of Pure Reason*: "It is one and the same spontaneity which in the one case, under the title of imagination, and in the other, under the title of understanding, brings combination into the manifold of intuition." Note to B 152. Kant, Immanuel, *Critique of Pure Reason*, transl. by Norman Kemp Smith, New York: St. Martins, 1965, pp. 171f

Metaphors in the discourse on architecture
If one speaks of metaphors in the discourse on architecture, then one doesn't need the large-scale hypothesis of a Jencks, that architecture is a kind of language. The metaphoricity, then, consists only in the use of concepts in the description of works of architecture that stem from other domains. Such linguistic behavior can stem from the above mentioned embarrassment of not having a true conception of architecture as a particular art but it can also help to render more articulate the effect a work of

Image 13: Charles Jencks, *The Languageg of Post-Modern Architecture*, 1977

architecture provokes. Obviously many examples, introduced by Jencks as architectural metaphors are, to be precise, metaphors in the discourse about architecture. If one calls the concrete grid of a multistore parking garage a cheesegrater,[12] this is a purely linguistic procedure: where one explains to somebody else short and concisely the impression of this façade.

In fact, this perspective will articulate the representation the parking-silo and at the same time imply a negative connotation. Equally there is a way of comparing Jörn Utzon's Opera house in Sidney to "turtles making love," which is a purely linguistic metaphor. It manages to clearly explain to somebody the uncommon shape of the roof and at the same time to express the surprise of the observer confronted by this work. But to call it a "mixed metaphor" as Jencks does, because it symbolizes "the growth of a flower over time – the unfolding of petals, fish swallowing each other"[13] is questionable. This argument seems to stem rather from the need of the architectural critique to look everywhere for meaning. In any case, it presumes that architecture is a language. Should we assume that the architect Jörn Utzon wanted to communicate something to the later observers of his works? This hypothesis would be dismissed by the ambiguity of the alleged symbol. Utzon has rather created a spatial form and therewith shaped the space of the Opera-house and its context. Through this, the observer feels in a particular way, he experiences certain impressions. We could say that the shape of the roof creates a certain atmosphere.

Atmospheres are spaces with a certain mood.[14] In order to characterize the atmosphere of a building, it seems that one needs again certain metaphors. So for example one could say to define the suggestions for movement contained by an architectural form, that they are *emergent* or *rapturous*, or even *sublime*. Yet, it is important to hold onto the fact, that these are not metaphors – that would imply that the corresponding terms would come from somewhere else. This is not the case. Rather the characters of atmospheres are attributed to the atmospheres themselves and to the objects that produce them. In fact they predicate properties of things not as their determination, but as their ecstasy, as well as the impressions, that a visitor will

---

12 | Jencks 1977, p. 40
13 | Ibid., p. 43
14 | For this concept see my book *Architektur und Atmosphäre*, München: Wilhelm Fink Verlag, 2006

experience. One can call a man stormy, or the weather or the shape of a roof, in any case it concerns the impression that people experience in their proximity. Particularly revealing are the examples of *bright* and *sweet*. To call a valley or garden scenery bright is not the transfer of a condition of the mind to an object of nature – that would be absurd: should a valley have a soul? – but the characterization of one's own condition while looking at the valley. In the case of sweet one can even demonstrate that the term – at least in German – originated not in sugar-sweated aliments, but in the pleasant par excellence.

Therefore there exist a lot of terms for the characterization of works of architecture, that appear to be metaphors, while in reality, they characterize the humors and dispositions, the synesthesias that one experiences in the environment of these works. However also symbols belong to the creators of atmospheres, but not symbols in the way Jencks has them, as he equates them with metaphors. Symbols are conventional signs. Those signs thus have to be historical and socially habitualized. There exist many elements of Christian architecture, for example the cross or the gothic ogive, that applied somewhere else, imply a religious atmosphere. Therewith we have entered the discussion on whether there is in architecture, that is in its works, a use of forms that we can reasonably call metaphorical.

Metaphors in architecture seen as language
Without any doubt there are also processes of communication in architecture, and it is not mistaken to say, that architecture turns towards a public through its work. Therefore the diagnosis of Jencks, that postmodern architecture – in contrast to modern architecture – is more turned towards the general public. But not every communication is mediated through symbols – one has only to think about bodily communication the way the philosopher Hermann Schmitz discussed it in his phenomenology.

Linguistic communication though is communicated symbolically – precisely by meaningful word – and normally it is related to an object. I say: normally, because exclamations don't need an object. Direct addresses namely don't have an object, they have an addressee, thus again we have here in the metaphorical speech the transfer to something that is outside language. Still, statements need a statement-object. But the object of a statement doesn't need to be a sensual object; it can also be an idea, or any other abstract. It is probably something like this that Jencks has in mind, when he considers architecture as a language: namely a communication mediated by symbols. Without doubts we have examples for that. But it would be a pity, if we would identify architecture or even only postmodern architecture with that. It would lose all contact to the tradition of architecture as the art of spatial forms.

The examples that fit the conception of Jencks can be easily found in Venturi, Scott Brown and Izenour's *Learning from Las Vegas*.[15] It is the *decorated shed* that meets the idea of Jencks. The term already suggests that there is a resignation on architectonic spatial design. Instead, there is a façade design that works with brand-symbols, characters and illumination. Here architecture becomes commercial art.

Now in fact it is correct, that postmodern architecture implies the return of decoration, after its condemnation in modernism, from Loos to Bauhaus. At the same time one has to admit, that architecture also serves to stage – the staging of power, of religiosity or of democracy and art. But at the same time this does not mean that it has to do without its own instruments for the benefit of symbols. And this also doesn't imply that decoration and instruments of staging have to be at any prize symbols or even metaphors. A flat roof doesn't "mean shelter and psychological protection," as Jencks suggests,[16] one can say at best that it suggests security, that is, it contributes to the creation of an atmosphere of security. Nor can we consider decoration as an architectonic metaphor. If for example the perception of a house suggests the impression of a face and this effect is amplified by decoration, then this decoration is not a metaphor for the face, but an articulation of the sight of a *face*. The discussion on metaphors appears to be the strongest, when it concerns the transfer of elements of style on modernist's buildings. Because here, in the words of Jencks, it is the question of *transfer* of elements from one code to another – if one can consider architectonic styles as codes. An ionic column in a modern building is not a metaphor for something else – as the lion for the audacious, aggressive warrior – but a symbol, that creates along the conventions an atmosphere

---

15 | Venturi, Robert, Scott Brown, Denise, Izenour, Steven, *Learning from Las Vegas, [1972], revised edition: The Forgotten Symbolism of Architectural Form*, Cambridge/Mass.: MIT 1977

16 | Jencks 1977, p. 63

of festivity and solidity.[17] This distinction is important because in the first case the architect has to presuppose the readability of the metaphor by his public – that is in general education – while he can bear in the second case on the immediate – even though culturally encoded – impression.

Image 14: Venturi, Robert, Scott Brown, Denise, Izenour, Steven, Learning from Las Vegas, Cover, 1972

Conclusion
The usage of metaphors in language has an appealing character. That is also the reason for the original use of metaphorical discourse in esthetics.

---

17 | Jencks 1977, p. 55, has an example which through his obviously being mere facade denies the emotional impression one may get.

A metaphor is an uncommon use of words, it is a terminological innovation. It therefore normally endows a new, surprising view and thus implies a cognitive function. And it achieves an accentuation and in many cases an illustration of the discussed object that it puts in the context of another domain.

Metaphors are thus not only an ornament of speech, but, in fact, the dynamic of the development of a language is considerably influenced by the constitution of metaphors. That implies that metaphors are, strictly speaking, only metaphors in their first utilization. Through repetition their appeal quickly disappears and they are then only words like others. An example for such dead metaphors is in German *Blatt* – leaf, page. This word was originally came from the realm of plants and blossoms, today it is used without any charm for almost anything that is flat: saw blade, rudder blade, a sheet of paper. The word atmosphere was in the 18th century a metaphor coming from meteorology, today it has basically two meanings: that is, *upper atmosphere* and *tempered space*, so that is a duty to explicate the relationship of the two.[18] Another destiny of metaphors is to become a way of speaking. One recognizes in it a certain strangeness, but without being able to understand it, still the way of saying lives on as an understandable concept. Examples are – I'm sorry but they work only in German – *Ich komme auf Schusters Rappen* or *den inneren Schweinehund überwinden*.[19]

These are all procedures inside language. If we are discussing architecture proper, talking about metaphors in architecture is indeed a metaphor. If metaphors concern expressions, which appear in the discourse about architecture, they are harmless and move inside the domain of the common. In that case they don't need any further justification, besides the warning, that metaphoric expression implicitly covers the incapacity, to speak directly about architecture wording its particularities. If one doesn't describe the elements of architecture only metaphorically, but instead calls these elements themselves metaphors, then the whole discourse is a metaphor. In

---

18 | See my article "'Mir läuft ein Schauer übern ganzen Leib' - das Wetter, die Witterungslehre und die Sprache der Gefühle," in *Goethe-Jahrbuch* Nr. 124, 2007, Göttingen: Wallstein, pp. 133-141

19 | The dictionary (Dr. Karl Wildhagen's German-English Dictionary, Wiesbaden: Brandstetter, 1972) says that "auf Schusters Rappen kommen" is equivalent to "on Shank's mare" and that "den inneren Schweinehund überwinden" is equivalent to "overcome one's baser feelings" or "the devil inside."

fact this discourse translates a word that actually corresponds to phenomena of language, on works of architecture. This is similar to Roland Barthes who has spoken of a language of fashion.[20] Thereby he has reconstructed the elements of industrial textile production as a system of signifiers that do not have a corresponding signified. A collar, a sleeve doesn't mean anything. But they could have, in the totality of a costume, a certain radiation. What Barthes has accomplished thereby is to reveal the modular structure of textile design. Something similar results from architectural semiotics. It is therefore not by chance, that it has been developed during the age of industrial and modular construction. But it is something different, when architecture becomes marketing, as Venturi and the others have represented it. In that case the elements of architecture have a meaning, they are signs. Considered in the overall this architectural thinking – and its corresponding way of designing – means decay. Architecture then only sets signs and renounces its original task that is to design and construct spaces.

---

20 | Barthes, Roland, *Système de la mode*, Paris: Seuil, 1983

Référence métaphorique et référence métonymique

Philippe Boudon

En architecture, pour commencer, il me semble que la métaphore est une représentation iconique, accompagnée d'un commentaire, explicite ou implicite, qui apporte cette valeur métaphorique. C'est une représentation dans laquelle entrent plus ou moins de *verbal* et plus ou moins d'*iconique*. Mais je ne pense pas qu'on doive confondre l'iconique avec le métaphorique, lequel relève du verbal. Dans le langage la métaphore fait image, c'est pourquoi l'image en question relève du langage. L'image littérale – si je puis dire – n'est pas métaphore. Il ne suffit donc pas qu'une architecture fasse image pour qu'elle puisse être dite métaphorique.

Le canard de bord de route américaine de Robert Venturi pourrait peut-être être tenu pour quelque chose *comme* une métaphore, tout comme pourrait l'être la « baleine » de Renzo Piano à Paris. À ceci près que, s'agissant du canard, il n'y a pas besoin de commentaire car, si j'ose dire, il parle de lui-même, tandis que dans le cas de la baleine, d'une forme moins déterminée, il faut que soit énoncé le mot *baleine* pour qu'il y ait métaphore. C'est ce que je veux dire en déclarant qu'il y a plus ou moins de discours, de verbe, de texte, de langage et plus ou moins d'image.

Mais à vrai dire, dans le cas du canard, si l'on peut dire justement qu'il « parle» de lui-même, c'est bien parce qu'il est implicitement question de langage dans l'image du canard. Car on peut considérer que l'image du canard est là justement pour « énoncer » une sorte de proposition comme : « Ici l'on mange du canard ». S'il y a bien image, elle est cependant là *pour du langage*. Ma thèse est que la métaphore, pour *architecturale* qu'elle puisse

Image 15: Canard de bord de route américaine d'après Robert Venturi

Image 16: La « baleine » de Piano « coque en forme de dirigeable lui valant le surnom de baleine »

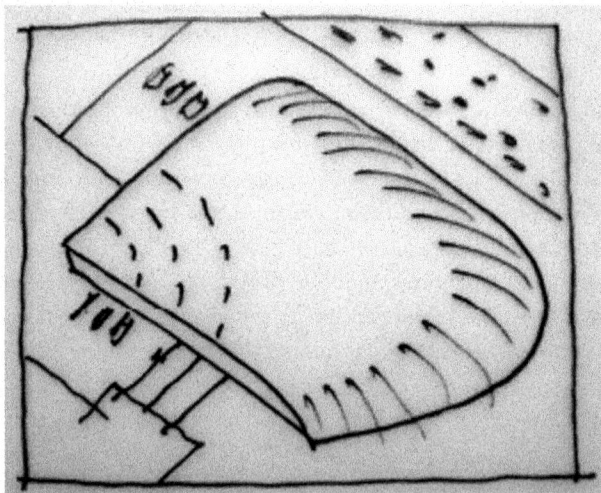

être dite dans certains cas, est de l'ordre du langage, d'un langage qui accompagne – explicitement ou implicitement – l'architecture, et qu'elle le reste. Un journaliste utilisait récemment à la radio l'expression de « métaphore architecturale » à propos de la question du juge d'instruction (actuellement débattue en France en matière juridique), et dont il venait de dire « qu'on l'avait fait sortir par la porte, et qu'il était rentré par la fenêtre ». Il n'est guère ici question d'architecture, on en conviendra, mais justement ce cas est intéressant car il met en évidence que l'architecture puisse en quelque sorte *soutenir* une métaphore, laquelle reste malgré tout une figure du langage. Dans ce cas, il n'y a pas grande spécificité architecturale, même si a été employée l'expression de « métaphore architecturale ». L'intérêt de cette petite histoire est pour moi de mettre en évidence la possibilité d'une métaphore dite *architecturale* alors même que l'architecture n'y joue guère de rôle spécifique, autre que celui de fournir cette image de portes et de fenêtres. Cette métaphore dite architecturale est très peu architecturale et plutôt ordinaire. Mais c'est justement à l'idée qu'une métaphore puisse être prétendue spécifiquement architecturale que j'ai tendance à m'opposer. Encore une fois, ce n'est là qu'une thèse, mais si on l'accepte, je pense qu'elle clôt la question : la métaphore est affaire de langage et non d'architecture, même s'il est question d'architecture dans un énoncé.

J'en aurais donc fini avec mon exposé (déjà !...) – en disant que la métaphore est et reste avant tout une figure de langage – qu'il s'agisse de canards, de baleines, de portes ou des fenêtres, si je n'avais utilisé moi-même le terme « métaphorique » en architecturologie, d'une façon que je vais préciser[1]. On verra dans mon exposé que 'métaphore' est un concept constitué en implication mutuelle avec celui de métonymie. Je distinguerai en effet la métaphore comme représentation mentale, difficile, pour ne pas dire impossible à définir, d'un concept propre à l'architecturologie et inspiré par la linguistique, *via* Saussure et Jakobson.

Mais auparavant j'illustrerai ma proposition introductive, à savoir que la métaphore est affaire de langage, et non d'architecture, par un dessin de Steinberg qui traduit graphiquement et dans l'espace la proposition: « ce bâtiment est une soupière ».

---

1 | Boudon, Philippe, « Modèle architecturologique et modèles linguistiques », in Vermandel, Frank (ed.), *Cahiers thématiques : Pratiques du langage*, Lille, Ecole d'architecture de Lille, Paris : Éditions de la Maison des sciences de l'homme, 2003, pp. 131-145

Image 17: Soupière d'après un dessin de Steinberg

Il ne diffère pas d'une métaphore verbale telle qu'on la trouverait dans la phrase: « son voisin était un ours ». L'image nous dit – je dis bien *nous dit* : « ce bâtiment est comme une soupière », ou encore « ce bâtiment est une vraie soupière ! » Autrement dit, bien que nous ayons affaire à une image, c'est du langage.

* * *

En *architecturologie,* maintenant, le terme « métaphorique » est utilisé comme concept, je l'ai dit, plus précisément *via* l'expression de *référence métaphorique,* laquelle se distingue d'une autre expression, par laquelle elle prend sens par opposition, celle de *référence métonymique*[2]. Dire qu'il s'agit d'expressions « conceptuelles », c'est rappeler que, comme disaient Gaston Bachelard et bien d'autres, un concept n'existe pas isolément, et que ces expressions s'inscrivent dans l'ensemble des concepts de l'architecturologie, celle-ci ayant pour tâche – pour le dire en deux mots – de conceptualiser ce que nous appelons *l'espace de la conception.* Je ne peux évidemment pas entrer ici dans l'ensemble des concepts architecturolo-

---

2 | Voir Boudon, Philippe, Deshayes, Philippe, Pousin, Frédéric, Schatz, Françoise, *Enseigner la conception architecturale, Cours d'architecturologie*, Paris : Editions de La Villette, Paris, 2000, p. 112

giques, mais il me suffira de considérer qu'en introduisant la métonymie au côté de la métaphore[3] nous sortons de l'isolement d'un concept supposé unique que serait la métaphore, pour passer à un système d'opposition, lequel associe, justement en les opposant, métaphore et métonymie, dans une sorte de micro-système.

Par ce terme d'*espace de la conception*, (l'objet, encore une fois, que l'architecturologie se donne de constituer) nous entendons le processus et les opérations qui mènent à l'édifice dans le travail de l'architecte. Travail que l'on tente de comprendre *via* les opérations qu'il suppose, plutôt que *via* l'observation de l'édifice une fois celui-ci construit, lequel n'est que la trace de ces opérations. Précision d'importance, car la métaphore prise comme figure du langage peut elle-même être considérée soit dans ses *effets*, soit dans sa production. Parler de conception est donc très différent de ce que serait parler de perception ou de réception. Charles Jencks, dans la section « métaphore » de son livre *Le langage de l'architecture post-moderne* soutient que « Moins un édifice moderne paraît familier au public, plus celui-là aura tendance à le comparer métaphoriquement à un édifice ou à quelque chose qu'il connaît... Ainsi quand les treillis en béton ont été utilisés pour la première fois en façade à la fin des années cinquante, ils ont été perçus comme des 'rapes à fromage' alors que dix ans plus tard, quand ils devinrent la norme dans une certaine catégorie de bâtiments, ils furent perçus en termes fonctionnels 'on dirait un garage'.[4] » Ce faisant il se situe dans l'ordre de la perception ou de la réception, comme on voudra, mais non dans celui de la conception. Il s'agit là d'un *effet* métaphorique de l'architecture, qui est légitime du point de vue de Jencks mais qui ne correspond pas au point de vue qui m'intéresse ici, celui de la conception[5]. Et lorsqu'il écrit encore que « Les gens perçoivent inévitablement un édifice par rapport à

---

3 | Suivant en cela Gérard Genette selon qui la métaphore est toujours un peu métonymie et celle-ci toujours un peu métaphore.

4 | Jencks, Charles, *The Language of post-modern architecture*, Academy Edition: London, 1979, p. 40

5 | Il est à noter que Charles Jencks dit appuyer sa thèse de la nature dichotomique du langage architectural sur plusieurs de mes ouvrages dont *Pessac de Le Corbusier (Lived-in architecture)* mais j'ai bien précisé dans la préface à la seconde édition de mon ouvrage le déplacement que j'avais opéré dans mon travail, de la réception à la conception. Or la métaphore est du point de vue de Jencks,

un autre édifice, bref ils le perçoivent comme une métaphore[6] », il se situe encore dans la perception.

Image 18: axe syntagmatique : la colonne

Mais qu'en est-il maintenant si l'on se situe non plus dans la perception mais dans la conception ? Les expressions de *référence métaphorique* et de

---

question de perception, tandis que je pose ici la question de la métaphore dans l'ordre de la conception.
6 | ibidem, p. 40

Image 19: axe paradigmatique : la classe des « chapiteaux »

référence métonymique m'ont été inspirées par le linguiste Roman Jakobson, lequel a utilisé les termes de métaphore et de métonymie pour désigner des figures de langage, ce, en partant lui-même de la fameuse distinction saussurienne entre *axe paradigmatique* et *axe syntagmatique*.

* * *

Le passage du *Cours de linguistique générale* dans lequel Saussure établit cette distinction passe par une illustration empruntée à l'architecture classique pour faire comprendre la distinction entre *axe syntagmatique*, dans lequel les rapports entre les mots sont, dit-il, des rapports *in praesentia*, et *axe paradigmatique* selon lequel les rapports sont des rapports *in absentia*.

Dans une colonne, dit Saussure, la base, le fût et le chapiteau sont dans un rapport *in praesentia* : c'est l'axe syntagmatique. Mais il est possible de substituer tel ou tel chapiteau à la place qui est la sienne, telle ou telle ou telle base à la place qui est la sienne : « base, fût et chapiteau ayant chacun leurs places respectives. Les chapiteaux sont donc rassemblés virtuellement dans une classe, un paradigme, et sont donc en rapport *in absentia* les uns avec les autres au sein de cette classe.[7] » C'est l'ensemble des éléments dits *chapiteaux* qui sont justement susceptibles de venir s'installer à la place du « chapiteau », ce qui n'est le cas ni du fût, ni de la base. Ainsi en va-t-il du langage dans une phrase qui, selon l'axe syntagmatique, enchaîne des mots en présence les uns des autres, tandis que peuvent venir s'installer à la place qui est d'avance la leur, des « articles », des « noms » ou des « verbes » termes qui désignent autant de classes structurant l'ensemble des mots de la langue. C'est l'analogie entre le double axe paradigmatique et syntagmatique, illustré par l'architecture classique, et défini par les opérations de « substitution » ou de « concaténation » qu'utilise Saussure pour se faire comprendre.

Or Roman Jakobson a étendu la distinction entre « substitution » et «concaténation» aux figures du langage c'est-à-dire, au-delà de la phrase, jusqu'au discours. Je rappelle son propos. Selon R. Jakobson, la métaphore est une figure de *substitution*, tandis que la métonymie est une figure de *contiguïté*, de *déplacement*. En effet, l'axe paradigmatique se caractérise en effet selon Saussure, on vient de le voir, par la substituabilité des mots dans le syntagme qu'est la phrase; et l'axe syntagmatique, comme son nom l'indique, est l'axe de la concaténation, l'axe de l'enchaînement, suivant les règles de la syntaxe, des mots dans la phrase. La métaphore est elle-même, pour Jakobson, une figure de *substitution*, tandis que la métonymie est une figure de *concaténation*. La métaphore établit des relations *in praesentia*, la métonymie des rapports *in absentia*.

Jakobson ne se prive pas d'étendre de façon *extralinguistique* la dualité *in praesentia / in absentia*, à d'autres domaines[8]. S'agissant par exemple de la peinture, il distingue la peinture symboliste par le fait que l'aspect paradigmatique y domine l'aspect syntagmatique tandis que dans le cas de la

---

7 | F. de Saussure, *Cours de linguistique générale*, (1916), Paris, Payot, 1995, pp. 170-171

8 | Jakobson, Roman, « Les deux aphasies du langage », in *Essais de linguistique générale*, Paris : Seuil, 1963

peinture cubiste, c'est l'aspect syntagmatique qui prédomine. Remplacer une rose par un lys dans une peinture symboliste est probablement plus grave que de remplacer une pipe par une guitare dans un Picasso. A l'inverse, déplacer la guitare dans le plan (syntagmatique) de la toile de Picasso pourrait être plus grave que déplacer le lys dans la peinture symboliste (...pour parler de façon figurée !) On pourrait, de la même façon, distinguer l'ordre paradigmatique de *l'harmonie* en musique, l'ordre syntagmatique de la *mélodie*. On retrouverait encore la distinction du côté du cinéma, en distinguant prise de vue et montage[9].

Mais m'intéresse surtout ici le fait que la dualité saussurienne paradigmatique/syntagmatique – établie à partir de la dualité *in praesentia / in absentia* – est étendue de façon *extra-linguistique* par Jakobson. D'où la possibilité qui m'est apparue d'étendre encore au domaine architectural cette dualité.

* * *

Image 20: « Axe historique » : succession syntagmatique Carrousel, Arc de Triomphe, Grande Arche

---

9 | Je n'insiste pas sur ces cas dont j'ai parlé dans les *Cahiers thématiques* de l'école d'architecture de Lille, op. cit. note 1 ci-dessus.

S'agissant d'architecture, je reprendrai le cas, que j'ai décrit ailleurs[10], de l'axe historique parisien – qui va du Louvre à l'arche de la Défense (à noter que le même mot *axe* peut être utilisé ici dans le même sens que celui employé par Saussure). Il met en relation *in praesentia* les objets architecturaux que sont l'arc du Carrousel, l'arc de Triomphe et la Grande Arche. Mais en même temps, chacun de ces éléments est en relation *in absentia* avec la classe, ou si l'on veut le *paradigme*, ou encore le *modèle*, des *arcs romains*, arc de Titus ou arc de Constantin. On retrouve bien là cette dualité entre axe syntagmatique des rapports *in praesentia* et axe paradigmatique des rapports *in absentia*.

Correspondant aux rapports *in absentia* et *in praesentia* en architecture, auxquels on peut encore faire correspondre mélodie et harmonie du côté de la musique, ou prise de vue et montage du côté du cinéma, comme je l'ai dit, on peut mettre en rapport *modèle* et *échelle* en architecture. L'idée de modèle architectural pouvant se trouver éclairée en quelque sorte par le modèle linguistique[11]. J'ouvrirai ici une parenthèse sur la relation que l'on peut faire avec l'idée de modèle. La base étant au fût et au chapiteau d'une colonne, ce que sont la base au fût et au chapiteau d'une autre colonne, le modèle « colonne » peut se définir comme associant les deux axes. Car on peut considérer que cet enchaînement est précisément ce qui fait qu'une colonne est une *colonne*. Le modèle est alors précisément la classe des objets qui peuvent venir prendre place à une place déterminée. Car si l'on suit Saussure, ce qui peut venir s'installer à une place déterminée, c'est ce qui relève de l'axe paradigmatique, – autrement dit le modèle – à savoir ce qu'on appelle respectivement « chapiteau », « base », « fût ». Au point que l'on peut se passer d'un chapiteau concret, ou d'un fût concret, pour peu que sa place soit déterminée, fût-elle vide... Ainsi en trouve-t-on l'exemple dans un bâtiment de la place de Catalogne, à Paris. Notons que, du côté du langage et en particulier celui, bien connu, des « Schtroumpfs », nous n'avons pas besoin de la présence de certains mots pour comprendre une phrase comme « *il a schtroumpfé dans sa trompette* »...

---

10 | Voir op. cit. note 1
11 | Voir là-dessus Boudon, Philippe, *Architecture et architecturologie II*, Paris : AREA, 1975 et Boudon, Philippe, *Introduction à l'architecturologie*, Paris : Dunos, 1992

Image 21: Un cas de présence-absence de colonnes, Place de Catalogne, Paris

Je n'aborderai maintenant que de manière très succincte la question de savoir si l'analogie qu'on trouve chez Saussure lui-même entre langage de l'architecture classique et langage à proprement parler – c'est-à-dire verbal – est elle-même de l'ordre d'une métaphore. La métaphore est en effet souvent comprise par les linguistes comme une analogie dont un des membres serait sous-entendu : *a* est à *b* ce que *c* est à *d*. Ceci nous entraînerait vers la redoutable question de l'architecture comme langage éventuel. Elle s'est maintes fois posée à en juger par le nombre d'ouvrages dans le titre desquels figure le mot langage. Que l'on pense au *Langage de l'architecture moderne* de Bruno Zevi, au *Langage de l'architecture post-moderne* de Charles Jencks, ou encore au *Langage classique de l'architecture* de John Summerson. De son côté on se souvient que Peter Collins avait consacré à *l'analogie linguistique* un chapitre d'un de ses ouvrages. Je terminerai toutefois en évoquant un cas d'usage du langage relativement à l'architecture.

Dans un article de journal récent on pouvait lire: « Avec cet immeuble-tour qui consomme peu d'énergie, l'écologie prend de la hauteur. La tour *Praetorium* est la première construction du plan de renouveau de la Défense à répondre aux critères de haute qualité environnementale. Elle mesure moins de 30 mètres.[12] » La contradiction de ce propos, portant sur une tour

---

12 | *Télérama – Sortir* 3122 -11 novembre 2009

Image 22: Tour Preatorium, quartier de la défense, Paris

qui n'est pas une tour, peut se comprendre seulement si l'on admet que ce n'est pas par sa hauteur que cet immeuble peut être qualifié de « tour » mais par sa *place* au sein des tours du quartier de la Défense. En d'autre termes, c'est l'aspect syntagmatique qui a pris le pas sur l'aspect paradigmatique et permis ce tour de langage (si j'ose dire) qui fait l'emporter la référence métonymique sur la référence métaphorique.

Naming Things
Terminology, Language Theory and Metaphorology from Alberti to Vignola

MATTEO BURIONI

In his doctoral dissertation Heinrich Wölfflin observes that the Bavarian Ministry of Finance seems to look at us with a "wrinkled forehead," whereas the Palazzo Strozzi has a rather benign outlook despite being completely rusticated.[1] The first building to which Wölfflin referred is no longer extant, as it was demolished by the Nazis to make place for a "parade route" to the *Haus der Kunst*.[2] It was a building designed by Jean-Baptiste Métivier and had a rusticated upper storey. According to Wölfflin, it seemed to frown at the passers-by. In his ground-breaking essay, Wölfflin tried to understand the phenomenon by which we tend to endow architecture with an anthro-

---

1 | I warmly thank Andreas Beyer, James Elkins and Alina Payne for their advice and Nele Putz and Leonore Bartko for their assistance with the revision of my English. "So können wir uns beim Finanzministerium in München des Eindrucks nicht erwehren, daß es die Stirn runzle, ein Palazzo Strozzi dagegen wirkt durch seine höhere Obermauer trotz Rustika nicht unmutig, sondern nur ernst-bedeutsam." Wöfflin, Heinrich, *Prolegomena zu einer Psychologie der Architektur*, mit einem Nachwort von Jasper Cepl, Berlin: Mann 1999, p. 34. The doctoral dissertation was first published as *Prolegomena zu einer Psychologie der Architektur*, München: Wolf 1886
2 | Götz, Christine, *Prinz-Carl-Palais. Vom Palais Salabert zum Sitz des Bayerischen Ministerpräsidenten*, München: Bayerische Vereinsbank 1989, p. 108 and p. 118. See also Rau, Hermann, *Jean-Baptiste Métivier: Architekt, Kgl. Bayerischer Hofbaudekorateur und Baurat (1781-1857)*, Kallmünz: Lassleben 1997, pp. 69-70

pomorphic physiognomy. Hereby, he ventured to establish "a Psychology of Architecture" highly indebted to the theories of *Einfühlung* by the likes of Robert Vischer and Johannes Volkelt.[3] Wölfflin's psychological approach to architecture was equally important for his subsequent *"bestsellers" Renaissance and Baroque* (1888) and *Kunstgeschichtliche Grundbegriffe* (1915). Their paradigmatic value can still be felt in Rudolfs Wittkower's *Architectural Principles in an Age of Humanism* (1948) as well as Erwin Panofsky's *Gothic Architecture and Scholasticism* (1951).[4] The importance of *translation*, in terms of historical terminology and tropes, in the context of a quest for "architectural principles" is still an open one.[5] After all would it be merely "metaphorically speaking" to say that the Palazzo Strozzi looks at us with a serious demeanor? Terminology is one of the most striking and interesting things about architecture. This terminology has been established over centuries in dictionaries and lexica.[6] It was devised to establish a common language, to educate the public and to control the discourse about

---

3 | See for a thorough study of *Einfühlung* Müller-Tamm, Jutta, *Abstraktion als Einfühlung: zur Denkfigur der Projektion in Psychophysiologie, Kulturtheorie, Ästhetik und Literatur der frühen Moderne*, Freiburg im Breisgau: Reimer 2005. See also: Vidler, Anthony, *The architectural uncanny: essays in the modern unhomely*, Cambridge MA: MIT Press 1992

4 | It is as if Panofksy wanted to refute Wöfflin's skeptical questions about the purported link between Gothic Architecture and Scholasticism in his *Renaissance and Baroque*. See Wölfflin, Heinrich, *Renaissance and Barock. Eine Untersuchung über das Wesen und die Entstehung des Barockstils in Italien*, München: Theodor Ackermann 1888, pp. 61-62. The recently discovered "Habilitationsschrift" by Erwin Panofsky with the title "Gestaltungsprinzipien Michelangelos, besonders in ihrem Verhältnis zu denen Raffaels" serves to underscore the Wölfflinian undercurrent in Panofsky's work. For Wittkower see Payne, Alina, "Architectural Principles in the Age of Modernism," in *Journal of the Society of Architectural Historians*, 53, 1994, pp. 322-342

5 | Payne, Aline, *The Architectural Treatise in the Italian Renaissance. Architectural Invention, Ornament and Literary Culture*, Cambridge: Cambridge University Press 2000; Clarke, Georgia, *Architecture and Language. Constructing Identity in European Architecture*, Cambridge University Press 2000

6 | The only systematic study of architectural terminology is Szambien Werner, *Symétrie, goût, caractère: théorie et terminologie de l'architecture à l'âge classique 1550-1800*, Paris: Picard 1986. For Italy see Nencioni, Giovanni, "Sulla

architecture. Why is it that terminology was and still is so important in architecture? Architectural discourse and theory have been haunted by the obsession to name building parts correctly. Sometimes this compulsion to name has come with destructive political implications as in the case of the Swiss ban on "Minarets", somehow reducing the implication and breath of value of an architectural member (e.g. it's long shared history with the bell tower) to one single highly distorted meaning. A secure connection between "words" and "things," between "res" and "verba," seems to be central to the practice of architecture.[7]

The eyebrow of the portal from Vitruvius to Alberti
In describing Ionic portals, Vitruvius says that a *supercilium* (brow or eyebrow in English) must be affixed above the door opening (*lumen* in Latin).[8] Dating back as early as the Renaissance, scholars have been disagreeing about what exactly this *supercilium*, this eyebrow, means in Vitruvius' text. Pierre Gros, editor of the most recent edition, argues that Vitruvius designates the lintel as an "eyebrow."[9] This interpretation is illustrated in Fra Giocondo's 1511 edition of Vitruvius and it can also be found in the marginal note of Guillaume Budé's copy of the treatise.[10] The commentary of the edi-

---

formazione di un lessico nazionale dell'architettura," in *Bollettino d'informazioni*, centro di Ricerche Informatiche per i Beni Culturali 5, 1995, pp. 7-33

7 | Foucault, Michel, *Les mots et les choses: une archéologie des sciences humaines*, Paris: Gallimard 1966; Borst, Arno, *Der Turmbau von Babel: Geschichte der Meinungen über Ursprung und Vielfalt der Sprachen und Völker*, Stuttgart: Hiersemann 1957-1963, 4 Vol.; Demonet, Marie-Luce, *Les voix du signe: nature et origine du langage à la renaissance (1480-1580)*, Paris/Genève: Champion 1992; Maclean, Ian, "Foucault's Renaissance Episteme Reassessed: An Aristotelian Counterblast," in *Journal of the History of Ideas*, No. 59, 1998, pp. 149-166

8 | Vitruvius, *De architectura*, ed. by Pierre Gros, Torino: Einaudi 1997, Vol. I, pp. 388-389, IV, 6, 2

9 | Vitruvius (as note 6), vol. I, p. 330, note 164

10 | Vitruvius, *De architectura per Iocvndvm solito castigatior factvs cvm figvris et tabvla vt iam legi et intellegi possit*, Venezia: Ioannis de Tridino, alias Tacuino 1511, f. 40r, IV, 6, 2; *Hoc in volumine haec opera continetur [Vitruvius, De architectura libri decem edente Johanne Sulpicio]*, Roma: G. Herolt 1486 [Bibliothèque Nationale de France, Signatur: Rés. M-V-48 (1)], f. 61r (Marginal annotation by Guillaume Budé)

tion by Pierre Gros offers an explanation. Vitruvius found the term in his Greek sources (οφρυς) and there a relation between body and building was obviously intended. This is quite probable as the term *supercilium* seems not to have been used by any other writer of classical Latinity in the context of architecture. In the dictionary of Forcellinus there is only one meaning of the term that helps us to understand Vitruvius' use. It can mean the upper delimitation of a landscape and corresponds to our *horizon*.[11] This is also the solution adopted in the commentary by Daniele Barbaro: "*Supercilium id est superlimitare, & est lapis supra antepagmentum superius.*"[12] Barbaro stresses the double meaning of the term: *supercilium* therefore means the upper delimitation of a sensory perception and a concrete architectural member, the lintel. In Vitruvius' idiosyncratic use, the Latin term designates a sensory perception and an essential architectural member. In his treatment of the Ionic portal, Leon Battista Alberti does not use the term *supercilius*. Apparently he disapproved of the idiosyncratic use of language and of the unclear rhetorical status of the term. He then transferred the metaphor to include an auditory dimension. "The Ionians, on the other hand, [...] included, at the top of both jambs and below the thick band of covered mutules, little projecting ears, as I would call them, because of their resemblance to that breed of dog with a keen scent and a fine sense of hearing."[13] With the addition of "as I would call them," Alberti makes the metaphor explicit. Alberti nonetheless avoids using a term to identify the architectural member. As the eighteenth-century English translation by James Leoni was eager to point out, these building elements are called "consoles" by architects.[14] The door posts then are envisaged as the watch dogs of the house. The auditory dimension of doors seems to have been

---

11 | Forcellino, Egidio, *Totius latinitatis lexicon opera et studio Aegidii Forcellini lucubratum [...] auctam et emendatam a Josepho Furlanetto*, Prato: typis Aldinianis 1858-1875, 6 Vol., Ad Indicem

12 | Vitruvius, *M.Vitruvii Pollionis De Architectura Libri Decem Cum Commentariis Danielis Barbari [...]*, Venezia: Francesco Franceschi 1567, p. 141

13 | Alberti, Leon Battista, *On the Art of Building in Ten Books*. translated by Joseph Rykwert, Neil Leach and Robert Tavernor, Cambridge: MIT Press 1988, p. 225

14 | "Besides this, at each End of the Entablature, on the Outside of the Jamb, under the Drip, they made a Sort of Ears, as we may call them, from their Resemblance to the handsome Ears of a fine Spaniel, by Architects called, Consoles." Alberti, Leon Battista, *Ten Books on Architecture by Leon Battista Alberti*, trans-

a quite familiar concept in Alberti's time. The motif of eavesdropping at a closed door is something that often arises in novels and paintings of his time. A miniature attributed to Lorenzo Monaco shows the descent of the Holy Spirit with a few bystanders that ostensibly hold their ears to the closed door.[15] In the well-known *Novella del Grasso Legnanaiulo*, the protagonist, the fat wood carver, holds his head against the door of his own house and is convinced that he can hear himself walking and talking around his house.[16] The reason why Alberti chose to transfer the metaphor to the auditory dimension can thus quite easily be explained by these examples. But there is more to Alberti's correction of Vitruvius. In Alberti's eyes the language of Vitruvius was a complete rhetorical shipwreck. It was probably a metaphorical catachresis in the Greek language from which Vitruvius took the terminus. This Greek meaning could not be transferred into Latin. Instead Alberti made the metaphor explicit and reached a rhetorically satisfactory result.

This instance of the metaphorical shift from visual to auditory sensation in explaining the Ionic portal is entirely representative of Alberti's approach to language. He did not seek a normative, classificatory denomination of architectural terminology, but a terminology that worked rhetorically. He was more interested in adapting the Latin of Vitruvius to the usage of the best Latin writers of antiquity and to the everyday use of his own time. Like for Lorenzo Valla, the use of words, *consuetudo*, was central to establishing their meaning.[17] As a consequence, clear-cut terminology in our modern sense was not a central objective of Alberti's architectural theory. He sought

---

lated into Italian by Cosimo Bartoli and into English by James Leoni, London: Edward Owen for Robert Alfray 1755, p. 152

15 | Kanter, Laurence B. et. al. (eds.), *Painting and Illumination in Early Renaissance Florence 1300-1450*, Ausst.-Kat. Metropolitan Museum of Art, New York 1994, p. 242

16 | *Novella del Grasso legnaiuolo nelle redazioni dei codici Palatino 51 e Palatino 200*, di Bernardo Giambullari e di Bartolomeo Davanzanti, ed. by Antonio Lanza, Firenze: Vallecchi, 1989; *Novella del Grasso Legnaiuolo*, ed. by Paolo Proccacioli, Parma: Guanda 1990. See Bach, Friedrich Teja, "Filippo Brunelleschi and the Fat Woodcarver: the anthropological experiment of perspective and the paradigm of the picture as inlay," in *Res*, Nr. 51 2007, pp. 157-174

17 | Waswo, Richard, *Language and Meaning in the Renaissance*, Princeton: Princeton University Press 1987, pp. 88-112; Monfasani, John, "Was Lorenzo

a coherent rhetorical approach to architectural language which he found by establishing his own terminology. At the beginning of his *Elegantiorum libri*, dedicated to the appropriate use of Latin words, Lorenzo Valla compares his endeavor with the construction of a triumphal arch. Paying tribute to someone who erects a triumphal arch with columns and all pertinent parts and then dedicates the building to a deity or semi-deity, Valla himself erects two columns which he does not dare call "arches." As *opifex*, he dedicates these twelve-foot high columns to his colleague Giovanni Tortelli. With his own hands he chisels a likeness of Nicolas V and puts it at the summit of the arch.[18] While this optimistic and laudatory simile opens the book, Valla is not willing to close the work on an accordingly positive note. In a concluding letter to Tortelli, he likens his endeavor to a vast, cavernous and sinuous labyrinth that was almost impossible to master.[19] Valla apologizes for not having mentioned the problems of his lexical project earlier and explains that at the beginning of a book all self-contempt should be avoided (*vitandus est enim in principio maxime comptemptus operis*). These contrasting analogies that the eminent philologist Lorenzo Valla postulates for his own work on the Latin language are exemplary. On the one hand, it is the aim of a lexical project to establish a firm base for the correct use of language (and architecture); on the other hand, they get inextricably entangled in vaster epistemological and linguistic questions that have no simple solution.

The same is true for Alberti's built architecture, which defies a normative approach to architectural terminology and architectural composition.[20]

Valla an Ordinary Language Philosopher?" in *Journal of the History of Ideas*, Nr. 50, 1989, pp. 309-323

18 | Valla, Lorenzo, *Laurenti Vallae Elegantiarum Libri sex [...]*, Argentorati: Matthiae Shurerii 1517, f. BBiii v.

19 | Valla 1517, f. 209v

20 | Syndikus, Candida, *Leon Battista Alberti. Das Bauornament*, Münster: Rhema 1996; Burns, Howard, "Antike Monumente als Muster und als Lehrstücke. Zur Bedeutung von Antikenzitat und Antikenstudium für Albertis architektonische Entwurfspraxis," in Forster, Kurt W., Lochner, Hubert (eds.), *Theorie der Praxis. Leon Battista Alberti als Humanist und Theoretiker der bildenden Künste*, Berlin: Akademie Verlag 1999, pp. 129-156; Bulgarelli, Massimo, *Leon Battista Alberti 1404-1472. Architettura e storia*, Milano: Electa 2008, pp. 39-51. For a performative use of the metaphor of the living building in Alberti see Burioni, Matteo, "Be-

In his Palazzo Rucellai, for example, he does not use a real superposition of orders like the Coliseum, his main reference for the composition of the facade, does. Instead he uses a simplified Doric order for the ground floor, a Corinthian order adapted from the Mausoleum of Hadrian for the first storey and a roughly hewn Corinthian adapted from the Coliseum for the upper storey. The Corinthian from the Mausoleum of Hadrian is therefore the most elegant capital used in the facade and this capital helps to stress the importance of the *piano nobile* in the house of the Florentine merchant.

Image 23 : Leon Battista Alberti, Palazzo Rucellai, 1448-1450

gründungen des Gemeinwesen. Performative Aspekte frühneuzeitlicher Palastfassaden," in Beyer, Andreas, Burioni, Matteo, Grave, Johannes (eds.), *Das Auge der Architektur. Zur Frage der Bildlichkeit in der Baukunst*, München: Wilhelm Fink Verlag, 2011, pp. 288-319

The architectural vocabulary of the facade is taken from the best sources of antiquity and it is used according to the custom (*consuetudo*) of the present time. The expedient use of visual citations of recognizable antique sources dispensed Alberti of the burden to "name" the building parts he cites. He did not need to worry about what to call this Corinthian capital, he just cited it and in so doing vested his building with all the formal and semantic connotations attached to the antique element.

While "order" as a normative concept is central to later architectural practise and theory, this is not the case with Alberti. For him custom and use were central to establishing and maintaining "order"; an order that is therefore not imposed, but that arises from the use of language and architecture. If we want to cloth the argument in a theoretical garment, we can refer to Hans Blumenberg's *Theory of Metaphor*.[21] "Order" can therefore be termed an "absolute metaphor." According to Blumenberg, this is a defining metaphor that is not explained, but serves as the structure of a whole discourse. In a second step, we can leave the discussion about the "absolute metaphor" of "order" for a moment (I will come back to that) and have a look at how Alberti himself uses metaphors. In his theory, Alberti seems not to be interested in establishing "order" as a leading metaphor. He is more interested in the metaphors that according to Blumenberg structure our everyday life and everyday language, thus metaphors that are inescapable and which – to once again quote Blumenberg – "we live by."[22]

Polyperspective terminology in the Hypnerotomachia Poliphili
The *Hypnerotomachia Poliphili*, published in 1499 in Venice, marks a turning point in the approach to language and architectural terminology.[23] The

---

21 | Blumenberg, Hans, *Paradigms for a metaphorology* [1960], translated from the German with an afterword by Robert Savage, Ithaca (N.Y.): Cornell University Press 2010; Haverkamp, Anselm, *Die Ästhetik der Rhetorik*, München: Fink, 2007, pp. 153-160

22 | Blumenberg, Hans, "Geld oder Leben. Eine metaphorologische Studie zur Konsistenz der Philosophie Georg Simmels" [1976], in Blumenberg, Hans, *Ästhetische und metaphorologische Schriften*, ed. by Anselm Haverkamp, Frankfurt am Main: Suhrkamp 2001, pp. 177-192

23 | For architectural terminology in the Hypnerotomachia see Bredekamp, Horst, "Der 'Traum vom Liebeskampf' als Tor zur Antike," in Beck, Herbert, Bol, Peter C. (eds.), *Natur und Antike in der Renaissance*, Frankfurt am Main: Liebighaus, 1985,

Image 24: *Hypnerotomachia Poliphili*, 1499

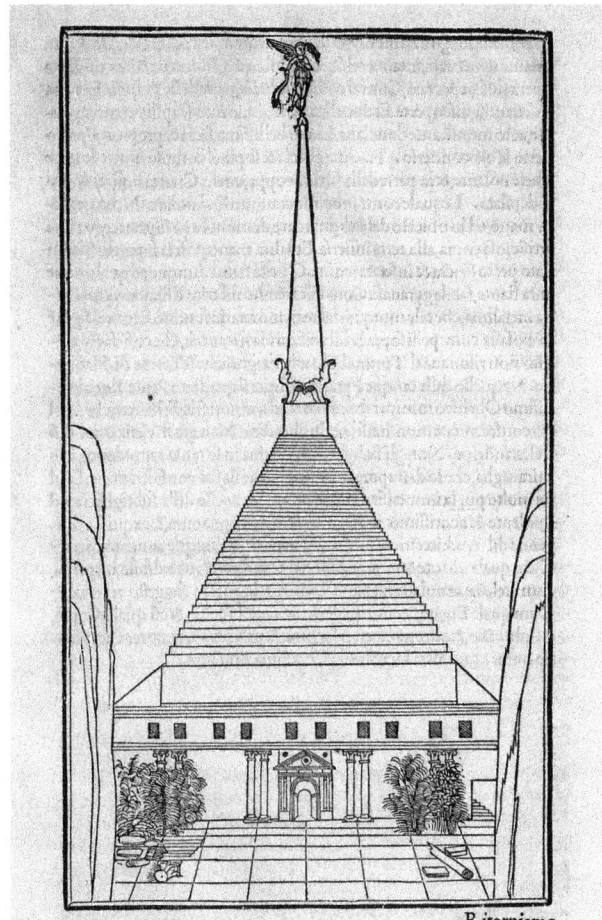

pp. 153-172; Furno, Martine, "L'orthographie de la porta triumphante dans l'Hypnerotomachia Poliphili de Francesco Colonna: un manifeste d'architecture moderne?" in *Mélanges de l'École Française de Rome. Italie et Méditerranée 106*, 1994, pp. 473-516. See Burioni, Matteo, "Das Ich der Baukunst. Traumwandlerische Architekturen in der Hypnerotomachia Poliphili," in Beyer, Andreas, Simon, Ralf, Stierli, Martino (eds.), *Zwischen Architektur und Imagination*, München: Fink, 2013

terminology in the *Hypernotomachia* changes according to the standpoint of the speaker. The polyperspective narration breaks with the humanist illusion that the past can be recovered. Antiquity is lost forever. But let us turn to a central episode in which the protagonist of this architectural dream, Polifilo, stands in front of a mausoleum which he then ventures to describe. I quote the new English translation by Joscelyn Godwin: "Without a doubt, I lack the knowledge that would allow me to describe it perfectly, especially since in our time the proper vernacular and native terms peculiar to the art of architecture are buried and extinct, along with the true men."[24] Poliphilo ostensibly utters these dead words in his cumbersome description of the wonderful, indescribable monument. He uses four words to name the base of the pyramid. Following the Vitruvian usage he calls it a *"plinthe"* and following Alberti's terminology he continues by naming it a *"latastrus"*. He also adds the Italian circumlocutions *"quadrato"* and *"pedamento."*[25] The text therefore seems to suggest that the denomination of architectural elements is dependant on the standpoint of the viewer. The architectural description opens up a polyperspective narrative space. To denote the columnar orders, he introduces the rare word *"columnatione"* that is only used by Alberti in his architectural treatise. In the ongoing description, he expresses many technical terms for seldom applied words and terms that had never before been used in this way. Thus, the text ostensibly declares the death and irrevocable loss of antiquity. A wonderful example is the use of "metope" to denote the front of the pyramid that Polifilo describes.[26] This is complete nonsense as "metope" only makes sense in the context of the Doric order where it features in the frieze alternating with triglyphs. However, the commentary to the recent Italian edition by Mino Gabriele notes that in the description of the pyramid of Cheops, Herodotus applies the word "metope" to denote the front of the pyramid.[27] The Hypnerotomachia then features dead and buried words from far-flung reach-

---

24 | Colonna, Francesco, *Hypnerotomachia Poliphili*, ed. by Marco Ariani und Mino Gabriele, 2 Vols., Milano: Adelphi 2006, Vol. I, p. 31 (f. bIIIIr); Colonna, Francesco, *Hypnerotomachia Poliphili: the strife of love in a dream*, translated by Joscelyn Godwin, London: Thames & Hudson 1999, p. 31
25 | See the notes in Colonna, Francesco, *Hypnerotomachia Poliphili*, ed. by. Giovanni Pozzi/Lucia A. Ciapponi, 2 Vol., Padua: Antenore 1980, Vol. II, pp. 58-64
26 | Colonna 1999, Vol. I, p. 31 (f. bIIIIr)
27 | Herodotus, *Historiae*, 2, 124. See Colonna 1999, Vol. II, p. 580, note. 7

es of the corpus of Roman and Greek literature. These words are encased like precious gems in the text of the *Hypnerotomachia*. The word "metope" is simply not comprehensible if the Italian word *"fronte"* had not been added. The *Hypnerotomachia* therefore seems to postulate that the name given to things depends on the standpoint of the beholder. The label attached to a building element can only be understood if supported by a given culture. The humanist project to recover antiquity and apply the appropriate words to the corresponding building elements has failed. It is only possible to confront the diverse labels attached to things and emphasize the pertinence of these words by linking them to an original context that gave them a distinct meaning. Consequently, there can be no true terminology since it changes in relation to the cultural horizon of the speaker. The antiquarian project of the Renaissance is radically criticized in the *Hypnerotomachia*. The language of antiquity is dead, it cannot be revived.

Order disputed between Michelangelo and Sangallo
After the death of Antonio da Sangallo the Younger a dispute arose over the completion of the Palazzo Farnese in Rome. It focused on the design of the monumental cornice that defines and delimitates the upper storey of the building. After Michelangelo had presented a first version of this monumental cornice as a wooden model in real-life proportions on the actual facade to Pope Paul III, a harsh critique was voiced against Michelangelo's

Image 25: Antonio da Sangallo the Younger and Michelangelo, Palazzo Farnese

design by the workshop members of Antonio da Sangallo.[28] Antonio da Sangallo had planned to add a big cornice to the palace commensurate to its height, but the building element designed by Michelangelo was much bigger and appeared a monstrosity to the Sangallo camp. In his letter to Pope Paul III the workshop member of Sangallo criticized that "the cornice is so heavy that it threatens to pull to the ground the whole facade. The cornice is too big for the facade and one should see that it does not overshadow the whole facade."[29] This critique is underpinned by extensive citations from Vitruvius' treatise on architecture. In the eyes of the Sangallo camp, the cornice was a kind of upper frame that delimitates the facade. Sangallo was convinced that it was possible to reach a "true reading" of Vitruvius that could solve all terminological problems. Thus, his conception of order was normative. The monumental cornice which Michelangelo designed was not proportionally related to the building, but was designed to be perceived in the larger context of the city. It was meant as a kind of "crown," that permitted one to distinguish the Palazzo Farnese, as the pope's palace, from all other family palaces in Rome. Michelangelo's design could be legitimized by using the original Latin word that Vitruvius used for the cornice: *"corona"*. *"Corona"* in Latin means cornice, but can also be understood as "crown". Therefore, in Michelangelo's eyes, the monumental cornice of the Palazzo Farnese was not justified by any reference to the "timeless Vitruvian rules" of architecture, but by a personal interpretation of Vitruvian terminology. Michelangelo's interpretation suited the patron. It was justified by the papal idea of power, the *plenitudo potestatis* that should manifest itself in the architectural projects of the pope. Two conceptions of "order" coincided in the middle of the sixteenth century with the design of the Palazzo Farnese. Sangallo's conception of "order" was conceived according to a normative interpretation of Vitruvius, whereas Michelangelo's was conceived according to a personal interpretation of Vitruvius. Sangallo tried to establish normative rules of architecture that

---

28 | Frommel, Christoph Luitpold, *Der römische Palastbau der Hochrenaissance*, 3 Vols., Tübingen: Wasmuth 1973, Vol. I, pp. 110-101; Frommel, Christoph Luitpold, "La construction et décoration du Palais Farnèse," in *Palais Farnèse*, ed. by École Française de Rome, Roma: École Française de Rome 1981, Vol. I,1, pp. 125-174, p. 161

29 | Pagliara, Pier Nicola, "Alcune minute autografe di G. Battista da Sangallo," in *Architettura Archivi – fonti e storia 1*, 1982, pp. 25-52, p. 33 [translation by MB]

legitimate the discipline and render it autonomous. Michelangelo countered this idea and gave visibility to an idea of "order" that referred to the political power of the pope. He sought to compare his artistic freedom to the sovereignty of the pope.[30]

History of concepts and fantastic figures
Returning to Wöfflin, the question arises if the physiognomic investment in a building front is not dependent on the geographical and historical specific genesis of the term *"façade"*. The term *"façade"* was unknown to the architectural language of antiquity. Vitruvius uses the term *"frons"* which is translated as "forehead" and was applied for the street front of the building.[31] The change of the concept from "frons" to *"faccia"* seems then to indicate a change in the complete outlook of architecture. The facade is the face of the building. It gives the building a recognizable and public appearance. If we want to take a closer look at the meaning of *"faccia"* during the Renaissance, we can have a look at the definition of Lorenzo Valla. He distinguishes between *"facies"* and *"vultus"*: "The face is an image of the body."[32] Whereas *"facies"* is related to the body, *"vultus"* is related to the movements of the soul. So the physiognomic investment in the front of the building is somehow dependent on the raise of the concept that the building should have a "face." Following the work of Reinhard Koselleck, Bernhard Jussen and Jaques Guilhaumou, a history of architectural concepts could be realized.[33]

---

30 | Bredekamp, Horst, "Zwei Souveräne: Paul III. und Michelangelo; das motu proprio vom Oktober 1549," in Satzinger, Georg, Schütze, Sebastian (eds.), *Sankt Peter in Rom 1506 – 2006*, Beiträge der internationalen Tagung vom 22. - 25. Februar 2006 in Bonn, München: Hirmer, 2008, pp. 147-157
31 | See "Fassade," in *Reallexikon der Deutschen Kunstgeschichte*, ed. by Zentralinstitut für Kunstgeschichte München, begonnen von Otto Schmitt, 10 Vols., Stuttgart: Metzler 1937-2003, Bd. 7, Sp. 538-543 (Wolfgang Prohaska)
32 | "facies est quasi fictura et effigies corporis," in Valla, *Elegantiae*, 1517 (as note 16), f. 115r
33 | Koselleck, Reinhart, *The practice of conceptual history: timing history, spacing concepts*, Stanford: Stanford University Press 2002; Jussen, Bernhard, *Der Name der Witwe. Erkundungen zur Semantik der mittelalterlichen Bußkultur*, Veröffentlichungen des Max-Planck-Instituts für Geschichte 158, Göttingen: Vandenhoeck & Ruprecht 2000; Guilhaumou, Jacques, *Discours et événement. L'Histoire langagière des concepts*, Besançon: Presses Universitaire de Franche-

A particular use of architectural terminology is therefore dependant on and informed by the contemporary idea of language. This can be shown by a comparison of the approaches of Alberti and Valla. For both custom, *consuetudo*, was the leading and central concept. Following the apparent loss of certainty envisaged by the architectural romance of the *Hypnerotomachia Poliphili*, an ever more pervasive idea of order took hold of architecture. This leading concept of order was then irrevocably put in question by the architecture of Michelangelo. At the end of the century, the imposition of order was no longer invoked in the name of timeless "rules of architecture" as it was by the members of the Sangallo supporters, but it was increasingly thought of as an arbitrary and personal imposition. In this vein, Vignola established a new rule for the architectural orders, but he did explicitly state that he "found it" and even ostensibly prefaced the work with his own effigy.[34] The same could be said of Andrea Palladio, who provided an incomparably accurate account of the architecture of antiquity and at the same time displayed his oeuvre as an exemplary role-driven architectural planning mode. The systems of Palladio and Vignola with all their weight and authority are both very personal creations that do not hide their auctorial dimension.[35] Neither of them claimed to have found the "rules of architecture" or that such rules could ever be found outside of the personal oeuvre of the architect. These timeless rules, which for a short period some architects of the Renaissance were confident of being able to establish, turned out to be a

---

Comté 2006. For architectural history see Oechslin, Werner, *Stilhülse und Kern: Otto Wagner, Adolf Loos und der evolutionäre Weg zur modernen Architektur*, Zürich: gta verlag 1994; Forty, Adrian, *Words and buildings: a vocabulary of modern architecture*, London: Thames and Hudson 2000

34 | Thoenes, Christof, "Vignolas 'Regola delli cinque ordini'," in *Römisches Jahrbuch für Kunstgeschichte* 20, 1983, pp. 345-376

35 | See Beyer, Andreas, "Opere senza giorni: i 'Quattro Libri'; un'autobiografia," in Barbieri, Franco, Battilotti, Donata et al. (eds.), *Palladio: 1508 - 2008. Il Simposio del cinquecentenario*, Centro Internazionale di Studi di Architettura Andrea Palladio, Venezia: Marsilio 2008, pp. 199-201. For the biography of the architect see Burioni, Matteo, *Die Renaissance der Architekten. Profession und Souveränität des Baukünstlers in Giorgio Vasaris Viten*, Berlin: Mann 2008; Burioni, Matteo, "Biographie als Theorie: der Wagemut des Architekten bei Vasari, Bellori und Félibien," in Oechslin, Werner, *Architekt und/versus Baumeister: die Frage nach dem Metier*, Zürich: Gta-Verlag 2009, pp. 30-39

futile endeavor that could only be understood as the personal rules of each individual architect. The terminology and language theory of the Renaissance also had its ludic aspects and two little known French architectural theorists put forward such a highly erudite *"divertissements"*: Hugues Sambin and Joseph Boillot.[36] Sambin in his *Oeuvre de la diversité des termes dont on use en Architecture* features a carnivalesque *détournement* of architectural order in a seemingly orderly fashion. He presents fifteen orders of Hermes of his own creation. We do not know much about this interesting architect, but he seems to play with the double meaning of "terme" in French. It can mean "herme" or it can mean "term or concept".[37] So while the idea of columnar order is subverted by his endless variants of herms, at the same time the language of architecture is absurdly enriched with an abundance of new creations. The same is true of Joseph Boillot, who, to the contrary, invented a whole range of animal herms. He thought it not appropriate for human beings to bear the weight of an edifice and with this good proposition he ventured to envisage a whole new system of columnar order. His treatise features almost all animals as herms. The animals are ordered in an ascending order culminating in the ape. These two lesser figures are representatives of a moment of great experimentation in architectural thinking.

A similar combination of rationality and fantasy that we have encountered in these two French figures of the late sixteenth century is present in the Paris of the nineteenth century. As the wonderful last book of the American medievalist, Michael Camille, shows, the great theorist and restorer,

---

[36] See Choné, Paulette, "Faire le Beau pour faire la paix considérations sur les bêtes dressées de Joseph Boillot (1592)," in Enenkel, Karl A. E., Smith, Paul J. (eds.), *Early modern zoology: the construction of animals in science, literature and the visual arts*, Leiden: Brill 2007, pp. 567-601; Gulczynski, Henri-Stéphane, "L'Oeuvre de la Diversité des Termes' de Hugues Sambin, à Lyon en 1572," in Deswarte-Rosa, Sylvie (ed.), *Sebastiano Serlio à Lyon: architecture et imprimerie*, Lyon: Mémoire Active, 2004, Vol. I, pp. 462-465. See also Gartenmeister, Marion, "Karyatiden. Zu selbstreflexiven Tendenzen in der Architektur," in Beyer, Andreas, Burioni, Matteo, Grave, Johannes (eds.), *Das Auge der Architektur. Zur Frage der Bildlichkeit in der Baukunst*, München: Wilhelm Fink Verlag 2011

[37] The double meaning of "terme" is suggested by the introductory sonnet of Estienne Tabourot see Sambin, Huges, *Oeuvre de la diversite de termes, dont on use en Architecture, reduict en ordre*, Lyon: Jean Durant 1572, p. 5

Image 26 & 27: Huges Sambin, Oeuvre de la diversite de termes, dont on use en Architecture, eduict en ordre, 1572; Joseph Boillot, Nouveaux portraits et figures de termes pour user en l'architecture, 1592

Viollet-Le-Duc, who studied Gothic architecture, designed a whole set of new fantastic creatures for the balconies of Notre Dame de Paris according to a rigorous and systematic plan.[38] These new creations were monsters of reason as they were backed by the art historical acumen and authority of the great restorer and scholar Viollet-le-Duc. It is only in recent times that the paternity of these fantastic monstrosities has been recognized. Architecture and architectural history should acknowledge that they are continuously producing "monsters," fanciful terms of their own choosing, artfully concealed behind the veil of disciplinary language.

Image 28: Emanuele Viollet-Le-Duc, Gargoyle

---

38 | Camille, Michael, *The gargoyles of Notre-Dame: medievalism and the monsters of modernity*, Chicago: The University of Chicago Press 2009, pp. 4-50

From Design Generator to Rhetorical Device
Metaphor in Architectural Discourse

ROSARIO CABALLERO-RODRIGUEZ

"In architecture as in medicine or law, 'learning the language' is inseparable from mastering the craft as a whole."
Thomas Markus, Deborah Cameron 2002[1]

"Much of the interest of [architecture's] critical vocabulary goes into the choice of particular metaphors to structure thought and experience. [The question is] why have some metaphors succeeded better than others?"
Adrian Forty 2000[2]

As postulated by what is known as the Contemporary Metaphor Theory (CMT) after Lakoff & Johnson's *Metaphors We Live by* (1980),[3] metaphor plays a critical role in the ways knowledge is organized in our mind. Because of metaphor, information from one familiar or concrete domain of experience (the metaphorical 'source') is 'mapped' onto a less familiar domain

---

[1] | Markus, Thomas, Cameron, Deborah, *The words between the spaces: buildings and language*, London: Routledge, 2002, pp. 2-3
[2] | Forty, Andrew, *Words and Buildings. A Vocabulary of Modern Architecture*. London: Thames & Hudson, 2000, p. 43
[3] | Lakoff, George, Johnson, Mark, *Metaphors We Live by*, Chicago & London: Chicago University Press, 1980

(the 'target') which is conceptualized in terms of the former – a definition that borrows the 'transfer', 'carrying over' meaning of the original Greek term *metapherein*.

Interestingly, architecture has been systematically used in understanding and verbalizing notions and activities outside its realm. One such metaphor is THEORIES ARE BUILDINGS[4] whereby the abstract notion THEORY is construed as having *building blocks, foundations* and *frameworks* (i.e. as requiring some sort of *buttressing*), and is qualified as *strong, solid* or *standing* when successful or as *shaky* and *falling apart* when less so. Likewise, human cognition, language, relationships, feelings, and products of human creativity (e.g. music) are often discussed as having an *architecture* – which, again, involves using building language when referring to their more specific 'components' and traits. In other words, architecture and buildings provide the immediate, tangible sources in our understanding of more abstract experiences and concepts or targets – as suggested by the language used to discuss them.

However, while the role of architecture as a productive source in our metaphorical construal of the world is well documented in CMT, the metaphors concerned with architecture itself – i.e. where architecture is the target – remain largely underexplored regardless of the fact that architects have always used concepts and entities outside the architectural realm in order to think of and discuss their practice.[5] In this chapter I survey some of the

---

4 | Following CMT conventions, the metaphors under discussion in this paper are rendered in SMALL CAPITALS, and the metaphorical language from and in the examples in *italics*.

5 | But see: Ackerman, John, Oates, Scott, "Image, text, and power in architectural design and workplace writing," in Duin, Ann Hill, Hansen, Craig J. (Ed.), *Non-academic Writing: Social Theory and Technology*, Mahwah, NJ: Lawrence Erlbaum Associates, 1996, p. 81-121; Caballero, Rosario, *Re-Viewing Space. Figurative Language in Architects' Assessment of Built Space*. Berlin & New York: Mouton de Gruyter, 2006; Caballero, Rosario, "The role of metaphor in architectural appreciation: A look at reviews from the 19th and 20th centuries," in Radighieri, Sara, Tucker, Paul (Ed.), *Point of View. Description and Evaluation across Discourses*, Rome: Officina, 2009, p.69-95; Markus, Cameron 2002; Medway, Peter, "Writing, speaking, drawing: The distribution of meaning in architects' communication," in

most salient metaphors in architectural discourse. My discussion is theoretically anchored in CMT, and mostly draws upon data retrieved from a 132-text corpus of architectural reviews since this is the discourse context where metaphor's ubiquity and instrumental role in the discipline may be best appreciated.

Metaphorical sources and targets in the language of architects
In architecture metaphor *is* knowledge: it is used from day one by architects, and informs all the stages of building design. Thus, metaphor helps architects think a building and translate their preliminary ideas into drawn form, motivates a fair amount of architectural jargon, and plays a critical role in post-construction assessment discourse practices. Metaphor's role as design *trigger* or *primary generator* (Darke 1979)[6] in the early stages of thinking a building is addressed in the passage below, where Zvi Hecker explains how one of his projects started to take shape:

"The school was designed in a form of a flower [...] since *its seeds orbit the sun and the sun rays illuminate all of the schoolrooms.* [...] Walls *rose* and the building began to *emerge.* In time it became evident that *the school*, whilst under construction, *was gradually transforming into an intricate city. Streets and courtyards followed the paths of the orbits and the infinitesimal traces of the sun rays.* [...] The building was nearing completion when an uncertainty arose. By now the construction resembled neither a sunflower nor a city but *a book whose open pages carry the load of the construction.* Building a book was not our guiding principle, and experts had to be consulted as to the

---

Sharples, Mike, Van der Geest, Thea (eds.), *The New Writing Environment: Writers at Work in a World of Technology*, London: Springer Verlag, 1996, pp. 25-42; Medway, Peter, Clark, Bob, "Imagining the building: Architectural design as semiotic construction," in *Design Studies* 24, 2003, pp. 255-273

6 | Darke, Jane, "The primary generator and the design process," in *Design Studies* 1, 1979, pp. 36-44; see also Goldschmidt, Gabriela, "Visual displays for design: Imagery, analogy and databases of visual images," in Koutamanis Alexander, Timmerman, Harry, Vermeulen Ilse (Ed.), *Visual Data Bases in Architecture*, Aldershot, UK: Averbury, 1995, pp. 53-74; Lawson, Bryan, Shee, Ming Loke, "Computers, words, and pictures," in *Design Studies* 18, 1997, p. 171-183; Casakin, Hernan, Goldschmidt, Gabriela, "Expertise and the use of visual analogy: Implications for design education," in *Design Studies* 20, 1999, pp. 153-175

cause of the continually mutating images. Following a lengthy Talmudic debate, the school was eventually found to be built correctly. It was acknowledged that the sunflower, when transplanted from the Holy Land to Berlin evolved naturally into a book. [...] Oblivious to these transformations were only the school children. They had to discover themselves how *the sunflower* absorbs the light into its *deeply cut canyons* and reflects it upon the *pages of an open book*, and how in turn *the House of the Book becomes a city of streets, courtyards and places to hide*. [...] the House of The Book is not the building of a School, but *a landscape of our childhood dreams*."[7]

Images 29 & 30: Zvi Hecker, School, Berlin, 1992

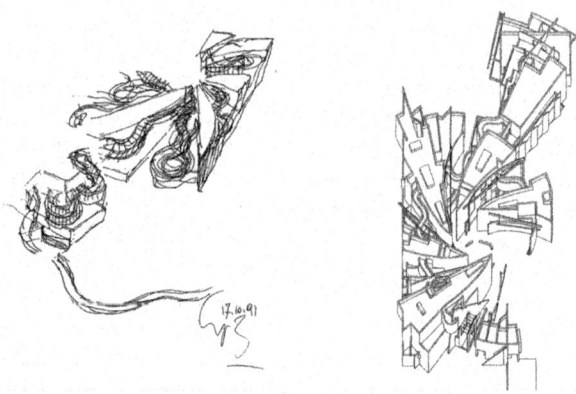

This example illustrates how Hecker's initial ideas gradually evolved into new ones, a process that involved the use of different metaphors: what starts as a *sunflower* turns into *an intricate city* and ends up being *a book* –an evolution also suggested in drawings and plans. This mixture of metaphors also focuses on diverse aspects of the building at issue, from its visual properties (e.g. streets as *canyons* and supporting elements as *book pages*) to the more abstract and/or symbolic concerns underlying its design (the bookish and/or dreamlike quality of the final ensemble). The latter role is the topic of the ensuing sections.

---

7 | Text and drawings provided by Hecker Studio, *Heinz-Galinski-Schule Jewish Primary School Berlin*, Dcbln-01\50.PBLC\pblc.project\pblc.jews\jews_text\ jews_20050215_building of the school_EN.doc

Metaphor and architectural jargon

A fair amount of architecture's jargon is undeniably metaphorical – a quality nevertheless 'obscured' by the conventional status of professional language. Most metaphors in architecture draw upon the natural sciences, cloth making and textiles, spatial mechanics, linguistic interaction, and music (Forty 2000; Caballero 2006). Thus, insights from the natural sciences elaborated architects' long-standing anthropomorphic views of space, foregrounding the functional and structural properties of built artefacts and motivating terms such as *skin, skeleton, bowels* or *circulation* among others. Buildings' functional properties are also informed by spatial mechanics, whereby elements in a building are often referred to as its *mechanisms* or *mechanics* (e.g. Le Corbusier's views of houses as *machines for living*). Finally, structural linguistics underlies views of buildings as intelligible and readable *texts* which result from the correct combination of *lexical* devices in accordance with *grammatical* rules. Other metaphors come from such different activities as cloth making (e.g. *cladding, jacketing, sheathing, sheeting, curtain wall*) and music (*rhythm*). Finally, and in accordance with the visual concerns of the discipline, any entity with a clear shape is also recurrently used to refer to building elements. Table 1 displays some of the metaphorical jargon found in architectural texts:

Table 1. Metaphorically motivated jargon

Metaphorical frames	Metaphors and examples
ORGANIC	BUILDINGS ARE LIVING ORGANISMS *skin, membrane, skeleton, rib, haunch, hip, footer/footing, blister, fatigue, bleeding*
TEXTILES	ARCHITECTURAL PRACTICE IS CLOTH MAKING *stitch, weave, thread* BUILDINGS/CITIES ARE CLOTH *city's/building's fabric, tightly-knit (spaces)* BUILDING ELEMENTS ARE PIECES OF CLOTH/CLOTHING *cladding, jacketing, sheath(ing), sheeting, curtain wall, apron, blanket, sleeve*

LANGUAGE	ARCHITECTURE IS LANGUAGE
	imagery, lexicon, vocabulary, syntax, idiom
	BUILDINGS ARE TEXTS
	vernacular
MACHINE	BUILDINGS ARE MACHINES
	machine, mechanisms, mechanics
MUSIC	ARCHITECTURAL PRACTICE IS MUSICAL PRACTICE
	choreograph, orchestrate
	BUILDINGS ARE MUSICAL PIECES
	rhythm
SHAPES (geometry/alphabet)	
3-D OBJECTS	*I-beam, I-joist, J channel, V-truss roof valley, saddle, box, barge, butterfly/ sawtooth roof, ring beam, half-barrel/ barrel/corbel/fan/groin/net/spiral vault*

The twofold dimension of architecture as a craft and art, i.e. as driven by both aesthetic and intellectual concerns, is reflected in the various metaphors informing architectural language, which may be concerned with abstract knowledge (*conceptual* metaphors), visual knowledge (*image* metaphors) or a mixture of both. Consider the following example:

"The walls of the wedge-like form *are clad* entirely *in a* delicately translucent glass *skin*, so that the building is perceived as a series of elements encased within *a shimmering membrane*."[8]

Here *clad* instantiates a textile metaphor and refers to the architect's intervention in the building. In turn, *membrane* and *skin* are informed by a biological metaphor, and focus on the visual properties and function of the building's outer surface. Put differently, *clad* and *skin* appear to instantiate two conceptual metaphors whereas *membrane* would illustrate an image metaphor. However, distinguishing between the visual and non-visual information in architecture is a tricky issue since many expressions combine both 'types' of knowledge in agreement with the idiosyncrasy of the discipline. In fact, irrespective of their conceptual bias, both *clad* and *skin* retain an unmistakably visual 'flavour' – a knowledge combination best

---

8 | "Manchester Metropolis," in *The Architectural Review*, April 2000, italic by RCR

illustrated by such conventional terms in architectural jargon as *skeleton* or *rib*, both combining physiological (abstract) and anatomical (visual) information.

A more sensible approach, then, involves paying attention to the general functions covered by different metaphors, that is, whether they focus on the processes undergone by architects to achieve particular design solutions or on the products of their work (i.e. buildings).

Focus on process versus focus on product
Process-focused metaphors draw attention to the combinatory procedures involved in architectural design, portraying them in terms of seemingly related practices. Some such metaphors are ARCHITECTURAL PRACTICE IS CLOTH-MAKING, DESIGNING A BUILDING IS EXPERIMENTING, ARCHITECTURE IS LANGUAGE or ARCHITECTURAL PRACTICE IS MUSICAL PRACTICE, as exemplified below:

"The delicacy with which [the architect] *has stitched the new to the old* recalls Foster's work at the Royal Academy."[9]

"Eric Owen Moss, *the architectural alchemist* who turns base buildings into sites of revelation, *has conducted another brilliant experiment* in Culver City, California."[10]

"Holl studies *architecture's rhetoric*; he uses typological conventions and elements to create new meanings. In the Cranbrook science center, Holl begins with *the basic vocabulary of foursquare enclosures* infiltrated by oblique angles at facade openings."[11]

"Through carefully *choreographed* handling of light and fastidious attention to detail, Kalach *orchestrates* an extraordinarily lyrical spatial and sensual experience."[12]

---

9 | "Pastoral Idyll," in *The Architectural Review*, February 1999, italic by RDC
10 | "The Glass Fantastic," in *Architecture*, March 2000, italic by RDC
11 | "Between Typology and Fetish," in *Architecture*, March 1999, italic by RDC
12 | "Mexican Labyrinth," in *The Architectural Review*, July 2000, italic by RDC

These metaphors rest upon rich knowledge schemas which include procedures, agents, and products (i.e. cover a broad scope of topics); hence, their linguistic instantiations may suggest a concomitant view of architects as CLOTH-MAKERS, EXPERIMENTERS, WRITERS or COMPOSERS/CONDUCTORS and of buildings as TEXTILE ARTEFACTS, EXPERIMENTS, TEXTS or MUSICAL PIECES irrespective of whether the expressions refer to both in such explicit terms. In other words, given their all-encompassing quality, many process-focused metaphors subsume product-focused metaphors. All in all, however, most product-focused metaphors draw upon *organic, inorganic,* and *motion* sources, and are used to refer to, describe and assess buildings according to (a) their functional or 'behavioural' properties, and (b) their external appearance.

Inorganic metaphors are basically concerned with external appearance, i.e. carry visual information – the exception being the metaphor BUILDINGS ARE MACHINES. Among the diversity of sources used for conveying what buildings and building elements look like, we find common, everyday-life objects (*hairpin, umbrella, fan*), terms denoting shapes of diverse sorts (*box, pinwheel, surfboard*), and even food items (*baguette, wedding cake, blancmange*). The following examples illustrate the richness of some such sources:

"The green glass wall [the rear facade of a café] becomes transparent [...]. *An aviary without birds or a fish tank without fish*: one is forced to look at a detritus of bogong moths, palm leaves, cigarette packets and grime."[13]

"[T]he basic parti of the bank building is *a three-sided doughnut,* with corridors that triangulate around a light well."[14]

"[The residential wing] subdivides into *three dormitory pods* along a west-facing veranda, with east-facing verandas between *each pod*."[15]

Indeed, a large amount of architectural jargon appears to be motivated by visual metaphors: from nouns used to refer to structural elements in a building (*slit, box, strip, pod, star*) or noun + noun compounds concerned

---

13 | "Chifley Square," in *Architecture Australia*, 1998, italic by RDC
14 | "Hidden Assets," in *Architecture*, February 2000, italic by RDC
15 | "Between Two Worlds," in *Architecture*, August 1999, italic by RDC

with types of such elements (*bowstring truss, ring beam, wheel arch, saw tooth roof, V truss*). Both – referential and classifying – uses respond to the visual, aesthetic bias of architectural practice.

Other recurrent terms dealing with buildings' external appearance draw upon animal or plant sources, and instantiate the metaphor BUILDINGS ARE LIVING ORGANISMS (organisms which are often specified as human). This is the case of adjectives *muscular, masculine, feminine, strong, sinewy, lithe,* or *sexy,* all of which highlight form rather than function:

"A linear bar capped by a huge roof, the [building] is *muscular* yet precise, like the sport itself."[16]

"[T]he tower is a chromatic apparition of saturated red and blue, with a *litheness* and depth not evident elsewhere in Legorreta's *stout* forms."[17]

Nevertheless, the main focus of organic metaphors is buildings' functional and/or 'behavioural' traits. The most conspicuous – and long standing – metaphor is BUILDINGS ARE PEOPLE whereby buildings are presented as susceptible to having moods and personality, playing social roles, or having kinship relationships with the buildings in their surroundings. This is suggested whenever buildings appear as the syntactic subjects of verbs prototypically related to human activities (e.g. *speak, succeed, seek* or *aim*) or are qualified as *friendly, brooding, ungainly* or *unassuming,* to list but a few of the personifying adjectives found in building assessment). This personification of buildings is illustrated below:

"Despite its size and location, *the building doesn't engage its neighbours; rather, it politely turns its back to them.*"[18]

"This building, *which steadfastly refused to pretend it was old but never wore its newness with pretension,* is now an historic monument and canonic work of modern architecture."[19]

---

16 | "Shooting Star," in *The Architectural Review,* October 2000, italic by RDC
17 | "Chromatic Cloister," in *Architecture,* February 1999, italic by RDC
18 | "Light Wash," in *Architecture,* October 1999, italic by RDC
19 | "Back to School," in *Architecture,* January 2000, italic by RDC

A final recurrent metaphor in architectural texts is FORM IS MOTION. This is instantiated by verbs such *climb, rise, step, fly, hover, meander, emerge, cling* and the like, and reflects a long-time concern in the discipline with architecture that 'moves'.[20] The following examples illustrate this dynamic rendering of buildings:

"Based on a boomerang shaped plan, the new building *steps down* from a prow at its south end *to embrace* a new public space."[21]

"The new library *eases* gently into a Wild West landscape of rolling forested hills and snow-capped mountains."[22]

"One geologically contoured part of the building *heaves up* from the site [...] while another part *thrusts* toward the intersection [...]."[23]

Here particular spatial layouts (the metaphorical targets) are seen as reminiscent of the kind of movement expressed by the motion verbs (the metaphorical sources). In other words, perception and understanding of spatial arrangements and topologies derives from a more basic understanding of particular ways of moving.

In sum, the difficult, elusive nature of space, and the complexities involved in its handling for human use appear to lie at the heart of architects' reliance on metaphors of diverse sorts, as attested by the long lineage of some of the most recurrent metaphors in contemporary architectural communication. These co-exist with more ad-hoc, often visual, metaphors – both 'old' and 'new' types being, nevertheless, an intrinsic part of the discipline and the discourse around it.

---

20 | Caballero, Rosario. "FORM IS MOTION, Dynamic predicates in English architectural discourse," in Thornburg, Linda, Panther, Klaus-Uwe, Barcelona, Antonio (eds.), *Metonymy and Metaphor in Grammar*, Amsterdam & Philadelphia: John Benjamins, 2009, pp. 277-290
21 | "Manchester Metropolis," in *The Architectural Review*, April 2000, italic by RDC
22 | "Rustic Regionalism," in *The Architectural Review*, June 1998, italic by RDC
23 | "Hidden Assets," in *Architecture*, February 2000, italic by RDC

The use of metaphor in reviewing space
Architectural reviews (ARs) are aimed at describing and evaluating built arrangements. These two rhetorical goals not only underlie the genre's textual organization around three distinct sections (Introduction, Description, and Closing Evaluation) and subsections within these, but also influence reviewers' use metaphor.[24]
Metaphorically motivated jargon is the most blatant case of metaphor used for descriptive purposes – a function intrinsically linked to its referential role. Metaphorical language – particularly, instantiations of visual metaphors – also reflects architects' constant handling of different dimensions and perspectives when representing and describing space, as shown in the following example:

Image 31: Peter Hübner, Horthaus Bremen, 1996

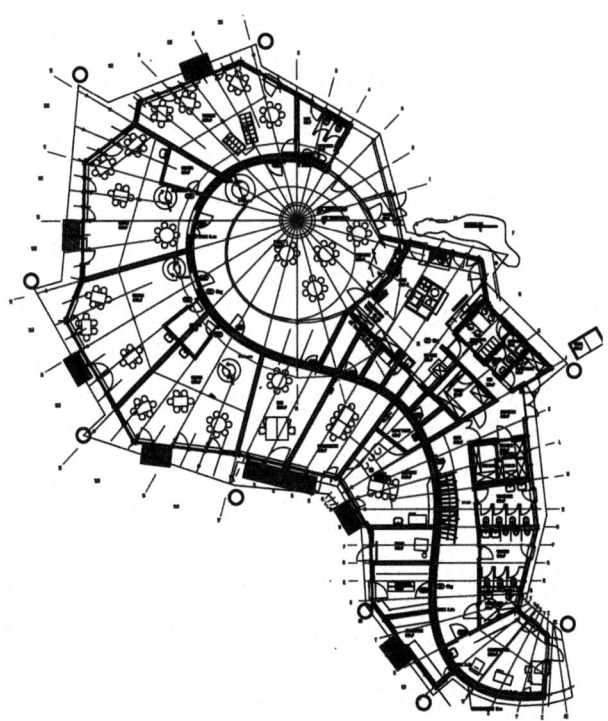

---

24 | Caballero 2006

"As a free-standing element, [a crèche in Bremen] needed to be curved for stability, and the curve chosen prompted the development of *a tadpole-like plan* with entrance and social centre in *the head*. In the developing narrative about the building *the serpentine wall doubled as a city-wall and as the remains of an imagined fossil creature – the Urtier. The thick, solid brick wall is visibly the spine of the whole, emerging naked externally in the tail.* It contrasts everywhere with the flimsiness of the timber parts that *butt up against it* [...] The combination of radial and linear principles in the plan allows transition between centrality in *the head* and a route distributing to either side in *the tail*. [...] The wall *runs* north-south. [...] The spatial organization presented to a small child could scarcely be simpler: from a distance *the building is a kind of mound or crouching creature* with very low eaves to bring the scale down."[25]

This building is first introduced in two-dimensional, flat terms ("tadpole-like") in agreement with the shape suggested by its ground plan. Likewise, its two furthermost extremes are later referred to as the "head" and "tail" respectively. The shift towards three-dimensionality occurs by qualifying the central wall in the complex as a "spine emerging naked," and by comparing it to a "mound or crouching creature." These metaphor clusters are usually found in the Description section of ARs and in the captions of the visuals accompanying the main text.

Metaphor is also an evaluation tool, and this role is often textually marked in ARs. For instance, reviews often open with a metaphor, and the frame thus set is further elaborated throughout the ensuing text. Together with this, metaphor also helps reviewers to 'negotiate' their views (and assert their authority) in the genre. The next example illustrates these evaluative – both 'textual' and interpersonal – roles of metaphor:

"[Architect's comment] This was a great opportunity to further explore my theories relating to *the parasite* in architecture. [...] As a form, [the roof] *bites* into the thirties structure and *clings* to the ground inside the courtyard. *Growing* from this position, it *surges* towards the north; splintering the light with glass, shade cloth panels and zincalume-clad wings. These materials combine the flesh-like fragility of cloth with the idea of *exoskeleton* in the

---

25 | "Lyrical Geometry," in *The Architectural Review*, April 1998, italic by RDC

shells and *steel*. [...] *It is analogous to the growth of a large fig tree.* Unlike minimalist modernism, it shows *the struggle of structure through space*.

[Reviewer's comment] Goodwin calls his new work *a 'parasite'*. It's actually a roof which has *a strong narrative*. [...] In this case, *this 'parasite'* is at work under the building, *in the bowels* of the structure, *emerging* to engage the very insides of the building with the unsuspecting passer-by. [...] *The roof is an organic response to the need for the entire building to mark the passing of time.* It creates a dynamic tension. [...] Richard Goodwin, metaphorically, *has dumped the guts on the footpath.* [...] this building is not what you see. It has *beating*, pumping services lying just below *its skin*. No longer can the neat and poised exterior of the Union Hotel conceal the truth; *the underbelly of this building has been scratched and the parasite has emerged. A parasite that exposes the real goings on of this place: of the stench of fifty years of beer and cigarettes, of the tales told, of the jokes had, of the human passing. Scratch below the surface and the spirit of this building will disgorge.*"[26]

Here a roof is assessed by its architect and a reviewer – both following an organic metaphor, yet exploiting it in a different way. The title provides a

Image 32: Richard Goodwin, *Parasite*, 2004

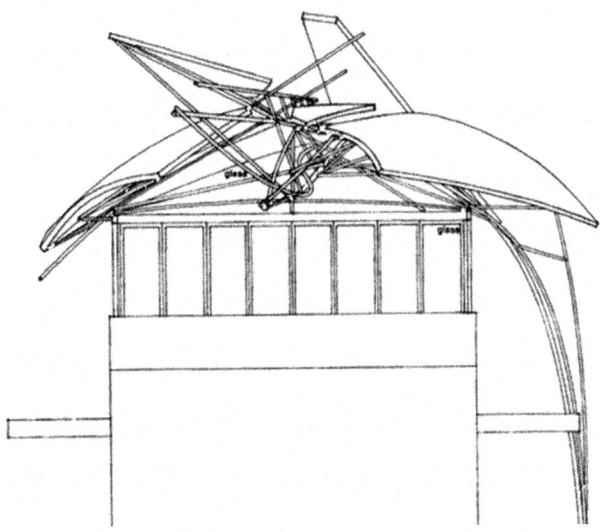

26 | "Parasite," in *Architecture Australia*, 1999

visually-biased initial assessment by borrowing the architect's own 'parasitic' views (reinforced by drawings which show a huge spider-like metal structure grafted on top of a building). In contrast, the reviewer's commentary mixes both abstract and visual information: although he appears to follow the architect's metaphor throughout the text, he adds his own appreciation of the building as having 'intellectual' needs. This is done through a language metaphor (the roof's having *a strong narrative*) which may well have been used to allude to the long-standing time-space commonplace in architecture (*the need for the entire building to mark the passing of time*). As a result, the building is somehow personified, a human construal which co-exists with the architect's more animalistic portrayal. Moreover, by foregrounding the abstract qualities of both roof and building the reviewer's explanation leaves images aside (which, as pointed out, are faithful to the PARASITE metaphor).

The interplay of metaphors in ARs may, finally, be explained as ultimately geared to achieving the same goal: creating the illusion of objectivity in an essentially subjective genre aimed at an audience as knowledgeable as the reviewers. For instance, authors often mitigate visual metaphors by using lexical hedges ('a kind of', 'metaphorically'), cautionary quotes (*'parasite'*, *"feminine"*) or by attributing them to the architect at issue (i.e. quoting them). In other words, since the genre's audience can 'read' both the visuals and text in ARs and, hence, contrast the information provided in both as well as agree or disagree with the reviewers' views, visual metaphors need to be 'downplayed' to avoid confrontation. In contrast, metaphors concerned with abstract properties (e.g. the roof's having *a narrative* in Example 18) appear to be more authoritative and less hedged: given the impossibility of comparing the assessment thus articulated with the visuals in the texts, the audience's disagreement remains a personal matter.[27]

Concluding remarks
Together with exploring what aspects of architects' worldview are construed in figurative ways, in this chapter I briefly discuss the discourse staging of those metaphors, i.e. how and why architects use metaphor in a particular genre of their discourse interaction. Metaphorical language has been seen as meeting the ideational, textual, and interpersonal needs of architects

---

27 | For a detailed discussion, see Caballero 2006

and, more specifically, reviewers, according to the specific demands of the discourse context under analysis. The figurative data here discussed bring to light a shared and culturally specific ontology built upon metaphorical sets largely acquired and learnt to manage through socialization and repeated use. Metaphor is, then, both a conceptual and a socialization tool, and one that is partly acquired and effectively put to work through discourse interaction.

Skins in Architecture
On Sensitive Shells and Interfaces

SUSANNE HAUSER

The notion of the openings and closings of surfaces, and thus of the body, has shifted in the past decades. This does not only apply to the human body and its skins, but also to the openings and closings of other bodies, for example those that emerge within artistic and architectural spatial reflections, processes and designs. There are of course highly metaphorical processes involved – this can be said with certainty – but in what respect? Who is transferring what concept to what other place and discourse? And besides: What is a metaphor?

1.
There are different ways of understanding metaphors. My version refers to some linguistic and philosophical discussions, findings and conclusions mainly of the 1960s, when metaphors turned out to be not just an improper or merely "tropical" use of otherwise clearly expressible notions but instead something much more dangerous and creative.

As long as metaphors are interpreted as a way of creating an accidental and contingent analogy or substitute for a "proper" expression to be removed after use from the universe of communication without any surviving traces, metaphors seem to be just meaningful terms on leave from their usual duties. Since the 1960s the discussion of metaphors focuses on their highly dynamic qualities – traditionally well known but until then somewhat ignored.

One of the decisive steps in the process of their reevaluation in linguistics was the discovery that their meaning – in written and in spoken language alike – was context-sensitive. The relevant context for the understanding and comprehension of a metaphor could imply other words and sentences and also certain traits of the situation of their use.[1] This meant that the discussion of metaphors had to leave the realm of the dictionary. Not just words, but texts, sentences, narrations, situations and even full-grown discourses with their practical and material conditions had to be taken into consideration in the interpretation of metaphors.

Another remarkable step in their reevaluation was the discovery that metaphors quite often functioned as a way of expressing something that had no other way of being expressed and that had not been expressed ever before. This applied for example to crucial and yet not fully (in terms of "concepts") expressible ideas in the history of thought and technology. It also applied to basic philosophical notions, to fundamental convictions in the sciences and to their changes.[2] Metaphors turned out to be a way, and sometimes to be the only way of actively making sense: as a way of creating, stabilizing and conveying meanings and knowledge.

The general movement towards a more dynamic understanding of metaphors also affected the concept of everyday language in linguistics. In a widely discussed book *Metaphors we live by* its authors, with a theorctical background in cognitive linguistics, argued that our way of creating concepts is basically and generally metaphorical: Once productive and groundbreaking metaphors are constantly turning into "dead" metaphors and thus into "normal" expressions whose metaphorical qualities pass unnoticed in everyday communication. Thus metaphors are a central issue in understanding social processes and political thought – and we may add: in the creation of new concepts in design too.[3]

---

[1] | Cf. Weinrich, Harald, "Semantik der Metapher," in *Folia Linguistica. Acta Societatis Linguisticae Europeae*, 1 1967, pp. 3-17

[2] | Cf. e.g. Blumenberg, Hans, *Paradigmen zu einer Metaphorologie*, Bonn: Bouvier, 1960; Blumenberg, Hans, *Die kopernikanische Wende*, Frankfurt/M.: Suhrkamp 1965. Blumenberg's approach already implied a critique of the concepts of "metaphor" and "concept;" their relations were also discussed by Jacques Derrida, Paul de Man and others; see Haverkamp, Anselm, *Metapher. Die Ästhetik in der Rhetorik. Bilanz eines exemplarischen Begriffs*, München: Fink 2007

[3] | Lakoff, George, Johnson, Mark, *Metaphors we live by*, Chicago: University of Chicago Press 1980

The inability of structural linguistics to tame metaphors and the joint examinations of metaphors by linguists, historians and philosophers of language fomented distrust in any structural and static concept of language. Their discussions opened up the perspective of more dynamic approaches to meaning in general; they emphasized the basic role of metaphors in our ways of understanding the world and stressed their creative potential. Metaphors have to be seen as dynamic features, creating and/or conveying sense in any processes of communication and thus in creative processes of any kind.

2.
Talking about "skins" seems to be a quite common way of referring to the shell, the wrap, the covering of a building, to its outer walls in architecture.[4] That "skin" was a metaphorical expression too, however, did not pass unnoticed during the 1990s as some architects and architecture critics reanimated the metaphorical potential of the term in their references to walls and surfaces of buildings.

In 1993 Kenneth Powell and Rowan Moore published a quite voluminous book about the then recent projects by Grimshaw & Partners with the title *Structure, Space and Skin*.[5] Also in 1993, Maarten Kloos edited a small book on Dutch architecture: *Die Haut der Erde* (The Skin of the Earth), adopting the title of a project by Raoul Bunschoten – who was possibly quoting Marshall McLuhan and his description of information technology.[6] Marc C. Taylor's "Reflections on Skin" was published in several journals discussing recent architectural designs.[7] Alicia Imperiale's book on the newly disco-

---

4 | Using the expression "skin" in this respect may be more common in English than the use of the German term for "skin" which is "Haut"; I assume that the "Haut" keeps much more its status of a not yet completely "dead" metaphor.

5 | Powell, Kenneth, Moore, Rowan, *Structure, Space and Skin. The Work of Nicolas Grimshaw & Partners*, London: Phaidon 1993; German edition: *Struktur, Raum und Haut. Nicolas Grimshaw & Partners, Bauten und Projekte*, Berlin: Ernst & Sohn 1993

6 | See Kloos, Marten (ed.), *Die Haut der Erde. Architektur für ein neues Jahrhundert*, Berlin: Nishen 1993

7 | Taylor, Marc C., "Reflections on Skin," in *Columbia Documents on Architecture and Theory*, vol. 6 1995, pp. 13-18; a German version was published in 1995: "Überlegungen zur Haut," in *arch+* 129/130 1995, p. 113

vered "Surface Tension in Digital Architecture,"[8] published in 2000, showed impressive "skins," and in 2002 the Japanese journal "Architecture and Urbanism" published an issue on "Skin Architecture" with works by Libeskind, Alsop, and many others.[9] It is not by chance that Juhani Pallasmaa discovered "The Eyes of the Skin" in 1996,[10] stating the involvement of more senses than just one in the production and the use of architecture, and this is one of the keys to understanding what was going on.

The conceptual premises in the architectural reflection on outer walls and their surfaces were changing in the 1990s. The concepts of surfaces, of limits, of boundaries, of transparency, translucency and opacity were reconsidered and even transformed. A new kind of imagery emerged and it was not modern, not even post-modern, but truly different as it came along with a change of the metaphoric realm architecture – and not just architecture – was referring to when discussing boundaries: It implied a reinterpretation of the role of visuality and the other senses in architecture.

In the 1990s common ways of conceptualizing boundaries in architecture were discredited. The post-modern practice of adorning the surface of a building with meaningful items referring to a variety of sign-systems and/or historic or fictitious narrations was left behind as well as the traditional modern approach to a building's walls and shells. The modernist concept of surfaces, – of bodies, of buildings, even, in language theory, of sentences – was usually related to the question of transparency. The concept was focused on the eye and, in the figurative sense, on the eye's power to recognize and eradicate ambiguities and secrets. The related discussions of the materiality of boundaries and surfaces in architecture were and sometimes still are about concrete, steel and – this is the most important feature and material – about glass.[11]

---

8 | Imperiale, Alicia, *New Flatness. Surface Tension in Digital Architecture*, Basel, Boston, Berlin: Birkhäuser 2000

9 | "Skin Architecture. Works by Libeskind, Williams/Tsien, Oosterhuis, Ropa, Ricciotti, Alsop, Souto de Moura, UN Studio, Grimshaw & Nouvel," in *A+U* 02/10, 2002

10 | Pallasmaa, Juhani, *The Eyes of the Skin. Architecture and the Senses*, London: Academy Editions 1996; 2nd edition Chichester: Wiley-Academy 2005

11 | See Hauser, Susanne, "Transparenzen. Ein Essay," in Johanna Rolshoven (Ed.), *Hexen, Wiedergänger, Sans Papiers. Kulturtheoretische Reflexionen zu den Rändern des Raumes*, Marburg: Jonas 2003, pp. 143-156

As in the classical moderns, any discussion of surfaces in the 1990s dealt with borderline situations too. Thus the questions raised some 20 years ago happened to be just the same as the questions asked during the inter-war-period, in the 1920s and 1930s. What does interior and exterior mean? What does it mean physically? What does it mean to draw a line between private and public, intimacy and publicity, secrets and knowledge, nakedness and cover, protection and exposure? The answers, however, changed in 1990s: The qualities and positions on both sides of the boundary – which in modern notions of individuals and subjects are associated with transparency – no longer appear as opposites. Instead they now appear as possibilities and potentialities that come into play simultaneously and to varying degrees. They put bodies with weak or blurred boundaries into relationship with each other and transform them to different intensities.[12]

The eye and its gaze are disempowered. In the discussion of a "skin's" qualities, the focus lies not on walls and boundaries, which are created in respect to sensory perception at a distance. The discussion does not touch upon the ideal and visible accordance of outer appearance and interior structure, nor is it focused on the eye and the cognizance of a traditionally associated clarity and rationality. These forms of control, evidence, distancing and perspective have no impact on the skin. Skin is not transparent and not clear. Dealing with skins means dealing with multiple diffusion. Subjects, individuals and closed bodies are beyond the self-evident preconditions of a discussion of boundaries that involve skin. Speaking about skin brings other senses – especially touch, but also taste and smell – and their disruptive powers into play.

With skins in mind considerations of boundaries and surfaces are different from the outset. They are now associated with considerations of other sensual experiences. These considerations imply a redefinition not just of surfaces. Skins in all their possible meanings become a focus for a discussion redefining the building as such leading to a much more diverse redefinition of the body than any concept of boundaries and surfaces based on visuality. Thus whereas modernist debates on surfaces and borderlines

---

12 | Some of the following examples are discussed in Hauser, Susanne, "Die Haut als Zwischenraum," in Angela Lammert et al./Akademie der Künste Berlin (ed.), *Topos RAUM*, Nürnberg: Verlag für Moderne Kunst 2005, pp. 308-319

are focused on visual experience the interdisciplinary debate on skins took up new aspects. But what aspects and what kind of skins were involved?

3.
Whenever we are dealing with metaphors we are, as I mentioned before, not just dealing with words but with their rather elaborated contexts and situations often governing more than just one specialized discourse. To understand this it is useful to state, that it was not just architecture discussing surfaces at that time. During the 1990s media theory, cultural studies, biology and medicine, design and philosophy of nature were reconsidering surfaces and bodies too. References on the topic also included the fact that skin was the first human organ that can be manufactured to be functional via cell-breeding.[13] Surfaces, boundaries and skins thus invite us not only into debates on design and architecture in the 1990s, but also into anthropological ones.

The fine arts adopted the topic in quite convincing ways. There were challenging experiments to be observed commenting on the history of art, on older and recent images governing concepts of skins – displaying the potential of their conceptual richness, the fragility of supposedly self-evident knowledge about their qualities and the skins' multifaceted metaphorical power. Some of the images of skins in the arts were quite shocking in their display of mutilated and tortured bodies, suggesting processes of violence without restraint. I will restrict my examples to three comparatively harmless but nevertheless illuminating examples that refer to three kinds of critique of the body and the senses, of the image of the body and its skin.

Lilla Lo Curto and Bill Outcault used cartography software to extend and transform images of their bodies. This had the effect that their skin appeared as a two-dimensional surface on the two-dimensional surface of the picture. The identification of picture surfaces and skins is not unprecedented in the history of art. Michelangelo's face in the Sistine Chapel appears on a (painted) canvas, apparently loosely held like a cloth, and alluding to at his time contemporary images of skinned Christian martyrs, illustrations

---

13 | Lupton, Ellen, *Skin. Surface, Substance, and Design,* Catalogue ed. by the Cooper-Hewitt National Design Museum, Smithsonian Institution, London: Laurence King Publishing Ltd. 2002, pp. 47ff

of the Marsyas legend or of anatomic studies. Like Michelangelo's portrait the cartographic approaches disturb and blur the difference of image and body, of surface and action, of sensitivity and perception. Lo Curto and Outcault comment on their work: "selfportrait.map looks at the digital reordering of three-dimensional forms through a reshaping of the digitized body and offers an alternate way of representing the human figure by remapping its surface onto a set of simple shapes. The fragility and tenuous nature of our existence is a reoccurring theme in our work and, in the

Image 33: Lilla LoCurto, Bill Outcault: Kharchenko-Shabanova BS1sph(8/6)7_98, 1999

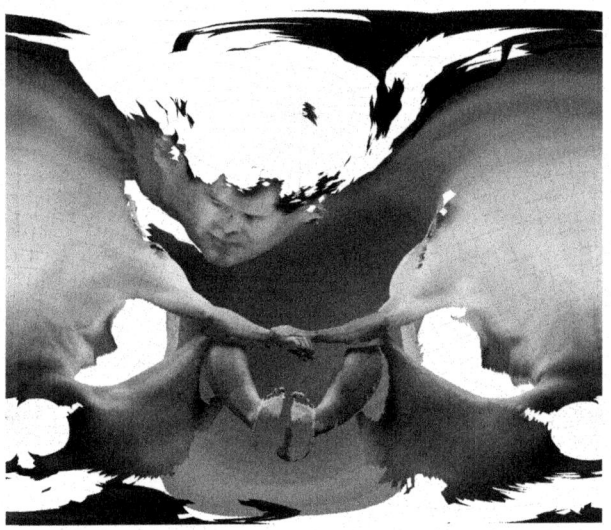

process of unfolding the scans, the computer generated a complex network of jagged seams and torn edges. Although stitching utilities exist that allow the projections to be repaired, we considered the holes and gaps to be evocative of both the landmasses of maps and the vulnerability of life."[14] This is a serious challenge of any distanced approach to images and to any concept of embodiment.

---

14 | www.locurto-outcault.com/pages/selfportrait.map.html, 3.11.2011

A second approach: In 2001 photographer Nicole Tran Ba Vang showed perfect female bodies with skins that had an uncanny way of being replaced and worn like masks or dresses. This may be read as an ironic comment on those perfect bodies of antiquity with tight fitting and unwrinkled skins, that were appreciated for example by Winckelmann who defined, in the middle of the 18th century, a new concept of art and art history as well as of subjectivity. Nicole Tran Ba Vangs's photographs may also be read as a

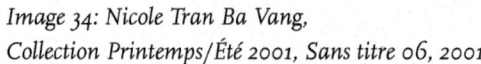

Image 34: Nicole Tran Ba Vang,
Collection Printemps/Été 2001, Sans titre 06, 2001

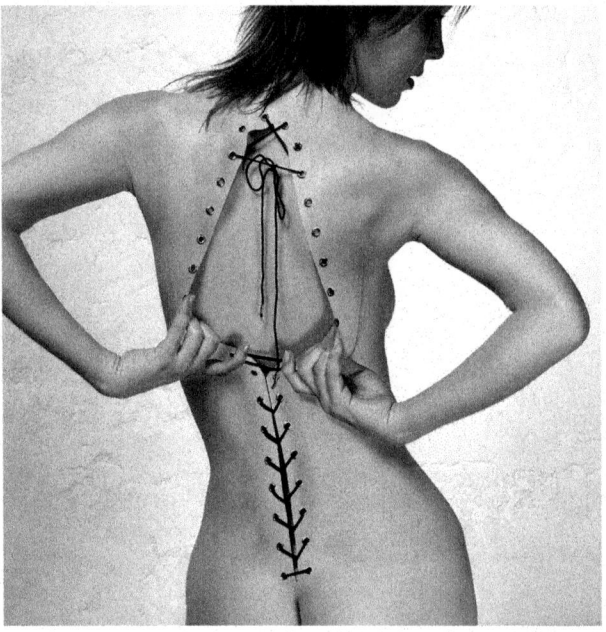

comment on the lost secret of nakedness, on the reduction of women and of female human bodies to hallstands, and on the enormous effort of presenting a visually perfect outside to the world: skins prepared to function as a pleasure for male eyes – revealing no truth, no real thing, showing nothing at all that is worth to be seen. This is a serious attack on the phantasms of the unmediated and penetrating visuality as conceived in modernist approaches to transparency.

A third example: In the last years of the 1990s Anthony Aziz and Sammy Cutcher showed bodies and faces that were covered with skin, enclosing the bodies all over and reducing their contact to the world to skin contact. During the first decade of their collaboration, their work "focused on the representation of the body in relation to new technology. Issues of anxiety, identity, transformation, mutation, and the increasing disappearance of the traditional boundaries between the organic and the artificial lay at the core of the series of works produced during this time."[15] Among these works were pictures showing "Chimeras" wrapped in a humanoid skin. In Greek mythology chimeras are known as monstrous beings composed of the parts of several animals: of the body of a lioness with a tail that terminates in a snake's head. The head of a goat arises at the center of the spine. In Aziz' and Cutcher's interpretation chimeras seem to come into existence as beings of an unclear status. They may be the outcome of dubious wet labs, of uncanny laboratories for genetic research, populating a new and yet incomprehensible world.

My selection is of course polemic as it singles out three very distinct topics: The question of the (digital) image as a physical entity and its complex relations to bodies; the question of the eye's role in the field of knowledge and cognizance; and the redefinition of the sphere of the living. These are just three approaches commenting on the imaginary and the imagery of the body and its boundaries but apt to illustrate some basic aspects of the change in the perspective on organic and informational processes.

The images question the possibility of the integrity and identity of the body. This turns the "skin" into a very powerful and productive metaphor. The metaphorical impact of skins of the 1990s was related to recent findings in biology and genetics, to the critique of the image and the neglect of the activities behind it. This also implied a critique of visuality and the neglect of the other senses in the production and reproduction of the environment. And a second field spread its conceptual framework too and added to the importance of the skin-metaphor at that time: Many a description of bodies and surfaces was inspired by information technologies and their definition and description of interfaces. This is also true for the images of skins discussed here. They were not just presenting ambiguities and questions of

---

15 | www.azizcucher.net/series.php, 3.11.2011

the digital age, of its surfaces and images; they used advanced and recently available digital technologies for image processing. Thus the production

Image 35: Aziz + Cucher, Chimera No. 8, New York, 1998

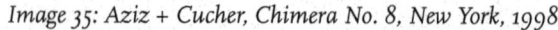

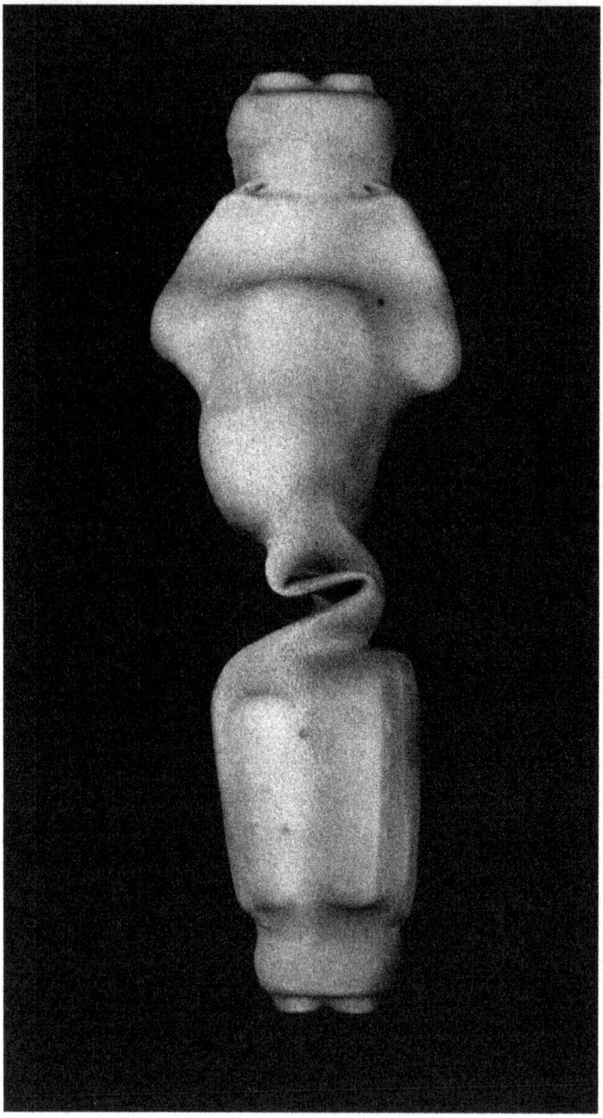

processes already created inseparable links between the world of the organic and the digital world, between bodies with questionable skins and information processes and their rapidly changing relations.

A striking illustration of the groundbreaking change in the imagery of bodies and skins of the 1990s reflected in the discussed examples and in many other fields, including architecture, comes from industrial design: In 1972 Mario Bellini designed a calculator for Olivetti, and on top he put a flexible and smooth plastic material. This was a mimetic way of referring to certain qualities of skins. In 2001 Sam Hecht presented a quite similar design, at least on first sight – but now everything was different: This machine was able to localize the human hands operating it and to take their activity into consideration.[16] Organic and informational metaphors mixed: at the point of contact, at the "interface" called skin questions arise on type, mode and meaning, on reproduction and construction of processes of exchange that are mediated over many layers, many sensitivities and connections.

4.
"Skins" discussed in architecture are not just architectural but part of a wider reconsideration of boundaries and skins, of a wider imagery penetrating innovative ideas for designs. In the past two decades architectural practice has contributed to the general discourse on the body and its skins, to the interpretation of organic and information metaphors – from the creation of genuine architectonic concepts to the nearly mimetic translation of organic skins into façade constructions.

Translucence and changeability have challenged, if not replaced, modern transparency and permanence in buildings created within the past two decades.
    Glass is still an option, but its use and its functions have changed, not just on the level of its interpretation. The overlapping of various layers, covers and forms of shading, and several ways of reducing the passage of light and energy are endemic in buildings of the 1990s. The notion of a building shell as an irritating surface that can always be seen anew is one of the pos-

---

16 | Lupton, Ellen, *Skin. Surface, Substance, and Design*, Catalogue ed. by the Cooper-Hewitt National Design Museum, Smithsonian Institution, London: Laurence King Publishing Ltd. 2002, p. 40

sible approaches still referring to modernist options but relating them now to images of quite another type. Toyo Ito's famous *Mediathèque* in Sendai (2000) explicitly explored the transition between transparency and translucence, information and information, interior and exterior climates.[17] The use of profile glass and the overlapping of many layers create reflections and reflexes. They translate the topic of a virtual reality relativizing body, borders and perspective into real architecture.

Printed Glass, figured glass and overlaps produce ever changing visual impressions. Jean Marc Iba's and Myrto Vitart's extension for the museum in the Palace des Beaux Arts in Lille (1997) is one of the buildings making use of these possible effects. The architects created a new interpretation of what the depth of an architectonical object might mean and produced a new kind of façade that still refers to transparency without being transparent. The visual impression of the building reacts to its built environment and to any change of lighting conditions in a very sensitive way.[18]

Another approach to "structure, space and skin" was illustrated by Nicolas Grimshaw in his Lord Reilly Memorial Lecture of 1992: A photograph by Karl Blossfeldt displaying a snail's diaphanous shell with its fragile and strong structure combined with a picture of a delicate bat's wings function as icons defining the idea of architectonic structure and its relation to skins.[19] In the already quoted book on projects by Grimshaw & Partners the architectural adaption of organic images are illustrated mainly through façades made of glass and steel; in some projects textile fibers play a major role too. The relation of structure, space and skin reached a new level

---

17 | See Witte, Ron, Kobayashi, Hiroto (Ed.), *CASE: Toyo Ito - Sendai Mediathèque*, Munich etc.: Prestel 2002

18 | See the architects' metaphoric comment on their building: "The reflection realizes the interface between the old and the new. In setting up infinities of the depth, the mirror articulates a continuum with the built environment. The layered image of the Palais and its monochromes, with which the subject interfaces as both voyeur and actor, symbolizes the museum within the city." www.ibosvitart.com/en/orojet.php?id=43, 3.11.2011

19 | Grimshaw, Nicolas, "Struktur, Raum und Haut," in Powell, Kenneth, Moore, Rowan, *Struktur, Raum und Haut. Nicolas Grimshaw & Partners, Bauten und Projekte*, Berlin 1993, pp. 236-243

with the famous Eden Project in Cornwall (1995-2001). The buildings were among the first ones ever that were covered with foil, with blown up cushions made of ETFE, a transparent and very light material. This material

Image 36: Jean-Marc Ibos; Myrto Vitart, extension to the museum of the Palais des Beaux-Arts, Lille, France, 1997

marks a new approach; its use enables new forms, new visual effects and indicates "skinlike" haptic qualities that can be "felt" or imagined already by looking at photographs of the dome-shaped buildings.

Closed and tattooed or semi-opaque and multilayered surfaces develop their own visually manifest physical presence. The skeleton, and thus the construction is not primary any more, but the skin. This is shown in Jacques Herzog's and Pierre de Meuron's library for the University of Applied Sciences in Eberswalde/Germany (1999), a box whose façade of pale concrete and glass is covered all over with imprinted photographs. It can be read as one of the most prominent examples of this attitude. Thomas Ruff, the photographic artist who chose the historical pictures to be "tattooed" on the building's skin, also produced a congenial interpretation of this aspect in his multilayered photographic presentations of the library.[20]

---

20 | See Thomas Ruff's photographs in Mack, Gerhard, Liebermann, Valeria, *Eberswalde Library. Herzog & de Meuron* (= Architecture Landscape Urbanism 3), London: AAPublications, 2000

A theoretical approach challenging the depth of the (building) corpus was derived from embryology and followed a certain image of the (human) body. The concept sees the body emerge from the egg's fertilization through a constant inversion and involution of its surface. Everything here – bones, organs, cells – is skin; everything is surface. With this image, the cultural critic and philosopher Marc C. Taylor conceived and described bodies of any kind that are meant to be entirely surface, that celebrate not boundaries but rather express transitions and connections.[21] Terence Riley chose the imagery displayed in Taylor's text to comment on not exactly biological processes. Riley was interested in the fascination with continual surfaces devoid of depth in architecture, mainly associated with a certain geometric figure: the Möbius-strip, which shows no enclosed interior. Temporarily, in digital design's pioneering phase, it was a very prominent icon and form in architecture.[22] There are many Möbius-strips we have seen by now, also many Klein bottles, zero-volume bottles with a one-sided surface. We have also seen designs transforming these possibly embryonic structures into houses.[23] These designs merge the fascination of a continual surface and the new possibilities opened up by digital technology.

Discourses and practices tend to react to metaphors and their use depending on their own logic and in different ways. Sometimes this results in quite stupendous interpretations as in the case of the Aegis Hyposurface (1999-2001). It was designed for the Birmingham Hippodrome Theatre by Marc Goulthorpe of deCOi, together with a multi-disciplinary team, among them mathematicians and computer specialists. The design process started with the idea (or metaphor) of a physically reacting architecture. The designers developed a wall that could be reconfigured dynamically. Its surface was elastic, moved by a matrix of actuators. It was able to react to sound, movement, or touch in real-time. In an experimental way this project linked several domains of imagery and challenged the imagination of

---

21 | Taylor, Marc C., "Reflections on Skin," in *Columbia Documents on Architecture and Theory*, vol. 6 1995, pp. 13-18

22 | Riley, Terence, "The Un-Private House," in *The Un-Private House*, catalogue, New York 1999, pp. 9-38, pp. 29ff

23 | Possibly the most prominent among them is the Möbius House designed by UNStudio (1993-1998); see http://www.unstudio.com/unstudio/projects/mobius-house, 03.11.2011

spaces, objects, of borderlines, limits und surfaces: "The piece marks the transition from autoplastic (determinate) to alloplastic (interactive, indeterminate) space, a new species of reciprocal architecture."[24]

5.
Although the metaphorical potential of "skins" in the arts in general and particularly in architecture may not be fully exhausted, it is not a strikingly active potential any more. This is also true for the interpretations of the relation of biological findings, communication technologies and the arts associated with the skin-metaphor in the 1990s. The case of this metaphor once able to open up numerous references and options shows that the period of time when metaphors are able to inspire and to interpret creative solutions can be limited. It may run out when the questions that a metaphor helped to ask and to answer lose their importance or prominence; when they are in fact answered; when metaphors are not fashionable any more; when the related questions can be defined to such a degree in architectonic terms that a metaphorical approach, which always implies a reference to non-architectonic images and meanings, is not helpful any more in current processes; or when a special trait of the old metaphor becomes so important that another imagery, another metaphor replaces the old one. I assume that this latter possibility is what happened to the skins of the 1990s in architecture.

The irritating relation of bodies and information technology has lost its former acuteness and emphasis without being thrashed out. What remains is a specialized interest in architectural "skins" in their functional description, as a basis of translation processes in architecture and materials research.[25] This description and its technological interpretation became dominant at the beginning of the 21st century. Among its most prominent icons is Mike Davies' (Richard Rogers Partnership) polyvalent wall, a concept published in 1981 already and whose adaptive qualities Davies compared to

---

24 | http://www.sial.rmit.edu.au/Projects/Aegis_Hyposurface.php, 03.11.2011; cf. *dECOi book*, Catalogue of the Smectic State exhibition at FRAC, Orleans, Paris: Hyx Publications 2006

25 | Cf. e.g. Wymann, Jean-Pierre, "Fassade als Haut," in Schweizerischer Ingenieur- und Architekten-Verein (ed.), *Tec-Dossier Oberflächen*, Zürich: Verlags-AG der Akademischen Technischen Vereine 2006, pp. 22-25

the skin of a chameleon.[26] This design already implied a literal understanding of the skin-analogy, the translation of chosen and well-defined features into technological solutions and the justified rejection of features not to be translated: The analogy functioned as a model. This is a variety of analogies

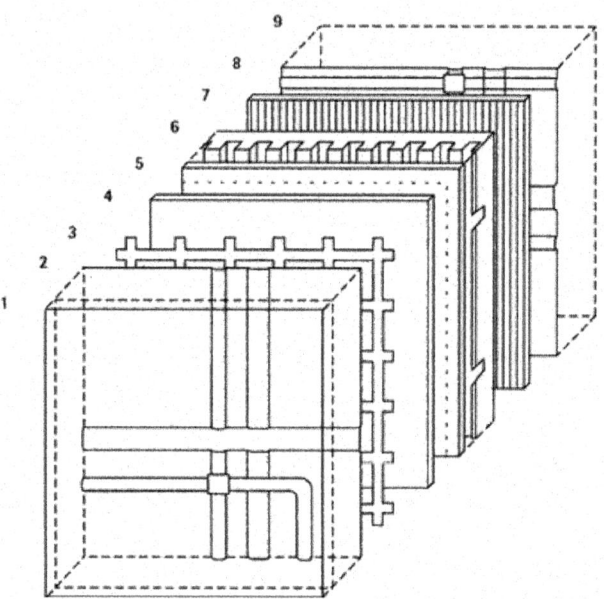

Image 37: Mike Davies, Polyvalent Wall, 1981

whose metaphorical status has been described as the special case of a "sustained and systematic metaphor." Processes based on this type of reading, understanding and translating analogies may be considered as a specialized type of metaphor-based creativity – and they definitely produce very interesting types of "skins." Their ways and potentials of reacting to certain environments and exigencies have changed dramatically during the last two decades. Materials and constructions with integrated digital and mechanical networks, among them glass, textiles and highly flexible high-tech membranes, react to light, heat, and touch as well as to mechanical stress. The most prominent expression in their discussion, however, is not "skin"

---

26 | Cf. Davies, Mike, "A Wall for all Seasons," in *RIBA Journal*, 88 (2) 1981, pp. 55-57 any more but the – equally metaphorical – reference to "smart" or "intelligent" materials and solutions. This announces a new imagery guiding and inspiring the conceptualization of buildings and their surfaces, an imagery yet to be analyzed in its implications and consequences.

A new Urban Question 3[1]
When, Why and How some Fundamental Metaphors were used

BERNARDO SECCHI

We are facing now a new urban question. Environment, mobility and growing social inequalities are the main issues defining the nature and character of this new urban question.[2]

It is not the first time in western history that an urban question has arisen as a knotty problem, a crux in the path of social and economic growth. We simply have to remember "the luxury controversy" during the XVIIIth century,[3] in fact a debate about where the capitalistic accumulation could and was taking place; the "housing question" in the middle of the XIXth century, in other words the contradictions in passing from artisan manufacture to the factory system of production with the unavoidable pro-

---

1 | I put this "3" in the title because in the month of November 2009 I gave three conferences in Paris (SFA), Zurich (ETH) and again in Paris (ESA) with the same title. The content of the three conferences obviously was different: the first one, in Paris, had its focus on the research we (Paola Viganò and I) did for the Grand Paris, the second one, in Zurich, was focused on the research the new urban question is asking to plan; the third one, again in Paris, is this one about "metaphors" accompanying the urban question in its long history.
2 | Secchi, Bernardo, *Une nouvelle question urbaine 1*, Colloque internationale. Le territoire dans tous ses états, SFA, Paris, 14 November 2009; Secchi, Bernardo, *A New Urban Question 2*, The Swiss Spatial Sciences Framework (S3F), Zurich, 18 November 2009
3 | De Salignac de La Mothe - Fénelon, François, *Les adventures de Télémaque*, Paris, 1699

letarian concentration in the industrial city; the *Grossstadt* question at the turn of the twentieth century, the main theme for Simmel, Kracauer and Benjamin,[4] or the first perception of the emergence of the crowd in the de-measured metropolitan space.[5] Finally, during the nineteen sixties and seventies, when Ford's model of labour organization becomes exhausted and disappears and at the same time the importance of individual autonomy emerges and, as a consequence, the importance of everyday life, a new urban question emerges based on the "right to the city" which is studied, as is well known, by Manuel Castells,[6] Henry Lefebvre[7] and Michel de Certeau.[8]

Roughly speaking, my hypothesis – just a working hypothesis – is that whenever the structure of the whole economy and society is undergoing radical change, an urban question emerges: at the very beginning of the industrial revolution; passing from artisan manufacture to the factory system; under Taylor-Ford labour organization; at its end and finally at the beginning of what Bauman calls the "liquid society,"[9] Beck the "risk society"[10] and Rifkin the "society of access."[11] In other words, when a growing individualization of society, a growing awareness of the scarcity of environmental resources and a growing confidence in technological progress and change

---

4 | Fuzesséry, S., Simay, Ph., *Le Choc des métropoles. Simmel, Kracauer, Benjamin*, Paris: Editions de l'éclat, 2008

5 | Riesman, D., *The Lonely Crowd*, New Haven: Yale University Press, 1948, 1953, 1961, 1969

6 | Castells, Manuel, *La question urbaine*, Paris: François Maspero, 1972 (engl. transl., MIT Press and Edward Arnold 1977)

7 | Lefebvre, Henri, *Le Droit à la ville, I*, Paris: Éditions Anthropos, 1968; Lefebvre, Henri, *Le Droit à la ville, II - Espace et politique*, Paris: Éditions Anthropos, 1972

8 | De Certeau, Michel, *L'Invention du Quotidien. Vol. 1, Arts de Faire*, Paris: Union générale d'éditions, 1980

9 | Bauman, Zygmunt, *Modernity and Ambivalence*, Ithaca, N.Y.: Cornell University Press, 1991

10 | Beck, Ulrich, *Risikogesellschaft. Auf dem Weg in eine andere Moderne*, Frankfurt am Main: Suhrkamp, 1986

11 | Rifkin, Jeremy, *The Age Of Access: The New Culture of Hypercapitalism, Where All of Life is a Paid- For Experience*, New York: Putnam Publishing Group, 2001

are building images, scenarios, policies and projects partially contrasting if not conflicting with one another.[12]

It is during these periods that we are unable to use plain discourse. Every one of these periods was in fact marked in the past by a set of metaphors trying to depict the real urban situation and its problems. The role of the metaphor, as is well known, is just this: to give a meaning to what we are provisionally unable to understand.[13] In fact, it is when we do not understand the situation that, in my view, we need strong metaphors and images. The ancient Greeks, for instance, had a better knowledge of the city than of the body. That is the reason why they used metaphors depicting the body as a city, made of different parts often conflicting with each other, in what was considered an illness. The human body, in the books of ancient Greek medicine, is where many fluids flow, mixing, conflicting and reciprocally reacting; it is a battlefield where different elements are struggling for power. The health of both the body and the city is assured by an absence of internal conflicts.[14] The body is where the stability of the equilibrium is represented, but it is also where the dynamics of the processes – similar to those taking place inside the polis – eventually aim at reaching equilibrium through a capacity to manage conflict by the doctor-urbanist.

In fact, since antiquity, the human body and the city have been metaphorically linked; but in antiquity, when the human body was the difficult entity to understand, it was the body to be like a city.[15] Since the Renaissance, on the contrary, it is the city that has become like a human body and this metaphor probably became the most pervasive and powerful metaphor in any discourse on the city. For me the reasons are clear: first we all have an everyday experience of our body, but more than this the city can be conceptualised as a human body as being made of different parts. Each part, as in the human body, has a form, a location and a role, but these three terms are not linked by necessity. By this I mean that nothing is saying that my hand,

---

12 | Secchi, Bernardo, *A New Urban Question*, The Swiss Spatial Sciences Framework (S3F), Zurich, 18th November 2009
13 | Lakoff, Georges, Johnson, Mark, *Metaphors We Live By*, Chicago: University of Chicago Press, 1980
14 | Vegetti, M., *Tra Edipo e Euclide*, Milano: Il Saggiatore, 1983
15 | Secchi, Bernardo, *La prima lezione di urbanistica*, Roma: Laterza, 2000

as a part of the city, has this form and is located here in order to do what I can do with my hand. It is true on the contrary that I can do this because my hand has this form and is located here. More than this, everybody can judge if the dimension of each part of a human body and of a city are correct or not. In the latter case, we are speaking using another metaphor: of London as a monster city for instance.

At the beginning of the industrial revolution, the rhetoric of the entrepreneurial spirit is the driver. As in Laugier,[16] who conceives the city as a forest: the maximum of difference between the elements and – as in nature –great homogeneity of the whole. And again, just to remember the most famous metaphors, during the first half of the XXth century, in a period of growing mechanization of the world,[17] the city is conceived as a "banal machine,"[18] a machine always answering in a predictable way to the different inputs. If I look to the discourse about the city,[19] I find two groups of metaphors (again a working hypothesis):

– The first speaks of the city in terms of some other field of our physical experience. The city as a forest, order and diversity, order on the whole and diversity in the details, at the beginning of liberalism and the entrepreneurial spirit; the city as a human body and the related metaphors,[20] a "natural" way to give a role to different parts of society: form, location and

---

16 | Laugier, M. A., *Essai sur l'architecture*, Paris, 1753
17 | Giedion, Sigfried, *Mechanization takes Command. A Contribution to Anonymous History*, New York: Oxford University Press, 1948
18 | Secchi, Bernardo, "La macchina non banale: una postfazione," in *Urbanistica*, No. 92, 1988
19 | The literature I'm exploring is limited to the last three centuries, from the XVIIIth century till now and is only the literature produced by architects and urbanists. But even with this limitation it is an immense literature. As a consequence, what I'm pointing out is a research program more than an accomplished research. In a quite arbitrary way I consider the preceding literature, since antiquity, very important to building a genealogy of many of the metaphors I'll mention.
20 | *The Living City* for instance (F.L.Wright), or the Saint Simonian metaphor of the urban infrastructure as an arterial and vein network.

function; the city as a banal machine,[21] the "functional" city, the importance of performances; the city as a factory, the social geography of the city reflecting the Taylor-Ford labour organization; the city as a playing field, the actors' interplay in building and using the urban space; the city as an expanding network, as a patchwork or a labyrinth, a new idea of personal and collective freedom in the expanding global world; the mobility network as a sponge or as a system of pipes hierarchically structured, looking for an order in the chaos of the contemporary metropolis, are only some of the main and well known ones.

– The second group of metaphors, working at a different, more abstract level, can be called conceptual metaphors and speaks of the city in terms of an abstract concept: continuity, regularity, order, transparency, equilibrium, process or fragment, patch. I can call them figures of the discourse, i.e. figures we frequently use speaking of the city. These figures, building a bridge between reality and a more abstract way to read and interpret it, had an important role for the physical project of the city and territory. The figure of continuity, for instance, oriented the majority of scientific fields of study throughout modernity, in the same way as the figure of the fragment orients contemporary thinking. Both had an important role concerning the way to observe, interpret and build the city. We find the traces of them not only in discourses about the city, but also in the physical constitution of the same modern and contemporary city. We find them in the discourses of architects and urbanists, but also of all the scholars crossing the depth of social movements. We find them in literature, in the visual arts as in vernacular language. They cross, meeting great resistance, the space between words and facts.

A progressive figure in the 16th century – when Descartes recognized it as the representation of a new form of rationality – is continuity, which I consider to be modernity's predominant one. It pervades five centuries of urban history and it embodies infinity in the 17th century, regularity and

---

21 | I utilize this term of the "banal machine" to distinguish this metaphor, typical of the Modern Movement, from the metaphor of the city as a "non-banal machine" taking into account uncertainty as in H. von Foetster, "Cibernetica ed epistemologia: storia e prospettive," in Bocchi, G., Ceruti, M. (eds.), *La sfida della complessità*, Milano: Feltrinelli, 1985

transparency in the 18th, order and hierarchy in the 19th when it finds its most complete and coherent representation in the linguistic unity of urban space in Europe's great capitals. Throughout its long history, continuity meets and refers to other figures without contradiction; it is enriched during mannerism, baroque, neo-classicism, romanticism and eclecticism, needless to say, because continuity is simultaneously a figure of urban as well as social space.

Although all modern thought was dominated by visual thought, continuity does not pervade only the figurative aspects of urban space, nor should the concept be understood in a restrictive way. The culture of modernity from the Renaissance until the 19th century is universalistic because it is saturated by the figure of continuity. For example, in terms of mathematical analysis, without this concept, infinitesimal calculus could not exist; and the contribution of this field to modern thought is commonly accepted. But even if we observe the history of the formation of various disciplines during this same period, we understand how important the figure of continuity was for all of them.

Most often, continuity is represented as the identification of an idea of freedom in the infinite possibility of circulation and subdivision of the real. For instance, the idea of the infinite subdivision of land lies at the origin of the middle-class demand for property rights and its market value. Great insistence was placed on the continuous, isotropic, infinitely divisible and permeable nature of the bourgeois city and less on the fact that it opposed the indivisible nature – even if only symbolically so – of lordly property rights, of civic uses and of the common rights of medieval society. To leave medieval property rights behind and enter into the modern bourgeois concept of ownership meant accepting the land's continuous divisibility as well as the infinite mobility of people and goods in physical, economic and social space. This same idea is linked to the ways in which trade mechanisms and the free market were conceptualised respectively as theatre and modus agendas of actors, each having infinitesimal dimensions in relation to the whole. This idea lies at the origin of the increasingly ordered division of labour and of specialized modern thought as opposed to the unitary thought of previous eras. It lies at the origin of the Fordist idea represented tangibly in the *Ford River Rouge Complex*, in the simultaneous organization of work and city, in total social synchronization. It is associated with an idea of democracy based on the subdivision of powers.

For a long time, the figure of continuity accompanied the emergence of the subject as opposed to the otherness of power and domination, its reduction to the isolated individual and removal of the collective subject. The figure of continuity meets great resistance along the path of its progressive conquest of western culture. Modern society will never be conceived as a regular and infinitely transparent perspective space – as a panopticon.

Image 38: Le Corbusier, *Précisions sur un état présent de l'architecture et de l'urbanisme*, 1930

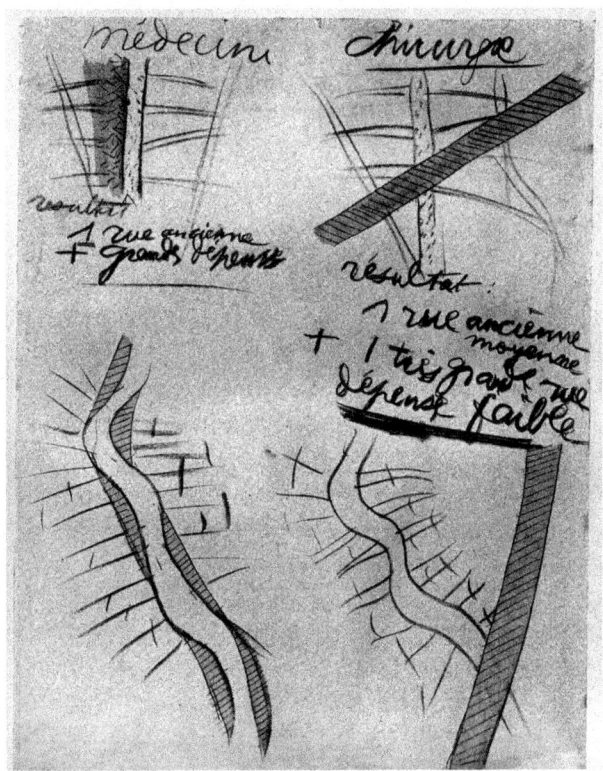

Within it, as within the modern city, aggregations will form or persist. Like fragments of past worlds, or germs of a future one, these aggregations, by constructing differences, will tend to compete with continuity for symbolic, physical and social space.[22] This resistance is also expressed in forms of the moral economies of the sub-classes and in forms of conflict;[23] or in forms of resistance to the homologation and codified equality of the industrial and juridical arrangements of the great modern states. This resistance is expressed in the exploitation of memory, in the formation of increasingly numerous minorities in the perennial search for identity, in increasingly sophisticated criteria of inclusion/exclusion. It is expressed in the substitution of a society of equals sustained by codes and constitutional pacts with a statutory society in which every minority, local or professional group is endowed – as in the pre-modern era – with its own recognized and specific statute. Progressively, the western world has become aware of both the destruction of local cultures and places of social life wrought by modernity as well as the limitations placed on the collective dimension implicit in the modern city; and poses resistance to these phenomena.

For this reason, we can identify two main phases in that period dominated by the figure of continuity – that is throughout all of modernity. In the first phase, in the words of Descartes, continuity is liberation and conquest; liberation from medieval constraints and conquest of a new bourgeois freedom. The second phase is dominated by anguish, fear of the infinity of equality and of the rift opened in society, and in individual consciousness. It is dominated by the anxiety over the idea of a society reduced to a continuous and homogeneous mass. This is why, between enlightenment and positivist historicism, the figure of continuity first becomes the search for transparency and regularity, permeability and infinite circulation; and later for order and hierarchy, for strong forms of rationality to which to refer. In the end, it becomes nostalgia.

In this passage, regularity plays a crucial role. It was interpreted between the 17th and 18th centuries as a guiding principle for urban space ordered like a fabric and transparent like glass. At the turning point between the 18th and 19th centuries, regularity becomes, with J.N.L. Durand[24] the systematic rationale for the architectural project and a condition for the

---

22 | Battisti, Eugenio, *L'antirinascimento*, Milano: Garzanti, 1989
23 | Thomson, William Irwin, *The Time Falling Bodies Take to Light: Mythology, Sexuality and the Origins of Culture*, St. Martin's Press, New York, 1981
24 | Durand, Jean-Nicolas-Louis, *Précis des leçons d'architecture données à l'École royale polytechnique*, 1809-13

construction of isotropic and homogeneous space in which the magnitude of modern industry unfolds.[25]

Regularity also becomes a measure of normality and deviance. On the one hand, it is anomalous, moving away from, or refuting, established order. In this sense, it can be considered pathological and so must be distanced, isolated and repressed. On the other hand, it is the substitution of the enlightenment idea of an irrepressible and meta-historic human nature with a kind of normality that can be empirically measured – thanks to developments in statistics. It is something that – in light of increasing information and its sophisticated manipulation – can be made to appear correct.[26] The 19th century brings with it the stamp of normality and becomes as obsessed with this concept as it does with its contrary.[27] In the modern city and society, great anguish and fear is expressed in the figure of concentration. On a much less abstract level than continuity, we find concentration in many disciplines; urban planning bears its mark.

"One of the most important events in the development of our culture," wrote Sombart in 1912, "is the rapid demographic growth of many cities beginning in the 16th century and the birth of a new kind of city: the city of hundreds of thousands of inhabitants, the Metropolis, which, towards the end of the 17th century, approaches the modern form of the city with millions of inhabitants like London and Paris."[28]

These metaphors are different from fragment, heterogeneity, dispersion, figures and conceptual metaphors that concern the way we look to the city.[29] What I am trying to say is that many of the metaphors in each group have built an influent metaphysic, unifying and orienting analogically the way of thinking of an entire historical period and establishing pertinent relationships between different aspects of the perception and interpretation of reality.

---

25 | Guillerme, Jacques, 1970; Szambien, Werner, *Jean-Nicolas-Louis Durand 1760-1834*, Paris: Picard; Huet, Bernard, 1984

26 | Canguilhelm, Georges, *Le normal et le pathologique*, Paris: Presses Universitaires de France, 1966

27 | Hacking, Ian, *The Taming Of Change*, Cambridge [etc.]: Cambridge University Press, 1990

28 | Sombart ,Werner, *Luxus und Kapitalismus*, 1912

29 | Secchi, Bernardo, *La prima lezione di urbanistica*, Laterza: Roma, 2000

An investigation of metaphors is thus, for me, a way to study the different collective imageries and rationalities: an articulated world of images, discourses and behaviours behind which we can recognize the ideologies of different actors and social groups and their relations to different physical urban situations. If we look only to the metaphors used by scholars in different disciplines it is a way to study different technical cultures and there we discover the communicative role of the metaphor, the way it links, also in a technical way, different disciplines and different research fields. Some years ago, for instance, Paola Viganò and I started to conceptualise the mobility networks as made by "sponges" and "pipes." As is well known, we have available to us some simulation models for the traffic running in a pipe (models using a hydraulic metaphor) but not for the traffic in a sponge. We asked some mathematicians to help us. They were studying the capillary irrigation of the brain and started to conceive a mobility network in the same way. In this way, the brain became a metaphor for a territory irrigated by a capillary network of mobility and vice-versa.[30]

For instance, an investigation of metaphors is also today a way to discover two main concepts, hierarchy and isotropy – they too often used as metaphors – and thereby a long battle of power against democracy. Hierarchy obviously is the figure of a central power with its ramifications, the image of the social organization and of the city as a tree (another powerful metaphor).[31] But the city and society can be conceptualised in a different way, not as a tree[32] but as a highly connected and isotropic network for instance. Isotropy is, in our view, the figure of democracy, of an open society and of a city without privileges. To use isotropy and not hierarchy as a fundamental concept in designing the city today has to do with a strong political engagement against any form of exclusion and inclusion.

---

30 | Secchi, Bernardo (ed.), *On mobility. Infrastrutture per la mobilità e costruzione del territorio*, Venezia: Marsilio, 2010
31 | G. Lakoff, M. Johnson 1980
32 | Alexander, Christopher, "A city is not a tree," in *The Architectural Forum*, April- May 1965, pp. 58-61

Semper's Metaphor of the Living Building
Its Origins in 18th-Century Fetishism Theories
and its Function in his Architectural Theory

CAROLINE VAN ECK

The metaphor of the living building is one of the oldest and most persistent in architectural discourse. The metaphor of the stones that speak is a topos that occurs in classical Latin oratory, for instance when Cicero in his speeches calls upon the stones of the Forum to cry out in outrage. In John Ruskin's analysis of the Gothic in *Stones of Venice*, not only the ornament grows and coils, and arches spring or meet; but the main task of architecture in general should be to look well, act well and speak well. We also find visual varieties of such metaphors, for instance in Michelangelo's gradual transformation of the outline of a column into a human face, or in Serlio's gradual metamorphosis of rustication – called in fact by his Italian contemporaries *pietra viva* or living stone – into snarling animals in his *Libro Extraordinario*.

In this paper I will consider one of the most intriguing cases of this metaphor in the 19th century, Semper's claim that buildings, by their dressing and masking, negate their material – that is inanimate, stone nature – and become alive, to consider what impact such metaphors have on our conception of architecture, and ultimately, whether they actually are metaphors.

Semper was not the first to introduce the metaphor of the living building. Already in Alberti, the metaphor of the building as a body is very conspicuous and consistently thought through. But the function of these metaphors is different in Renaissance architectural theory from the way they are used in the 19th century. In Alberti's *On the Art of Building*, the comparison between a building and the human body allowed him to obtain access to a substantial body of theoretical, theological and scientific knowledge: about

Image 39: Sebastiano Serlio, Libro Estraordinario (1551), rustic gate no. XXIX

the mathematical structure of the universe, the role of the divine artifex, or the theory of humors. The body metaphor thus serves as one of his strategies to elevate the craft of building to the status of a liberal art. But in the 19th century the role and effect of the metaphor of the living building turns out to be quite different.

Semper
In this paper I will concentrate on one of the most puzzling, and in many senses most extreme case of a 19th-century theorist attributing life to a building: Gottfried Semper's statement in § 63 of *Der Stil* (1863), that a building

in order to become truly monumental, should negate, dress and mask its material character. This famous, and heavily metaphorical passage draws on the metaphor of the living building in many ways, for instance in applying to façades the terms normally reserved for human beings and more in particular women, such as dressing, *maquillage* or adornment.

For Semper, dressing and masking, *Bekleiden und Maskiren*, are among the oldest and most widespread of human activities; they are as old as civilization itself, and one of the wellsprings of the arts. Works of art, whether they be paintings, operas or buildings all in some way are the result of dressing and masking, and are best enjoyed in the festive mood of masked revelry: 'the haze of carnival candles is the true atmosphere of art.'[1] Art always dresses and masks, and should be viewed as if it were part of a theatre festival, not in the sober and clear light of everyday reality. That is, architecture is not only a monumental representation of a momentous act, offering the viewer the decoration and dressing of the structural parts by making use of forms that represent the primitive crafts of mankind. It is also, by this very act of dressing or masking, a negation of matter and even reality itself. This is necessary for the development of a repertoire of forms created freely by man and endowed with symbolic meaning.

Now both dressing and masking suggest a formal language based on human forms and artefacts, but what can Semper have possibly meant by this appeal to negate matter and reality, particularly where architecture, that most material and practical of all arts, is concerned? An answer is suggested by one of the most intriguing passages in *Der Stil*, where human concerns suddenly intrude upon architectural theory: Semper's abrupt quote of Hamlet in *Der Stil*: "But what was Hecuba to him?" This occurs in the middle of a long note to § 62 that also includes the famous remark that the true atmosphere of art is the twilight of carnival torches. Reality and matter need to be destroyed for form to emerge as a significant symbol, and as an independent human creation. When Phidias created the reliefs for the tympana of the Parthenon, he hid all traces of the material he used to represent the gods: 'As a result his gods come to meet us, make us enthusiastic, alone and in cooperation, first and foremost as expressions of purely human beauty and greatness.' Semper then asks again: "What was Hecuba to him?" and next argues that as in Phidias' "stone dramas," the Greek

---

1 | Semper, Gottfried, *Der Stil*, Zurich, 1863, § 62, p. 250, note 85

tragic and comic poets developed the original Bacchic mask play, changing the proscenium into the frame of the picture of an immense part of human history that is not past, but will happen again "as long as human hearts" beat. Although he never lived to complete it, Semper intended to show in the fourth part of *Der Stil* that Greek architecture succeeded in making the viewer forget means and matter, 'how it appears and acts, and is sufficient unto itself as form'.

Here we finally get a clue to what Semper may have meant with this almost obsessive repetition of Hamlet's question. The actor in the play Hamlet has performed in Elsinore is so carried away with his role that he forgets himself and becomes the part he plays, even though he is playing the role of a woman who died long ago and in a foreign country. Just so works of art in order to truly become art, need to destroy, or rather deny reality through representation, or in Semper's words, through dressing and masking. Dressing and masking, one might say, are representations; they are no longer the space or structure they represent, but their sign, and as such have a different ontological status. Their representational function as signifiers replaces the material, practical function of the spaces they cover.

Architectural dressing, that is, is not just a representation of the four basic crafts that are the origin of architecture. It is the final step completing the transformation of a building into monumental architecture, when it becomes architecture proper and uses materials for figurative representation or *bildliche Darstellung*.[2] It is also a denial of material reality that paradoxically greatly enhances the presence of the work of art, be it a drama or a building. It makes the building appear and act upon the viewer, makes it alive and humanizes it. Throughout *Der Stil* passages occur in which architecture is described as if it were a living structure, in which the artistic expression of the conflict between pressure and counter pressure animates the building's appearance. In the case of Greek temples the use of a 'veil of paint' masks mechanic necessity and transforms them into 'dynamic, even organic, forms, a matter of endowing them with a soul [...].'[3] At the same

---

2 | Semper 1863, § 63, p. 250

3 | F.i. Semper 1863, § 164, p. 728; and § 78, p. 379. Semper here is clearly indebted to Schopenhauer's view of architecture as an animated system of the conflict between load and support in *Die Welt als Wille und Vorstellung*, § 35; cf

time, the theatrical mode which Semper advocates implies both a dematerialization of architecture (it no longer simply is, but represents itself not as a material artifact, but as a cultural being), and the oscillation between presence and representation, acting and enacting that is characteristic of a theatrical performance.

Image 40: G. Semper, Burgtheater Vienna, 1873-88, showing the masking of the constructive parts by intensive rustication thematizing

This raises at least two questions: how are we to understand the fictionalization Semper advocates? And what is the fiction monumental architecture offers? To answer these questions we have to consider the intellectual genealogy of Semper's ideas on dressing and thereby denying the material reality of architecture.[4]

As Mari Hvattum has recently shown, Aristotle's thought was a crucial intellectual influence on Semper. Whereas classical and neo-classical doctrine had presented imitation as the means through which the classical

---

Semper, Gottfried, *Style. Style in the Technical and Tectonic Arts; or, Practical Aesthetics*, introduction by H.F. Mallgrave, translation by H.F. Mallgrave and M. Robinson, Los Angeles: The Getty Research Institute, 2004, p. 39

4 | For a more extended treatment of these issues and Semper's intellectual forebears see my "Figuration, Tectonics and Animism in Semper's *Der Stil*," in *Journal of Architecture* 14/3, 2009, pp. 325-37

tradition was kept alive and passed on to new generations, Semper redefined imitation as Aristotelian *mimesis*, the representation of significant human action. In the case of architecture these were not as in the *Poetics*, the dramatic plots of Greek mythology, but the four basic crafts connected with the four elements that formed the origin of human society: the hearth, the earthwork mound, the woven enclosure, and the wooden roof.

Semper also appropriated the terminology Aristotle used to define what distinguishes living organisms from dead matter. According to the latter they are organic unities structured so that the parts can fulfill a purpose that existed as *telos* or form shaping matter before the organism itself came into being. But Semper then used this teleological terminology, which is about the *purposes and functions* of organisms or artifacts, to talk about the *formal* properties of artefacts. By the same stroke he removed the artwork from the real world of purposes, functions and uses. But this caused him a problem that would return in various forms throughout his life, and which he would never solve: whereas his analysis of the historical development of art aimed to set out the rationale of change in terms of political, cultural and material factors, it in fact concentrates entirely on formal aspects.[5] Or, put slightly differently, Semper's transformation of the Aristotelian and Kantian analysis of organisms and artefacts in terms of fitness for purpose into a language of formal analysis contributed greatly towards the status of art works as autonomous microcosms obeying their own organic principles of figuration; but at the same time separated them completely from the endeavors, desires and needs of human reality.

Reconstructing some of the intellectual origins of Semper's theory of style helps to put his substitution of *Stoff* in the sense of material for *Stoff* in the sense of subject matter in a wider context: it is the consequence, or perhaps one might say a symptom, of his failure to forge a connection between the formal properties of art works, buildings and artifacts, of which he was such a subtle and eloquent analyst, and the social, political and cultural conditions that surrounded their making. This formalism or 'compression of meaning', as Hvattum has called it, can thus be understood as a result of the application of Aristotle's definition of tragedy as the imitation of significant action to architecture's dressing and masking as the imitation

---

5 | Hvattum, M., *Semper and the Problem of Historicism*, Cambridge: Cambridge University Press, 2004, pp. 47-57, 87-114 and 149-5

of significant form while limiting the latter's significance strictly to space, tectonics and structure.

At the same time, his adaptation of Aristotle's definition of living beings in terms of teleology or fitness for purpose made it possible to project life unto the inanimate forms of architecture. As we have seen, architecture teems with life in *Der Stil*, and at times it seems as if the significance of built form resides almost exclusively in its animated representation of structural conflicts. The ultimate fiction of architectural masking, and therefore denial of matter and reality, would thus be that inanimate stone can be represented as animate by means of fictional representation.

Animate architecture and fetishism
Usually the attribution of animation or even life to buildings by Semper is placed in the tradition of the German aesthetics of *Einfühlung* or empathy. According to its best-known proponent Friedrich Theodor Vischer, the vital properties we think we experience when looking at nature are in reality projections of our own feelings and thoughts. When we admire windswept clouds or trees bent by age, we lend our bodily sensations, feelings and thoughts to nature and in the process of doing so give it life and even a soul.[6] Empathy was taken up by his son Robert, who considered the symbolic animation of form as the result of empathy, defined by him as the 'projection of one's own bodily form – and with this also the soul – into the form of the object.' Vischer's aesthetic and psychological researches were the inspiration of a series of late 19th-century studies into the experience of art and architecture, culminating in Heinrich Wölfflin's *Prolegomena zu einer Psychologie der Architektur* of 1886.[7]

But Semper's attribution of life to architecture can also be given another context, that of French 18th century research into the origins of religion, particularly the Président de Brosses' study of fetishism, *Du culte des dieux fétiches, ou Parallèle de l'ancienne religion de l'Egypte avec la religion actuelle*

---

6 | See f.i. the discussion of *Einfühlung* in Vischer's *Kritische Gänge*, 1847, vol. 5, p. 45

7 | On 19th-century German aesthetics of architecture based on empathy see R. Vischer and others, *Empathy, Form, and Space: Problems in German Aesthetics, 1873-1893*, introduction by H.F. Mallgrave and E. Ikonomou, Los Angeles: The Getty Research Institute 1994, in particular pp. 17, 21-22, and 28

de Nigritie (1760). In these early essays in anthropology, the attribution of sentient being, personhood and agency to shells, stones or plants was not considered as an aesthetic response, but as animism: a manifestation of the primitive mind's tendency to superstition. This way of looking at the origins of art was taken up by the Piedmontese *érudit* Octavien de Guasco, a friend of Montesquieu in *De l'usage des statues chez les Anciens* (1768). From the outset he distances himself from the traditional artistic or antiquarian study of antiquity.[8] Religion is the origin of sculpture. Iconic sculpture in the shape of man or animal is born from fear and superstition, because these were the motives which made primitive man venerate the aniconic monuments nomadic tribes had erected when they took leave of each other on their wanderings. Guasco gives examples from the entire world, from Japan to northern Europe to illustrate this custom and its transformation. These monuments, originally erected as signs of human will, first became the place where the human spirit resided, and next the god itself.[9] Motivated by the same fears and superstitions which led primitive man to attribute to stone and wood the agency of living persons, aniconic statues were gradually replaced by statues in the shape of man. The aniconic objects were believed to be animated by the divine spirit.[10]

Through the use of the human form to shape cult statues, the tendency to attribute life, personhood and agency to these inanimate objects was strengthened. Idolatry was thus kept alive because the human appearance of statues led the believer to attribute the mental characteristics that go with human form to these statues.[11] Thus fear and superstition first led to the belief that inanimate stone was animated by divine spirit, next to the

---

8 | Guasco, O., *De l'usage des statues chez les anciens. Essai historique*, Brussels: chez J.L. de Bourbers, 1768. On Guasco see: Griener, P., "Ottaviano di Guasco, intermédiaire entre la philosophie française et les antiquités de Rome," in Norci Cagiano, L. (ed.), *Roma Triumphans? L'attualità dell'antico nella Francia del Settecento*, Roma: Ed. di storia e letteratura, 2007, pp. 26-51; on Guasco and Quatremère see : Sarchi, A., "Quatremère de Quincy e Octavien Guasco: abozzo per una genesi dello *Jupiter Olympien*," in *Ricerche di Storia dell'Arte* 64, 1998, pp. 79 – 88, in particular pp. 82-3
9 | Guasco 1768, p. 17
10 | Ibid., p. 29
11 | Ibid., p. 34

development of figurative sculpture, and culminated with the creation of anthropomorphic statues.

Now one of the few texts Semper quotes with approval was by an author much influenced by De Brosses and Guasco, Antoine-Chrysostome Quatremère de Quincy's book on polychromy: *Le Jupiter Olympien [...], ouvrage qui comprend un essai sur le goût de la sculpture polychrome* of 1815. Even though Semper felt Quatremère had not gone far enough in his conclusions, he approved of the latter's argument that ancient Greek architecture and sculpture had been covered in color, that the pure white surfaces of

Image 41: Frontispice of A.-Chr. Quatremère de Quincy, *Le Jupiter Olympien*, 1814

their statues and temples were a classicist fiction. The Greeks' use of color was only the culmination of a tradition that linked their work to the art of the oldest civilizations of the Middle East. Adding layers of paint, incrustation and dressing, all of which were so conspicuously displayed by the Olympian statue of Jupiter, are all manifestations of the primitive and universal human instinct for dressing and masking.[12]

Yet when we turn to Quatremère's book we find a slightly different interpretation of the use of color, which nonetheless throws some light on the possible meaning of the metaphors of dressing and life, and the fictionalizing of architecture they imply, in *Der Stil*. As we have seen, adding a veil of paint to buildings animated them, and even gave them a soul. But for Quatremère this worked in a slightly different manner, and with different effect. To begin with, the connection between sculpture and religion for him is manifest and profoundly connected to the actual nature or meaning of religious statues. Greek sculpture was not the expression, as it was for Semper, of autonomous human creativity or pure human beauty and greatness. In ancient Greece there was no such thing as autonomous art: '[the art of sculpture] was religion's favourite art, and the most docile servant of its wishes.'[13]

For Quatremère as for Semper polychromy was the result of an innate urge of primitive man to associate color and form; but for the former it did not become the dressing through which matter and reality were denied; on the contrary, its purpose was to strengthen the mimetic illusion of statues to the point were viewers believed the statue was alive, not an image, but the god it represented. This served the needs of religion very well: statues

---

12 | *Style* § 61, p. 242. On Semper's views on polychromy see most recently: Pisani, S., "'Die Monumente sind durch Barbarei monochrom geworden.' Sempers Vorläufigen Bemerkungen über bemalte Architektur und Plastik bei den Alten," in Nerdinger, W., Oechslin, W., (eds.), *Gottfried Semper 1803-79. Architektur und Wissenschaft*, Munich: Prestel Verlag and Zurich: GTA 2003, pp. 109-16. On the polychromy debate in 19th-century sculpture and Semper's role in it see Blühm (ed.), *The Colour of Sculpture 1840-1910*, Zwolle: Waanders 1996, in particular pp. 18-19

13 | Quatremère de Quincy, A.-Chr., *Le Jupiter Olympien [...], ouvrage qui comprend un essai sur le goût de la sculpture polychrome*, Paris: Firmin Didot 1814, p. xxiii

that through the use of colour seemed to be alive exercised a very strong agency on their viewers, instilling in them a sense of presence that was the stronger for the simple character of their representation.

The use of polychromy, different materials, and clothes strengthens the suggestion that the representation is actually what it represents. Such identification undermines the imitational character of these statues, because for Quatremère true imitation is based on the use of different materials in the representation from what it represents, but at the same time very much strengthens the illusion of reality and living presence.[14] This use of materials that are identical to the being represented supports another human tendency, to confuse a sign or representation with what it represents.[15]

Image 42: Head of the emperor Augustus, Roman, about 27-25 BC, found in Meroe, Sudan. Bronze, with inlaid eyes of mother of pearl. Height: 47.75 cm.

There are significant differences between Quatremère and Semper on the nature of art and the implications of polychromy for its reality. For Quatremère polychromy undermines the reality of a statue as an autonomous work of representational art but is essential for suggesting the living presence of the being the statue represents, whereas for Semper polychromy

14 | Ibid., p. 2
15 | Ibid., p. xxiii

– as any other kind of dressing or masking – is the condition of its status as an autonomous work of art. But comparing their views on polychromy does throw some light on the question, in what sense Semper can have meant that masking or dressing negates matter and reality, whether we are to understand his attribution of life to buildings as merely a metaphorical way of speaking.

When Semper and Quatremère's views on polychromy are put next to each other it becomes clear how the fictionalization or denial of matter through representation may be said to work: through the suggestion of animation or even life. Dressing, in applying a layer of figurative form to spatial enclosure, often draws on the forms of living nature, and thus suggests life. For Quatremère, living presence is suggested because the polychromy and dressing of statues totally undermines their representational character as an imitation, and brings them too close to the being they represent. For Semper, dressing or masking gives life or even a soul to a building because by representing the conflict between load and support or dramatizing the crafts at the origin of architecture it animates dead, unmoving stone. But in both cases it turns out that the ultimate fiction, or denial of reality, is that of animating the inanimate.

Conclusion
How do these attributions of life to architecture function as metaphors? Can they even be said to be metaphors? What started in Alberti's use of the building-body analogy as a means of appropriating and integrating bodies of knowledge into architectural theory, or what Gernot Böhme has called the use of a metaphor as a transport of ideas, developed in the 19th-century varieties of the building as a living being metaphor into something quite different. In Semper's use of the metaphors of dressing, make up, acting and speaking, a much more radical line of thought can be discerned. We might call this not so much the metaphor of the living building, because the fictional aspect gradually dissolves, but rather a case of what the English anthropologist Alfred Gell has termed 'animacy': an object sharing not all, but a number of significant aspects of being alive with living beings, in this case the complex of dressing, movement, facial expression and speaking.[16] For Semper animacy had clear implications for architectural design: the

---

16 | Gell, A., *Art and Agency. An anthropological theory*, Oxford: Clarendon Press, 1998, pp. 96-122, in particular 118-20 and 121-2; cf my "Living Statues: Alfred

Semperoper or the Burgtheater for instance are based on a poetics and rhetoric of dressing, veiling, and negating materiality. Here the metaphor of the living building is no longer a matter of us speaking about architecture, but is changed into a design program and a poetics of architecture.

But there is another implication: the fundamental instability, not to say precariousness, the metaphor of the living building brings with it, in two ways. On the one hand, if the metaphor becomes too vivid, or the building too much alive, it ceases to be a work of art, it loses its artistic character as the creation of the human mind. This was noticed already in the 19th century, in discussions of polychromy or wax sculptures which, for instance for Quatremère de Quincy or Schopenhauer, by the very vividness of their imitation dissolved the border between realism and idealism, and ultimately between art and life.

But on the other hand, if a metaphor really works well, that is, evokes a very rich field of meanings not directly rooted in the object to which the metaphor is applied, the object looses its own essential character. If, to use Nelson Goodman's definition for a moment, a metaphor is an affair between a predicate with a past and an object that yields while resisting, its surrender may be too complete.[17] The essential character of architecture as the construction of space may be buried under the evocative charms of dressing, make up, gesture and speech. But Semper's use of the complex of meanings associated with the metaphor of the living building is not a case of straightforward use of metaphor. Instead of thinking of this metaphor in terms of a transport or attribution of meaning, it may make more sense to think of it in non-linguistic terms: in the classical rhetorical sense, first developed by Cicero and Quintilian, of *figurae*, figures of speech that, by giving a new shape or outline to a speech or work of art, animate the inanimate; both by the analogy with the human body and face or figure, and by the novel aspect they convey to objects.[18]

Gell's *Art and Agency*, Living Presence and the Sublime," in *Art History* 33/4, 2010, 642-660

17 | Goodman, N., *Languages of Art. An Approach to a Theory of Symbols*, Indianapolis: Bobbs-Merrill, 1968, p. 69

18 | Cf Quintilian, *Institutio Oratoria*, VIII.iii.62; VI.ii.32; IX.i.21 and VIII.v.34. see also Ps-Longinus XV.1. For a more extensive treatment of this issue see my

Considered in this light, the metaphor of the living building is not an attempt at transporting new meanings while speaking about language, but instead an attempt at escaping the linguistic constraints in order to preserve what distinguishes architecture from language: it is not enunciation but the construction of speech. Semper's use of the metaphor of the living building opens up new ways of conceiving the way a building addresses us, and acts upon us: not as some sort of truncated speech, but in a mode of address that is proper to architecture as a three-dimensional spatial art: it gestures, acts upon us, and draws us into its interiors.

Classical Rhetoric and the Arts in Early Modern Europe. Cambridge and New York 2007, Introduction and Chapters III and V

Organic Metaphors and Urban Causalities

BENEDIKTE ZITOUNI

Organisms and action patterns
What if city development were equated with that of an organism? What if the organism served as a metaphor for urban investigation? It might be worthwhile and it is a course that I have taken in my own work, concerned with the 19th century development of Brussels and its planning tools[1], but it requires much tact and caution. For metaphors, as the mathematical biologist Evelyn Fox Keller argues, are not models, not analogies, not simulations, not comparisons. They are vague, unstable and literary sometimes. They do not point to similarities that concern the entire set of characteristics of the two given systems but pinpoint only one possible similarity that is underscored for the sole purpose of stimulating the investigator in her explorations.[2] In other words, it doesn't matter whether the metaphor is true or not – of course we all know that the city is not an organism – but to posit that it is so might help us to investigate one specific subject with a little more imagination. It opens up the possibility for sidetracking, i.e. deviating from the perspective of urban studies and sociology into the field of biology and life sciences. The subject in need of such imagination and sidetracking, is, in my case, causality.

The hunch is an old one. Many authors concerned with cities have linked causality to biological findings and natural sciences. At the beginning of the 19th century, the Edinburgh School held eco-systemic and evo-

---

1 | Zitouni, Benedikte, *Agglomérer. Une anatomie de l'extension bruxelloise (1825-1915)*, with a foreword by Eric Corijn and an afterword by Bruno Latour, Bruxelles: Academic Scientific Press & VUB University Presss, 2010
2 | Fox Keller, Evelyn, *Expliquer la vie. Modèles, métaphores et machines en biologie du développement* [2002], Paris, Gallimard, 2004, pp. 137-138

lutionary views on cities in order to amend local surroundings and trigger civic action.³ In the 1920's, the Chicago School defined the city as an organic entity in order to show that it was not planned for and could therefore not be tackled by mere mechanical engineering or political programs.⁴ In the last decade, the Harvard Project links urbanism to cybernetics and to theories of complexity in order to show the functioning and patterning of urban regions.⁵ The city needs breadth of vision, the city is social metabo-

---

3 | Geddes, Patrick, *City Development, a Study of Parks, Gardens and Culture-Institutes*, Edinburgh: Geddes and Company; Birmingham: Saint George Press, 1904; Geddes, Patrick, *Guide-book and outline catalogue to the Cities and Town-planning exhibition*, Belfast, Cities and Town-planning exhibition; Geddes, Patrick, *Cities in Evolution*, London: Williams and Norgate, 1949, 1915; Thompson, Arthur, Geddes, Patrick, *Life: outlines of general biology*, London: Williams & Norgate, 1931, (see especially Book II, Chapter XIII: Towards a theory of life, pp. 1384-1440); an inheritance of this line of thinking can be found in the work of Lewis Mumford, *The City in History, Its Origins, Its Transformations and Its Prospects*, New York: Harcourt Books, 1989, 1961; see also: Novak, Frank (ed.), *Lewis Mumford and Patrick Geddes: the correspondence*, New York, London: Routledge, 1995; I thank Judith Lemaire of the Horta-La Cambre Faculty of Architecture at the University of Brussels (ULB) for bringing the Edinburgh School and Patrick Geddes to my attention.

4 | Park, Robert, "Introduction," in Anderson, Nels, *The Hobo: The Sociology of the Homeless Man*, Chicago: University of Chicago Press, 1923; Burgess, Ernest, "The Growth of the City: An Introduction to a Research Project," in Park, Robert, Burgess, Edward, McKenzie, Roderick, Wirth, Louis, *The City*, Chicago: University of Chicago Press, 1925; Park, Robert, "Introduction," in Thrasher, Edward, *The Gang: A study of 1,313 gangs in Chicago*, Chicago: University of Chicago Press, 1926; Burgess, Ernest (ed.), *The Urban Community: Selected Papers from the Proceedings of the American Sociological Society 1925*, Chicago: University of Chicago Press, 1927, pp. vii-ix; Park, Robert, "The Ghetto," in Park, Robert, *Human Communities, The City and Human Ecology – The Collected Papers of Robert Ezra Park*, Glencoe: Free Press, 1952 (1928), pp. 99- 101; Wirth, Louis, *Le ghetto*, Grenoble: Presses Universitaires de Grenoble, 1928, 1980, pp. 291-307; Park, Robert, "The City as a Natural Phenomenon," in Park 1952 (1939), pp. 118-127

5 | Koolhaas, Rem, "What Ever Happened to Urbanism?" in OMA, Koolhaas, Rem, Mau, Bruce, *S, M, L, XL*, Rotterdam: 010 Publishers, 1995, pp. 958-971; in Koolhaas, Rem & al., *Mutations*, Bordeaux, Barcelona, Arc en rêve: Actar, 2000, see:

lism, the city is chaos at work – in all three instances, there has been a need for sidetracking into biology or life sciences in order to describe intricate action patterns.

The organic metaphor gives us a sense of what causality may be like in a complex urban system. Causality, then, is the way in which action travels inside a system or set of interactions. This view is held by the French sociologists of translation, Bruno Latour amongst them,[6] and will be used throughout this presentation. So, rather than saying "the city works" and marvel at the beauty of it, the organic take here presented aims at getting into the meanders of the network and at checking how it works, where the action is traveling. To do so, I will confront my own work on Brussels to some considerations that come from the life sciences. More precisely, I will sidetrack, i.e. deviate, into the work of George Canguilhem and Donna Haraway – two philosophers of sciences – and of Jean-Jacques Kupiec and Pierre Sonigo – an embryologist and an immunologist who have been involved in genetic research. Furthermore, this presentation owes a lot to the work of the GECo – Groupe d'Etudes Constructivistes, the exact references of which are mentioned in a few footnotes. In a nutshell, the idea is this: I aim to show that life sciences and the biological investigations of vital processes can be of great use to urban investigations insofar as they highlight causal matters.

Self-preservation and vital connections
In an article about the immune system and AIDS, published in 1989, Donna Haraway writes: "Immunity can also be conceived in terms of shared specificities; of the semi-permeable self able to engage with others (human and non-human, inner and outer), but always with finite consequences;

Chang, Bernard & al., "Pearl River Delta," pp. 280-334; Boeri, Stefano, "Notes for a Research Program," pp. 357-379; Kwinter, Sanford, Fabricius, Daniela, "Urbanism: An Archivist's Art?", pp. 494-507; Kwinter Sanford, Fabricius Daniela, "Dossier," pp. 628-649; Belanger, Pierre & al., "Lagos (Harvard Project on the City)," pp. 650-720; Koolhaas, Rem, Cleijne, Edgar, *Lagos: How it Works (with Harvard Project on the City)*, Baden: Lars Müller Publishers, 2007

6 | Akrich, Madeleine, Callon, Michel, Latour, Bruno, *Sociologie de la traduction: textes fondateurs*, Paris: Presses des Mines, 2006; Latour, Bruno, *Reassembling the Social: An Introduction to Actor-Network-Theory*, Oxford: Oxford University Press, 2005

of situated possibilities and impossibilities of individuation and identification; and of partial fusions and dangers."[7] Instead of looking at immunity as an army defending the body against foreign invasions, Haraway thinks of it as an ecosystem that co-opts, captures, re-balances the bodily elements. Disease then becomes the failure to do so. In an article on the normal and the pathological, Georges Canguilhem likewise writes: "An alteration only becomes pathological when a living being, which until then had managed to stay in equilibrium with its environment, becomes troubled in its existence to a very dangerous extent. That which was adequate to the normal organism, i.e. in relation to its environment, becomes inadequate and perilous to the modified organism."[8] Again, disease is not viewed as a victorious battle of the invaders over the organism's defense armies, but rather it is taken as a matter of vital connections gone wrong. The organism is forever changing, it is involved in a constant renewal of physiological orders[9] and it is sick when one of these changes doesn't allow it to interact adequately with its environment, when one of the alterations doesn't allow it any longer to re-establish a new coherence and to reinvent a new self.[10] The partial fusion has gone wrong; the next individuation can't come about.

One might take this to be a mere issue of political correctness or of semantics, but in fact, both quotations show that it is not so obvious to know where causality stands, i.e. it is not always clear how action is distributed and where it is traveling inside a complex system (that is the meaning of causality here). On the one hand, with the battle imagery, there are two fronts acting and reacting one upon the other. On the other hand, there are

---

7 | Haraway, Donna, "The Biopolitics of Postmodern Bodies: Constitutions of Self in Immune System Discourse" [1989], in Haraway, Donna, *Simians, Cyborgs and Women: The Reinvention of Nature*, New York, N.Y.: Routledge, 1991, p. 225

8 | Original French version: "Une altération dans le contenu symptomatique n'apparaît comme maladie qu'au moment où l'existence de l'être, jusqu'alors en relation d'équilibre avec son milieu, devient dangereusement troublée. Ce qui était adéquat pour l'organisme normal, dans ses rapports avec l'environnement, devient pour l'organisme modifié inadéquat et périlleux." Translation is mine, slightly shortened for the purpose of the presentation. Canguilhem, Georges, *La connaissance de la vie* [1965] Paris: Vrin, 2006, pp. 210-1

9 | Ibid., pp. 152, 165

10 | Ibid., p. 215

a fluctuating number of actions that interconnect and try to uphold themselves in constantly changing patterns. Viewing the organism in the latter way helps Haraway make a plea for a change in medical politics as well as in scientific investigation. She argues, convincingly, that it could partake in changing the experience of AIDS-patients and of doctors all along the medical treatment. For Canguilhem, the change allows him to move away from mechanical and deterministic biology to one that would put more emphasis on the organism's experience and the way in which organisms are creative and value-seeking entities, making sense out of their environment.[11] So, not only do the quotations show that an action's circulation is not given beforehand, that we do not know – even in medicine or biology – how the action circulates, but the quotations also show that each view on causality bears its own consequences, that each causality has its own possibilities and impossibilities as to how the field of investigation can be developed, both heuristically and politically.

Of course, within the social sciences there are many authors who emphasize the intricate process of collective action and structural changes. For instance, Michel Foucault showed us that it is worthwhile to look at power not as a mere possession but rather as something that is operated and transferred within the many shafts of knowledge practices and more recently Bruno Latour has shown us how each phase of an action pattern adds its lot of invention and of initiative.[12] But Haraway and Canguilhem, by way of their interest in biology, add an important element to this: the double argument of consistency and scaling. On each level of organic life – the organs, the body, the environment or other – consistency has to be

---

11 | Ibid., pp. 134, 146; Canguilhem, Georges, *Le normal et le pathologique* [1966], Paris: Presses Universitaires de France, 2005, pp. 186, 197

12 | Foucault, Michel, "Le corps des condamnés," in Foucault, Michel, *Surveiller et Punir* [1975], Paris: Gallimard, 2000, pp. 32-38; Foucault, Michel, "Cours du 14 janvier 1976," in *Il faut défendre la société* [1975], Cours au Collège de France, 1975, Paris: Gallimard & Seuil; Foucault, Michel, "L'oeil du pouvoir," in Foucault, Michel, *Dits et écrits* [1977], Paris: Gallimard, volume 2, 2001, pp. 190-206; Latour, Bruno, Hermant, Emilie, *Paris ville invisible*, Paris: Empêcheurs de tourner en rond & La Découverte, 1998; Latour, Bruno, "Irréductions," in Latour, Bruno, *Pasteur: guerre et paix des microbes suivi de Irréductions* [1984], Paris: La Découverte, 2001; Latour, Bruno, "Second source of uncertainty: action is overtaken," in Latour 2005, pp. 46-70

reached, be it by fusions, shared specificities, co-optation, invention or recreation[13]. On each level of organic life, scale is a matter of amplitude: how many elements of varying sizes are involved in the making of consistency; how far does the connected region go in terms of articulations?[14] In other words, when looking at organic life, we don't know beforehand the ways in which consistency is reached, nor its relative strength.

The double argument of consistency and scaling sets for a methodological requirement. When analysing organic life, i.e. consistency-in-the-making, one has to grant the power of initiative and of action to all the components involved. Kupiec and Sonigo call this the hypothesis of the liberated cells, which their book *Nor God, nor Gene* alludes to: "[...] the cells are subjected to the laws of evolution, not more, nor less [...] the cells form a society that is similar to those that we know at other levels [...] there is an ecosystem in each one of us, made of billions of microscopic little animals."[15] Or: "Let's grant some freedom to our cells, those billion microscopic animals that live within us and which, unknowingly, make us live, think, dream. Those unicellular animals do not live because they have to make us live. They live like us because they quite simply have to live. [...] The small doesn't make up the big, nor does the big make up for the small. The 'parts' and the 'wholes' have the same status."[16] Action and causal power

---

13 | On the matter of consistency, see the work of GECo - Groupe d'Etudes Constructivistes; Isabelle Stengers, 2007, "And if my body was a forest? Some pragmatic considerations," in *Life and Society*, conference held at the Max Planck Institute of Berlin on 3rd November; Debaise, Didier, "The Living and its Milieu," in *Process Studies*, volume 37, n° 2, 2005; and many other articles and papers by these authors. See also the current work of Olivier Thiery on Deleuze, Guattari, Ruyer and the life sciences

14 | This passage is inspired by Stengers, Isabelle, *L'invention des sciences modernes*, Paris: Flammarion (chapter 5, strength of laboratory sciences and eventfulness of demonstration devices), 1995, 1993; and by Latour, Hermant Emilie 1998, (the verbal figures: to dominate, to refer, to commensurate)

15 | Kupiec, Jean-Jacques, Sonigo, Pierre, *Ni Dieu, ni gène. Pour une autre théorie de l'hérédité*, Paris: Seuil, 2000, p. 129

16 | Original French version: "[...] les cellules sont soumises aux lois de l'évolution, ni plus, ni moins. [...] les cellules forment une société semblable à celles que nous connaissons à d'autres niveaux [...] Il existe donc un écosystème en chacun de nous, composé de milliards de petits animaux microscopiques" and

are thus returned to the cells which – under genetic pressure – had been deprived of it. Also, according to this stance, all instances of organic life have a purpose and rules of their own, none can be reduced to be the mere context or ingredient of the other, nor can they be defined as mere vehicles for an overall effect. Liberation means that there is no reason to treat agents of all kinds differently and that – as a matter of investigation – every agent should be upped onto the pedestal of purposeful – or as Canguilhem has it – value-seeking entity. But what does all this mean for urban investigations?

Growth and city-making
In my own work, looking at the growth of Brussels, I have purposefully granted the power of initiative and of inventiveness to all actors encountered in the city's and State's archives. No difference of causal nature was made between them: the State, the municipalities, the landowners, the entrepreneurs, none were bigger nor smaller than the others, none were frame nor ingredient to the others, none were omnipotent nor were they powerless. All were methodologically accepted as full-blown participants to the making of the city's extensions. Territorial consistency, then, made

---

"Cette liberté que nous revendiquons pour nous-mêmes, accordons-là aussi à nos cellules, ces milliards d'animaux microscopiques qui nous habitent et qui, sans le savoir, nous font vivre, penser, rêver. Ces animaux unicellulaires ne vivent pas sous la contrainte de nous faire vivre. Ils vivent comme nous, sous la contrainte de vivre tout simplement. [...] Le petit ne fait pas le gros plus que le gros ne fait le petit. Les 'parties' et les 'touts' ont le même statut." Ibid. p. 214

A similar interlocking as well as vitalist structure is mentioned by Canguilhem: "Du point de vue biologique, il faut comprendre qu'entre l'organisme et l'environnement, il y a le même rapport qu'entre les parties et le tout à l'intérieur de l'organisme lui-même. L'individualité du vivant ne cesse pas à ses frontières ecodermiques, pas plus qu'elle ne commence à la cellule. Le rapport biologique entre l'être et son milieu est un rapport fonctionnel, et par conséquent mobile, dont les termes échangent successivement leur rôle. La cellule est un milieu pour les éléments infracellulaires, elle vit elle-même dans un milieu intérieur qui est aux dimensions tantôt de l'organe et tantôt de l'organisme, lequel organisme vit lui-même dans un milieu qui lui est en quelque façon ce que l'organisme est à ses composantes. Il y a donc un sens biologique à acquérir pour juger les problèmes biologiques [...]." Canguilhem 2006, p.184

itself felt when closer analysis showed how maps, official letters and building permits circulated between the actors, how these documents were commented upon and interpreted, modified and imitated, forwarded and implemented until they held each other and the city's surroundings in a close wed/gridlock. In other words, action was traveling along the shafts of a city-making network and causes could be tracked down in a completely empirical manner. The findings are twofold: one can discover other causes as well as other territories.

Other causes: no God, nor gene but micro-undertakings. The city's extensions did not take their consistency by the enforcement of a national decree, a master plan or an action program. Nor were they the work of a few powerful landowners or the result of some general tendency to expansion and profit. This does not mean that there was no plan nor profit involved but rather that such causes cannot be relied upon to explain city growth and that they are always partaking in purposeful micro-undertakings. Thus, there isn't any automatic or theoretical rule in such matters; consistency is eventful and occurs when a series of actors is rescaled and gathered into a network of collaboration and co-optation[17]. This organic and Darwinist take on city growth has allowed me to underscore the performance of procedures and inscriptions. Brussels, like many Western cities perhaps, has grown along the abstract settings of administrative devices: technocratic regulations cast the horizon for political commitment; functional perimeters pave the way for planners' ambitions; sketchy dotted lines trigger construction sites and the rise of new neighborhoods. Very much like the magical circles engraved in tribal villages, the administrative frontiers have the power to change the behavior within their confines. If, as shown by anthropologists, land position and social status depend on the performance of rituals, then our modern city rituals are technocratic ones. The typical cogwheels of Western city-making involve cartographic instructions and assembly proceedings. At least, so it is suggested by the Brussels' case during the 19th century.

---

17 | This idea is inspired by Stengers, Isabelle, *Penser avec Whitehead: une libre et sauvage création de concepts*, 2002, pp. 57-71, pp. 181-183 (the event of endurance, prehension and eternal objects); see also Debaise, Didier, *Un empirisme spéculatif. Lecture de Procès et Réalité de Whitehead*, Paris: Vrin (eternal objects), 2006

Other territories: no two fronts, nor annexation but unwrapped strengths. Among local researchers, it is commonly said that Brussels suffers from its historical failure to annex all its municipalities into one central office. It is supposedly a fragmented city because it is run by 19 mayors and as many city-councils. But metropolitan regions do not necessarily arise through annexation and battles won over rural surroundings.[18] When one looks at consistency in the rare event of eco-systemic co-optation, not precluding in which way this must happen, other territories and unities may be discovered. For instance, Brussels was first unified by a stippled map: hypothetical line-ups of possible future houses were drawn onto rural land and gave way to an alignment of interests amongst civil servants, mayors and landowners. It was then assembled under the impact of a road maintenance law: in order to control local construction, municipalities registered land portions as quasi urban or "agglomerated" – i.e. comprising buildings that were not entirely isolated – and gradually they gave way to the delineation of one single Brussels "agglomeration". Next, the city was consolidated through landscape engineering: hilly surroundings were dug into, backfilled and leveled out in order to establish overall rail and road connections; over vast distances, the entire relief was streamlined. And so on. Each city beholds several layers of consistencies and strengths. The strength of alliances, the strength of the quasi city or city-to-be, the strength of a clearing, all these can be unwrapped by empirical investigation, as long as the powers of causality aren't limited to a few agents only.

For all that, whatever its causes and territories, city-making remains a closed system. It produces its own configuration, i.e. the outline of its core, its environment and its outer space. It does not involve everyone and everything, far from it. "What is peculiar to the living, is the making of its own milieu, the composing of its own environment" says Canguilhem.[19] Or: "Life is the submission but also the institution of an own milieu."[20] This milieu and its outline are defined by trial and error: "The living organism acts empirically. Life is experience, i.e. improvisation, use of occurrences;

---

18 | See also Zitouni, Benedikte, "Agglomérer plutôt qu'annexer: le cas de Bruxelles 1840-1875," in Bourillon, Françoise, Fourcaut, Annie (eds.), *Agrandir Paris 1860-1970*, Paris: Publications de la Sorbonne, pp. 148-164

19 | Canguilhem 2006, p. 184

20 | Canguilhem 2005, p. 185

it is an attempt in all its senses."[21] The organic take thus presented not only moves away from mechanical and deterministic views but also from open but vague considerations on city-making. It pleads for empirical precision, detection of cogwheels and strengths and weaknesses, recognition of singularity and open-ended outcomes. Each city growth is different. Nothing is determined as yet. Those, then, are the stakes: opening up the possibility for future experimentation. One cannot say what makes up a particular ecosystem, one cannot know what makes up the dynamics of a particular city, because in either case one cannot know beforehand where the action is traveling, how the patterns of action will arise and format the city's configuration.

Besides the genome
Urbanization is an intricate affair. Its analysis requires care and imagination. Again, this requirement can be taken from the afore-mentioned authors by way of some sidetracking. The recent writings of Fox-Keller, Kupiec and Sonigo show that some biologists are critical and disillusioned with the genetic claims made by their field. While acknowledging some merits, they underscore the shortcomings of genetic investigations. To an outsider like me, it seems that they are moving beyond or rather beside the genome. Biology has more to offer than genetics alone, they seem to say. Genetics itself should be reformed, they seem to imply. And that is interesting for the issue of causality. For there is an additional value which seems to lie in the investigative power of a hypothetical existence and of hypothetical abstractions. We are coming back to the initial phrasing: what if? Without getting into the empirical details, which would lead us astray, it seems to me that Fox-Keller, Kupiec and Sonigo pinpoint the problem of reification, i.e. regarding something abstract as a material thing, i.e. losing sight of the abstraction that was necessary to get ahead in the investigation and turning it into the guiding principle of reality itself. As I've already explained, Kupiec and Sonigo want to reintroduce Darwinism on each level of organic life. They want to get rid of the reductionist and Platonic views

---

21 | Original French version: "le propre du vivant, c'est de se faire son milieu, de se composer son milieu;" "la vie, étant non pas seulement soumission au milieu mais institution de son milieu propre;" "l'organisme vivant agit selon l'empirisme. La vie est expérience, c'est-à-dire improvisation, utilisation des occurrences; elle est tentative dans tous les sens." Canguilhem 2006, p. 152

held by their colleague geneticists who place the genes in a fortified place, in a reality zone that is more powerful than all the others. For each time a link between a gene and a particular behavior fails to appear, the geneticists call upon more complicated models and more elaborate explanations to make up for it, until they've even turned the gene itself into a selfish animal, thereby completing the picture of genetic hegemony. The problem here is not only that solely one cause and one action pattern is considered worthy of any attention. The problem is also that a fruitful tool of investigation – the hypothesis of the gene's existence first and of the gene's action afterwards – has become the guiding principle of reality itself.

On a less critical tone, Fox Keller emphasizes the worth of abstraction. She underscores the fruitful link that has existed between genetics and the use of metaphors from the start. According to her, metaphors played a very important role in genetics. By contrast, for example, experimental biology has rather worked with models, i.e. model organisms or exemplary organisms such as rats that carry the generic qualities which enable it to serve as a test case for many other animals (and generic doesn't mean general, for generality is much more connected to the models and simulations used in mathematical biology). So genetics is closely linked to metaphors. For a long time the gene served as a metaphor, a linguistic trope, different from a cell, different from an organism, because it could not be seen, nor identified yet in most of the organisms. It was the unknown element that had to be presupposed in order to make the investigations work. Then another metaphor, that of genetic information, had to be used in order to hold the gap between the gene and the behavioral or physical characteristics. There was a need to invent or to name the unknown in order to enable investigation to discover it. But one should never lose sight of the distinction between the tools and the results. For instance, genes do not send signals but to posit they did, helped to find out what their ways of impact really were. The signals are the tool of investigation; the discovered links and descriptions are the result. The more results there are, the more valuable the tool. In other words, the metaphor, the cause should not be reified.

Both books – *Nor God, nor Gene* and *Making Sense of Life* – make a plea against reductionism. Looking beyond, or rather around the genome, means that investigators should not mix the tools with the effects, the hypotheses with the reality, the metaphorical cause with all causality. In the same way, I presupposed the existence of consistencies and went out to look for them. Some empirical discoveries ensued but this does not mean that this one reality, the agglomeration, could shroud all other realities or modes of investigations. When we've discovered a causal pattern, there's still many more to pursue.

Metaphors as medium

Remains of War
Battlefields, Ruins and the Trick of Commemoration

ELISABETH BRONFEN

Hollywood has come to be known not only as a dream factory producing myths that register cultural desires and anxieties, but also as the communal site where an imaginary relation to the past, and, more specifically, narrations of the American nation, come incessantly to be played through. Personalized dramas, focusing on the trials and tribulations of individual characters we identify with not least of all because they are embodied for us by stars, serve to reflect upon national concerns. Particularly genre cinema has fulfilled the function of a common cultural ground which can be shared by a highly diversified audience, bringing to the screen stories everyone can relate to, regardless of their specific background. In the following essay, I will treat a particular genre, namely the war musical, not merely as a successful example of mass entertainment, but as a site of reflection and interrogation regarding the manner in which past military conflicts continue to haunt any attempt to rethink the nation in post-war culture. My claim is that the way a past war is imagined in retrospect, which is to say reconceived after all fighting is over, says much about the stories American culture tells itself to live with the memory of its military engagements. At the same time, given that fiction films always come after the event of war they restage on screen, they offer an imaginary reconception of the past recast in terms of the cultural needs of the present. They say as much about the war being cinematically re-enacted as about the world for which this reconception is intended.

As my case study I take Michael Curtiz' musical *White Christmas* (1954), focussing on the manner in which he revisits the Allied campaign in Monte Cassino, Italy, in 1944 by restaging it twice: first as the back story to a narrative about two successful Broadway entertainers, Bob Wallace (Bing Crosby) and Phil Davis (Danny Kaye), and then as a re-enactment of a Christmas troop show in the back yard of the man who used to be their commanding officer, Major General Waverly. Given that in this film, war is shown to spill over into peacetime, it is fruitful to read this military musical in relation to a point made by Michel Foucault in *Society Must Be Defended* (2003). Offering an inversion of Clausewitz' famous dictum that war is to be thought of as a continuation of politics by other means, he suggests, "we have to interpret the war that is going on beneath peace; peace itself is a coded war."[1] In the most obvious sense, the Cold War implicitly written into the world of Eisenhower's America is evidence of the residues of war in the political culture from which *White Christmas* emerged and which it speaks to.

Image 42: Michael Curtiz, White Christmas, 1954

Yet Foucault's proposition is more complex, claiming that the conflicts that structure the demand for and assertion of subjective rights during peace, recall the struggle for power installed by war. To follow his suggestion and look for a permanent war rumbling just beneath the calm order of peace, thus also means not forgetting that civil order, particularly the post-war prosperity of the 50s, is predicated on the power struggles of WWII. My second claim, therefore, is that the architecture of remains Curtiz has recourse to by re-capturing on screen a scene of war entertainment at Monte

---

1 | See Foucault, Michel, *"Society Must Be Defended." Lectures at the Collège de France 1975-1976*, New York: Picador, 2003, p. 51

Cassino, only to reduplicate this event on the home front a decade later, is grounded on a compelling spatial and dramaturgic embodiment of the interplay between war and peace, past and present Foucault gestures toward. In his re-staging of war, the ruin as architectural emblem of the remains of war, recalls a former battle zone but does so retrospectively. As such, it recalls a loss, namely the casualties of the battle that raged in its vicinity. At the same time, it also stands in for a gain, namely that the violence of war that produced it is over.

There is, however, a further issue at stake. Historical transmission requires an aesthetic refiguration that always already recycles previous visual formulas. When a film such as *White Christmas* depicts a particular war event, it inevitably recalls prior moments, during which a similar story had already been presented on screen. More to the point, when a musical clearly emerging from the visual style of the 1950s depicts a war scene that refers to an event that took place in Italy one decade earlier, it invariably invokes the musicals and combat films of the 1940s, produced and distributed as part of Hollywood's ingenious war effort, which at the time was aimed at both distracting the troops as well as boosting the moral of the men and women fighting for the nation overseas. As Robert Burgoyne notes, capable of "both recalling past usages and responding to the present in a new way," genre film serves as the principal vehicles for shaping and carrying social experience from one generation to another. Understood as "crystallized forms of social and cultural memory," genre films can be seen carrying with them a layered "record of their changing use."[2]

For *White Christmas*, this genre memory is explicitly written into the texture of the film in relation to the stars Bing Crosby and Danny Kaye, as well as the narrative that is told.[3] The film's title refers to the song "I'm dreaming of a white Christmas," which was a hit in 1942. The nostalgic portrait of yuletide festivities in a snow-covered landscape its lyrics evoke, bring into place the metaphor of home, in the name of which American

---

2 | Burgoyne, Robert, "Before the rain: ethnic nationalism and globalization," Conference paper, 1999

3 | See Robert Burgoyne's discussion of genre memory, a term he takes from Michael Bachtin, in his "Introduction," in Burgoyne, Robert, *Film Nation. Hollywood Looks a U.S. History*, revised edition, Minneapolis: University of Minneapolis Press 2010, p. 8

GIs were fighting in the European and Pacific theater of war. I will, therefore, be discussing a second architectural site, juxtaposing the war ruin, used both at the beginning and the end of the film as the set where "White Christmas" is performed, with the holiday home thematized by the song.

Since metaphor, in the way I am using it, involves the combination of two paradigms – battle front and home, past and present, war and peace – the issue of genre memory can be taken a step further, bringing into play a further set of doublings. Not only does Bing Crosby star both in Curtiz' post-war musical as well as Mark Sandrich's *Holiday Inn* (1942), in which he performed the song for the first time on screen. Rather, the post-war film *White Christmas* invokes and re-writes the story of the prior war-time musical, transporting it into the very civil world of peace predicated on the Allied victory at the end of WWII. The continuation of war at issue, however, foregrounds first and foremost a nostalgic remembrance of war. With the end of the war, the front, which, for 'the duration,' had come to represent an emotional bond for the fighting men, is forever lost. By re-invoking the front in the image of the battlefield ruin, serving as the stage back-drop for a moment of troop entertainment at home, however, this loss comes to be re-inscribed into the post-war cultural memory.

The first of the two films, *Holiday Inn*, based on show tunes by Irving Berlin, follows a classic musical narrative. Two show stars, (Ted Hanover) Fred Astaire and (Jim Hardy) Bing Crosby, are performing one Christmas Eve with their female partner Lila. Crosby has decided that he wants to leave the world of show business, and has bought a farm in upstate Connecticut. Once he realizes, however, that farming is something he is less skilled at than entertaining, he turns the farm into an inn, open only on holidays. Fortuitously, he is joined by Linda, who hopes to break into show business. Because Astaire, in turn, finds himself without a dancing partner the following New Year's Eve, he goes to visit his former partner, discovers the talents of his beloved and offers her a part in his new show. Ironically, it is not the fact that this new musical couple prove to be enormously successful on Broadway, but the idea of a holiday inn, hidden away in a quiet rural setting, which prompts a Hollywood producer to decide to make a film of Bing Crosby's venture. We must thus ask what this architectural metaphor, which the film deploys twice – initially as a site of retreat for its Broadway star and then as a site reconstructed in a Hollywood studio – represents.

The inn in Connecticut stands as a home away from home, a cozy site where you go only on holidays to celebrate time out from the ordinary. It is a heterotopic site, mirroring but also contesting the ordinary home. It is more perfect than home, a place where others cook for and entertain you, so you can give yourself over completely to leisure. At the same time, it is defined by its temporal limitation. It is a place you go to only on holidays.

Because the holiday inn Bing Crosby builds out of a ruined farmhouse is on the diegetic level of the film a site of recreation, but on the extradiegetic level from the start a movie set, only to be re-staged explicitly as such once the star goes to Hollywood to play himself in a film about his successful musical enterprise, Mark Sandrich quite self-consciously ties this architectural space to the site of cinema itself. Indeed, by reduplicating the inn as

Image 43: Michael Curtiz, White Christmas, 1954

a film set in a Hollywood studio, the cinematic quality of this architectural metaphor for a marked 'time out' from the ordinary comes to be foregrounded. For the narrative resolution the wartime musical *Holiday Inn* has to offer, it is important to note: It is at this reconstruction of the original inn in Connecticut, which is to say on a film set, that Bing Crosby is ultimately able to win Linda back. Even more poignant for the juxtaposition of home and front which Michael Curtiz' postwar refiguration of this wartime musical works with, are, however, the final shots of *Holiday Inn*. On the third New Year's Eve the film depicts, Crosby and Astaire, now joined by Linda as well as their first partner Lila, dance and sing together as two couples in a joint show number. The camera moves back to reveal the holiday inn from the outside, with heavy snow falling. It is this architectural metaphor – a home away from home during a winter holiday clearly marked as studio set – which *White Christmas*, in turn, resuscitates in its inaugural scene. It does so both in explicit reference to the WWII musical his audience would still have remembered a decade later in Eisenhower America, as well as the ideological notion of home, in the name of which the war against the Axis Powers had been fought in Italy.

Curtiz' post-war musical, *White Christmas*, in turn, begins with the title "Christmas Eve 1944" superimposed on a painted image of a small New England town, covered in snow. As the camera moves back we realize that this is the backdrop to a makeshift stage, set amid the ruins of Monte

Image 44: Michael Curtiz, White Christmas, 1954

Cassino. Two soldiers, played by Bing Crosby and Danny Kaye, are putting on a holiday show for their buddies, who are clapping along while enemy fire lights up the evening sky behind them. Just as Crosby begins singing "White Christmas," the commanding officer, Major General Waverly, arrives on the scene and sits down to observe his troops. Due to his war injuries he is about to be replaced by a new commanding officer and has merely returned to bid his boys farewell. The gaze with which he looks at his men, united in rapt silence as they listen to a song about the home they are fighting for, is doubly mournful. To him this particular performance reminds him of the home he is about to return to, even while it also anticipates what he is about to lose – the affective unity with his troops as this is obtainable only in war.

Poignant about Curtiz' *mise en scène* is the marked artificiality of the setting. The backdrop, in front of which Bing Crosby, who both during and after the war years had come to be identified with the song "White Christmas" stands, is a painting, invoking an all-American Christmas landscape. While this painted backdrop screens out our view of the actual front landscape, the ruins and rubble in the midst of which the soldiers have come together, are clearly a studio set. Indeed, the post card image of home is erected in front of another painted backdrop of war-torn Italy, which runs along the entire back wall of the set. We are on the front line, which is quite literally a site of contestation between two forces, struggling against each other. At the same time, the fact that this front has been turned into a stage signals that for the time of the performance, war is suspended by invoking an imaginary scene of a snowy holiday.

This architectural site – a stage, put up for the brief period of a Christmas entertainment which turns a battle zone into a zone of celebration – is, furthermore, juxtaposed onto another heterotopia, namely a painted image of home. While we hear war barrage in the background, the song's words sustain the metaphoric bridge between home and front, the civil world of peace and the world of war. The notion of home invoked by the song and architecturally depicted as a small all-American town, does not, in fact, exist except in our collective dreams, which are manufactured and sustained by Hollywood's dream factory. As such, the white Christmas Bing Crosby's lyrics bespeak is something we desire, which everyday life doesn't provide.[4] Put another way, the home invoked by this musical performance is not an actual site, but rather an affective space, architecturally produced in a metaphoric gesture by bringing together a postcard image with a makeshift stage and the war ruins it is embedded in. Crosby's front line yuletide entertainment comes to a spectacular end once Waverly has himself gotten on stage to officially take leave of his boys. His voice hesitates as he declares sadly that all he can say in parting is what a fine outfit he is forced to leave.

It is a moment marking loss, namely the bond between the commander and his troops, an affective moment whose energy comes to write itself into

---

4 | "White Christmas," was not written as a war tune yet because of its yearning, nostalgic tone it, too, hit the nerve of the wartime mood. See Woll, Allen L., *The Hollywood Musical goes to War*, Chicago: Nelson-Hall, 1983, p. 67

the set as well. With the help of the final marching number, in which all the soldiers, including those in the audience, declare in song that they would follow the old man wherever he goes because they love him, the parting officer is able to leave both this stage and the theater of war in general. As he moves through the audience, shaking hands one last time with individual men, the painted Christmas landscape diminishes, and we see it in visual contrast to the war ruins, captured in a long shot, yet equally artificial as the painting behind the stage. Then incoming enemy fire breaks up the entertainment. Indeed, if initially the ruined houses of Monte Cassino are

Image 45: Michael Curtiz, White Christmas, 1954

presented as stage props, the perfect surroundings for the 'time out' from war the entertainment affords, their mimetic quality is re-introduced with the incoming enemy fire. As the troops disperse to avoid bombshells, the stage set is bombed to bits and pieces. More importantly, what was before nothing other than a stage set turns into a potential danger. One of the walls is shown to be real. Its bricks actually come apart and it begins to collapse, threatening to smother Bing Crosby. Only because Danny Kaye comes to his rescue, does he survive.

What are the theoretical implications of the architectural metaphor I have been working with? As a trope, the concept *remains* conjoins several semantic paradigms. Literally, the word means to continue without change of condition, quality or place. The more common usage of the word, however, brings into play the question of loss. The word *remains* also refers to something left over after the removal, departure or destruction of others.

Remains of war, in turn, signify traces of battle; residues either still present after other people and things have been destroy, or metonymically referring to everything that is now gone, having been destroyed by war. There is, however, a further meaning to the word *remains*, bespeaking to something which is still left, invoking that something is still to be dealt with. The trope *remains* thus signifies a trace in a more specific sense, namely unfinished business. Finally, *remains* also refers to the way something endures, or persists; the prefix 're' signifying 'back,' while the root word 'manere' means 'to stay.' Indeed we might say, if *remains* as a word on the one hand refers to *what is left over* (and as such is still there), on the other hand it warns that something *has returned*.

Michael Curtiz' deployment of the architectural metaphor of the war ruin, conjoined with the metaphor of a mythic holiday home speaks to precisely this double sense of the trope 'remains of war.' As he restages the Christmas entertainment at Monte Cassino 1944, what comes to be performed is the fact that something is left over from the war; the memory of a blissful 'time out' from a particularly bloody battle during the Italian campaign. At the same time, given that it is precisely this scene of leave-taking which will be restaged a decade later in the general's backyard, we also have something which persists or endures. Since both the memory and the re-staging happen after the event, these re-visitations are explicitly figural. That the actual scene at Monte Cassino came to be destroyed by enemy bombs, is foregrounded by virtue of the fact that one of the walls proves to be of real bricks at precisely the moment that it topples down. Once this scene, so powerful in the affect it transports, is restaged at a country inn, the figural commemoration regains a material quality, acquiring both a site and a re-staging. As a metaphor, the word 'remains' thus invokes both the material and immaterial traces of an event of violence, to which, however, we have only indirect access.

Indeed, the reality of war has been displaced in more than one sense. Initially, it was re-encoded by turning the front into a site of entertainment, then by superimposing on this scene of 'time out from war' a painted image of home, which itself invokes the idea of a 'time out from the ordinary.' Finally, by destroying this first displacement such that not only the trauma of real war, but also the remains of this trauma, the ruins, disappear, we are left with an empty site which can now serve for a new cycle of displacements. This second cycle of displacements, played through in the final sequence of *White Christmas*, involves not only departing from the original site, the front line in Monte Cassino, but re-imposing this site of war onto a site at home, significantly once again on a stage. It is, thus, fruitful to bring the psychoanalytic notion of repression to bear as well on the re-enactment of the remains of war which Michael Curtiz' musical thrives on. One of Freud's claims, after all, is that repressed material inevitably returns precise because it consists of remains. More to my case in point, the affective experience of war is both what is *left over* after the veterans have come home to a renewed civil life, as it is also that *which persists*, indeed which *insists* on re-articulation. Furthermore, given that I am dealing with an archi-

Image 46: Michael Curtiz, White Christmas, 1954

tectural enactment of remains on screen, the metaphor 'remains of war' also invokes a displacement in relation to the filmic medium. The camp show is staged on a Hollywood set, recreating the front in Italy, but doing so in reference to the war musical *Holiday Inn*, even while it recaptures this entertainment scene a second time, on yet a different studio set in Hollywood.

What we thus have, as a battle zone remains, recalled and restaged a decade after the war is over, is a juxtaposition of two architectural tropes: an artificial stage on the front lines re-enacted on a second stage, now an artificial stage in the barn behind Waverly's holiday inn, both in fact stage sets in a Hollywood studio. The make-shift stage in Monte Cassino screens out the actual scene of war, which is indicated simply by virtue of the unrepresented blank behind the postcard image of home, painted on a sheet, shielding the soldiers looking at Bing Crosby (and implicitly us) from its sight. This real site of war is doubly phantasmatic, because though marked as unrepresentable by Curtiz' *mise en scène*, it is implicitly the site which allows the characters in the film (as well as the audience watching the film in 1954) to remember the actual war in Europe. My point is that only the complex architectural metaphor, welding together the stage of a camp show in the midst of war ruins and the stage in a holiday inn, redeploying these war ruins as props, can bring about an imaginary reconception of war. The marked artificiality of this re-imagination touches on the way a traumatic event from the past (the actual carnage of the battle at Monte Cassino) can be recollected: It can be re-visited with impunity by re-turning in imagination to the place at which it occurred, precisely because the war event has been re-encoded aesthetically. At the same time, I take as Curtiz' psychoanalytic point the fact that the place we return to, the place where the remains of war can come to be re-articulated, is in more than one sense displaced from the original site of occurrence. The metaphor as privileged rhetorical gesture touches upon what cannot be articulated directly, even while it indicates that only an indirect transmission is possible.

How, then, is the war entertainment, with which *White Christmas* begins, restaged in its closing sequence? After they have returned home from the war, Bing Crosby and Danny Kaye have become successful Broadway entertainers, while Waverly has had a hard time fitting into post-war America. In analogy to the character played by Bing Crosby in *Holiday Inn*, he has bought himself a farm in Vermont and turned it into an inn. When the two war veterans discover that their former commanding officer is close to bankruptcy, they decide to stage their Christmas show at his inn. To celebrate the 10th anniversary of the 151st Division, they have asked men from their former battalion to come up and re-enact the Christmas entertainment at Monte Cassino ten years earlier. As such, the repetition brings the front back home even while re-invoking the moment of parting.

When Waverly enters his barn theater, some of his former officers stand in attention while the soldiers' families in the audience energetically applaud. Then the curtain rises to reveal Bing Crosby, again leading his fellow performers in the song with which once already they had declared they would follow the old man wherever he went. There is, however, a significant difference. The backdrop is no longer a sheet, representing a snowy

New England town. Rather, at the center of the stage, we now see one of the bombed out buildings of Monte Cassino, which, during the opening sequence of the film, had stood to the left of the stage (indeed, we have the same studio set, used at the beginning and the end of the film). In the belated musical extravaganza, we are to surmise, the ruin has taken the place of the mythic representation of home, and indeed what the performers are commemorating with their song is not a white Christmas but their loyalty to their former commander. In other words, the war entertainment has now taken on the affective power of bringing a touch of home to the veterans, away from the front. Nothing – especially not a painted image of holiday home – needs to shield the audience's gaze from the war zone, because temporally removed by a decade and spatially translocated to Vermont, the battlefield of Monte Cassino can be included with impunity in this reduplicated frontline Christmas entertainment.

Once more, Waverly gets up on stage to speak to his troops, not, however, to take leave of them as he did a decade ago, but to express his gratitude that they have returned to him. The ruin at the center of the stage, in front of which the affective bond between Waverly and his men comes to be reinstalled, attests to the fact that the war remains unfinished business: Not, however, in the sense of a traumatic haunting, but rather as an affective memory, which those who shared the brief time out on Christmas Eve, 1944, are nostalgically moved by. The former major general is what has remained in their minds and has now been returned to them, even as, coming together once more, they embody for him emotionally the remains of war returned to him. Indeed, it is precisely this metaphorical notion of 'remains' which the ruin on stage explicitly invokes. What is returned to both the soldiers and their commander is affective memory as site. The force of this uncanny re-enactment is augmented by the fact that it is as transient as the original scene it invokes. No incoming fire breaks apart the ritual performance of unity as the ex-GIs come together in their shared rapture for a familiar song routine. Instead, once their performance is over, they join their families in the audience, and in so doing return once again to being civilians in Eisenhower's post-war America. The moment of bringing the site of advanced war action into one's own back yard, radically blurring the boundary between a war zone 'over there' and the 'here' of the home front, can not be sustained.

Curtiz' recreation serves to draw our attention back to the war, not in its actual atrocity, but rather in its magical moments of respite. Although a reference to Monte Cassino as one of the most brutal battles during the invasion of Italy, serves as the beginning and the end of *White Christmas*, it is important to bear the film's re-encoding of any actual advanced military areas in mind. Although war is evoked through musical memory, the hope this final show number responds to is a need to address something left over from the war, something which endures in the memory of those involved, yet something which can only be satisfied by the very displacement into entertainment which had evoked this affective capacity to movement in the first place. The actual drive of war can only find oblique re-articulation after the veterans have come home, as the capacity to movement which persists in the ritual repetition of a popular song on a stage, where frontline and holiday inn entertainment comes to be conflated.

Image 47: Michael Curtiz, White Christmas, 1954

In the final sequence of *White Christmas*, the uncanny splice between home and front lines is resolved as we return to the very first image of the film. As though the musical re-enactment had had a cathartic effect on nature itself, it has begun to snow. Seeking to include even the space outside the inn in their extravaganza, Crosby and Kaye push open the barn door so that the back of the stage now opens out onto Waverly's back yard. At the end of the finale, in which they join their female partners to sing "White Christmas," the back of the stage is lifted to reveal this white winter landscape, now once more a painted backdrop. As such we return to an embodied architectural metaphor: two sites juxtaposed. Not only does the inside of the barn theater open up to an outside scene, but the mimetic reality of the stage opens out to a painted back drop. The inn in Vermont, like the frontline at Monte Cassino, is again enclosed by a landscape painting, containing the piece we saw at the beginning of the film, but now stretching across the entire back stage.

Although the relation between imaginary home and war zone is now reversed, the latter has not been occluded. Instead, one might say, we have moved into a theater of memory. Not only is the world outside nothing other than a painted backdrop, rendering the holiday inn explicitly a film set. Rather, by metaphoric extension, the picture of a white Christmas home, stretched over the entire stage, has now taken the place of the ruin, which was there before, screening it out, but also recalling the conjunction of ruin and image of a white Christmas home in the first scene. What remains is a performance of architectural sites uniting home and front, yet doing so in a way that exposes both as nothing more, but also nothing less than picture postcards we dream of. The dream of something better to escape into, which the singing now evokes, is embodied by this architectural trope of a Christmas landscape inscribed by historical reality and genre memory. The rhetorical repetition Curtiz' *mise-en-scène* works with, suggests that if the military musical brought a touch of home to the front lines, it affectively recalls the war it was meant to detract from when it is re-enacted at home. Everyone is united not only in song, but in a nostalgia for a front line camp, which has become as much a site of fantasy as the white Christmas they were dreaming about while there. With this last tableau, *White Christmas* is cinema, celebrating its own metaphoric process.

Calibrating Metaphors and Tuning Places

RICHARD COYNE

Calibration and tuning
Calibration is a process of aligning a measuring instrument with a standard: for example, placing markings along a length of a wooden ruler that correspond to the markings on a standard length of steel. Scientific instruments, thermometers, electrical measuring devices, and touch screens require calibration. "Calibration" has currency as a term in many contexts. For example, judging panels in the assessment of UK university research are required to "undertake initial calibration exercises" to confirm that they are marking to the same scale and that they agree on standards.[1] This is presumably a social process where committee members develop a sense of each other's value systems.

The calibration of musical instruments is generally referred to as "tuning," a term also familiar in architecture. The architect Peter Eisenman writes about "fine tuning" in the context of a park design made up of overlaid site plans.[2] Design involves so many tweaks and tunings to bring building elements, grids and patterns into alignment, or to adjust them to the site or the particularities of the context.

In general terms calibration and tuning involve aligning two or more frames of reference. This adjustment can be treated instrumentally, as a geometrical and mathematical process, but it is also a social and psycholog-

---

1 | HEFCE 2010, *Units of assessment and recruitment of expert panels: guidance notes*, Bristol: Higher Education Funding Council for England, p. 12
2 | Kipnis, J., Leeser T. (eds), *Chora L Works: Jacques Derrida and Peter Eisenman*, New York: Monacelli Press, 1997, p. 77

ical operation. Certain theories of perception assume that we see the world and make observations through frames of reference, otherwise known as scripts, gestalts or schemas.[3] So calibration relates also to perception.

Calibration is an incremental process. Even the idea of a step change, the introduction of a radically new state in a system, can be described in terms of incremental adjustment. Think of the idea of the "tipping point," popularized in business literature.[4] Some small and inconspicuous change introduces a larger social result, as when changing the piped music at a bus station from pop to Mozart results in less loitering by groups of youths and less public disturbance. Of course, where it applies, the social conditions are already in place for such a small change to have this large-scale effect. As another case, if you keep tightening a guitar string beyond a certain point then the string starts to behave inelastically. You can't tune it down again. It may eventually break, or strain the tuning peg or guitar neck to breaking point. The subtle aspect of these incremental adjustments is that they do not necessarily *cause* the change. The change is in process, the conditions are set for the transition. As for a heavily loaded beast of burden, the incremental change can be the final straw that breaks the camel's back. Design involves so much adjustment and re-organization, often by degrees, which may in turn introduce sudden step changes, or the introduction of what we might think of as a new "concept." Design typically involves the adjustment of concepts relative to one another: the concept of a house with the concept of a machine; a hearth with an altar; a hotel with an art gallery. Such juxtapositions and adjustments are common currency in the architectural design studio.[5]

---

3 | Reddy, M. 1979, "The conduit metaphor: A case of frame conflict in our language about language," in A. Ortony (eds.), *Metaphor and Thought*, Cambridge: Cambridge University Press, pp. 284-324; Lakoff, G., *Women, Fire, and Dangerous Things: What Categories Reveal about the Mind*, Chicago: University of Chicago Press, 2003
4 | Gladwell, Malcolm, *The Tipping Point: How Little Things Can Make a Big Difference*, London: Abacus, 2000
5 | Tschumi, Bernard, *Architecture and Disjunction*, Cambridge, Mass.: MIT Press, 1994

Terms such as "concept" and "frame of reference" are similarly found in discussions of metaphor. The design theorist Donald Schon wrote about the "displacement of concepts."[6] As an example of this process he shows that amongst town planners, the metaphor of the city as a broken entity requiring reparation was displaced in the 1960s by the metaphor of the city as a community of competing interest groups. In working on a problem or a design task, one concept gets transformed into, or replaced by, another. In the town planning case the "broken" metaphor is transformed to the "competition" metaphor.

I propose here that calibration provides a good metaphor for the way such transformations operate. The philosopher Mary Hesse provides a useful account of such metaphorical transformations.[7] Metaphors relate closely to models, the latter being a formalized and structured presentation of a metaphor. A scientific model for example might consist of a series of variables or attributes. So the wave model is a structured way of relating attributes of source, propagation, reflection, etc. Her example is that of the transformation of models explaining the behavior of light. The propagation of light and the full spectrum of electromagnetic waves are analogous in many ways to the propagation of sound waves, in the way the waves seem to refract, reflect, and interfere. But the analogy breaks down when we think of the *medium* of propagation. Sound waves operate through a medium such as air. There is no detectable medium for electromagnetic waves. So other models are required to account for the behaviour of light. More advanced models are associated with concepts of fields, particles, and quanta, for example.

Think of any scientific model as entailing a series of attributes, some of which match the circumstances, and some that do not. Scientific models and observational circumstances get compared, aligned, and misaligned. In conventional scientific terms the experimenter may say that the model needs to be adjusted to fit the observations. However, some philosophers of science maintain that observations are already based on models. There is a sense in which scientists see what their models allow, and treat observations that do not fit as extraneous. For my purposes here it is helpful to

---

6 | Schön, Donald, *Displacement of Concepts*, London: Tavistock, 1963

7 | Hesse, Mary, *Models and Analogies in Science* [1963], Notre Dame: University of Notre Dame Press, 1970

leave to one side the problem of some external empirical model-independent condition to which models might refer[8] and to think of calibration as a process of adjusting models, frames or metaphors relative to one another.

Hesse's explanation of the "paradigm shift," the step change to a new way of thinking, is that the disanalogies in the model overwhelm the practical application of the model and render it inadequate.[9] A new model takes its place. We cannot readily ascribe a formula to this process, but the operation seems to involve the misalignment and realignment of two or more models. The models are impossible to align without some adjustment to the models, or the generation of a new model.

Aligning the terms in a metaphor
I hope by now that I've demonstrated the relevance of calibration and tuning to metaphor. Metaphors are subject to calibration one with another, as are the terms of a metaphor. At its simplest, metaphor involves the relationship between two terms: light as waves, house as machine. In the latter case "house" and "machine" have to be calibrated with one another, i.e. as the "house" frame is superimposed over the "machine" frame. The interaction theory of metaphor[10] suggests that human subjects do not need to analyze metaphors in order to understand them, as in the case of a scientist making use of a model of light. But it appears that the cognitive work in analyzing or unpacking a metaphor entails the identification of analogies and disanalogies, the discovery of moments where the frames align. In the case of "house as machine" metaphor this alignment will occur on the themes of efficiency, flows, and hygiene. The obvious disanalogies become occluded by the metaphor: warmth, protection and family.

The calibration of the terms in a metaphor is not restricted to bringing everything into alignment and thereby obscuring differences. It can be a creative process. Or at least calibration fuses with overtly creative practices. Sound artists and composers working with found objects, sensors, effec-

---

8 | Gregory, Bruce, *Inventing Reality: Physics as Language*, New York: Wiley, 1988
9 | Kuhn, Thomas, *The Structure of Scientific Revolutions*, Chicago, Ill.: University of Chicago Press, 1970
10 | Black, Max, *Models and Metaphors: Studies in Language and Philosophy*, Ithaca: Cornell University Press, 1962

tors, amplifiers and other electronic equipment will spend a great deal of time before a performance making adjustments, adapting, tuning and fine tuning. The enterprises of "hardware hacking"[11] improvisation with found materials, shares with Surrealism the practices of bricolage.[12] Moving objects into new contexts, juxtaposing objects in new combinations, inevitably involve adjustments of positions, adaptation, tunings and calibrations. Similarly, the play of metaphor is a creative process. Or, if you prefer, creativity is a metaphorical process.

Tuning
Irrespective of how calibration relates to metaphor in general, the calibration metaphor is useful in thinking about equipment, especially new, mobile communications technologies, such as mobile phones, hand-held navigation devices (GPS), cameras, signal receivers, and various recording devices.[13] Such electro-mechanical devices foreground the issue of calibra-

Image 43: Synchronising to maps via GPS

---

11 | Collins, Nick, *Handmade Electronic Music: The Art of Hardware Hacking*, New York: Routledge, 2006
12 | Chénieux-Gendron, J., *Surrealism*, trans. V. Folkenflik, New York: Columbia University Press, 1990
13 | McCullough, Malcolm, *Digital Ground: Architecture, Pervasive Computing, and Environmental Knowing*, Cambridge, MA: MIT Press, 2004

tion. Their manufacture and use requires adjustment and tuning. Tuning a radio is a kind of calibration. The early touch screens on PDAs (personal digital assistants), required the user to follow a particular procedure involving tapping the screen with a stylus at certain points in order to calibrate it. The current model of the Apple iPhone requires the user occasionally to wave the device through the air in a figure of eight pattern to reset its internal compass to the earth's magnetic field: a calibration exercise. Mechanical and digital clocks get adjusted and calibrated.

Image 44: View from clock tower in Prague. Clocks synchronise people's actions according to Lewis Mumford.

The historian Lewis Mumford described the clock as the defining technology that augured the industrial age.[14] Mechanical clocks require adjustment and calibration, but he also saw the clock as a defining technology that provided societal coordination. With the deployment of standardized time, and the mobility of time frames from one place to another, the clock enabled certain modes of organization, "the synchronization of men," enabling the work patterns and industrial and financial circulation of the developedworld. Think of synchronization here as a social kind of calibration, or a social tuning.

---

14 | Mumford, Lewis, *Technics and Civilization*, London: Routledge, 1934

Mobile phones[15] now largely supplant the functionality of portable clocks, time-pieces and wristwatches as coordinating devices. The enhanced functionality of ubiquitous smartphones combine time-keeping operations with communications, navigation, the delivery of media content, record keeping, image and sound capture, social networking, and general connectivity. Clock functions underlie the digital computational processes on which these devices are based. If clocks synchronize people's actions then ubiquitous digital media amplify and extend the means by which people coordinate their practices with one another. I describe this synchronization as a calibration or tuning process on the grounds that calibration and tuning provide potent metaphors that resonate with the current mobile digital milieu.

Entailments of the calibration metaphor
The calibration metaphor carries certain advantages, or entailments. Calibration is something we do with devices, or at least it is something that happens to devices. Designers and researchers often overlook calibration in the quest for seamless interfaces and interactions.[16] If you have to stop and calibrate an instrument then you bring it into conspicuous awareness. The user becomes aware of the seams, faults, and idiosyncrasies in the general field of interactions.

Calibration pertains to mobility. It is usually the case that transporting an electromechanical device requires that it be recalibrated. Gears slip and surfaces fall out of alignment in the process of being moved. The device may also have to be recalibrated to the new environment: temperature, magnetic north, and time zone. There is a further spatial aspect to calibration. Measurement standards are usually kept in a stable environment and in a stable location, a home base as it were, such as the Bureau International des Poids et Mesures (www.bipm.org). Calibration against a standard requires a return to the standard, a renewal, followed by an excursion back out to the field. Calibration implicates the relationship between the labora-

---

15 | Ito, Mizuko, Okabe Daisuke, Matsuda Misa (eds), *Personal, Portable, Pedestrian: Mobile Phones in Japanese Life*, Cambridge, MA: MIT Press, 2006
16 | Ishii, Hiroshi, Ullmer, Brygg, "Tangible bits: towards seamless interfaces between people, bits and atoms," in *Proc. CHI 97*, 22-27 March, Atlanta, Georgia, 1997, pp. 234-241

tory and the field; the military camp where the flag (standard) is kept and the front line; the home and the world outside.

Design can be considered as a calibration exercise: fitting the schema or plan to the site, overlaying grids, elements and patterns, and adjusting these to one another. Calibration also brings the conspicuous aspects of spaces and devices into relief, as well as revealing the ways people make adjustments to their environment. People adjust their world by opening windows, moving furniture and adjusting the sound system. How people adjust devices and environments is a design consideration, part of interaction design. Designers of successful consumer products such as iPhones pay particular attention to the way that the product is packaged, which impacts on the initial calibration of the device. Calibration becomes part of a consumer's "inauguration ritual." Think of the number of YouTube videos of an enthusiast unpacking their brand new iPhone from its box, and connecting it to the iTunes software on their laptop. Calibration draws attention to the lifecycle of the product, including its decommissioning, or decalibration, when all data is erased and it is returned to its factory settings ready to be traded in.

The tuning metaphor
The related metaphor of tuning introduces further entailments. Tuning suggests a less mechanic and more human set of practices than calibration. Musicians tune their instruments to a standard, but also to each other's instruments, and to each other's playing.[17] Tuning and retuning occur throughout a performance as players make small adjustments to fingering and blowing. Music theorists and composers have devoted much attention to the formation of musical scales, and the adjustments necessary to navigate across keys. The so-called "well-tempered scale" is testimony to the necessity within musical harmony to make adjustments.[18] Tuning is not incidental to music but inheres within its structures. The philosopher Martin Heidegger amplifies the human necessity to engage with tuning by

---

17 | Schutz, Alfred, "Making music together," in Arvid Brodersen (ed.), *Alfred Schutz, Collected Papers II: Studies in Social Theory*, The Hague: Martinus Nijhoff, 1964, pp. 159-178
18 | Murray Barbour, James, *Tuning and Temperament: A Historical Survey*, Mineola, NY: Dover, 2004

introducing the concept of "attunement," the maintenance of a mood or atmosphere.[19] Tuning invades and inflects human sociability as we think of tuning in, tuning out, and being in or out of tune with our peers, norms, the social milieu, and familial relationships.

The metaphor of tuning also provides ready access to the sonic aspects of ubiquitous electronic devices and media.[20] Smartphones typically include camera functions, but they have their origins as devices for the propagation of sound. Today's mobile hand-held devices represent a convergence between earlier transistor radios, personal stereos, Sony Walkmans, and MP3 players, with devices for talking to one another, ie mobile phones. Smartphones are sonic devices before they are game consoles, cameras, web browsers, personal organizers or navigators.

The tuning metaphor invites greater consideration of the sense of hearing, in place of the dominance of vision. In fact tuning engenders thought of how sound pervades the whole perceptual and spatial field. Murray Schaffer's book, *The Tuning of the World*, develops compelling arguments in favor of considering the whole environment through the sense of sound,[21] as do Jean-François Augoyard and Henry Torgue [22] at the Centre for Research on Sonic Space and the Urban Environment (CRESSON). There are similar moves in architecture.[23] The challenge is not simply to pay greater atten-

---

19 | Heidegger, Martin, *Being and Time*, trans. J. Macquarrie and E. Robinson, London: SCM Press, 1962

20 | Bull, Michael, *Sounding Out the City: Personal Stereos and the Management of Everyday Life*, Oxford: Berg, 2000

21 | Schafer, Raymond Murray, *The Tuning of the World*, Toronto: McClelland & Stewart, 1977

22 | Augoyard, Jean-François, Torgue, *Sonic Experience: A Guide to Everyday Sounds*, trans. A. McCartney and D. Paquette, Montreal: McGill-Queen's University Press, 2005

23 | Blesser, Barry, Salter, Linda-Ruth, *Spaces Speak, Are You Listening? Experiencing Aural Architecture*, Cambridge, MA: MIT Press, 2006; Coyne, Richard, "Creativity and sound: the agony of the senses," in T. Rickards, M.A. Runco and S. Moger (eds), *The Routledge Companion to Creativity*, Routledge: London, 2008, pp. 25-36

tion to the sonic environment, but to see how the world appears when viewed through the lens, earphone, or frame, of the sonic.[24]

Another calibration or tuning is required. When the sonic experiences, practices and devices of the world are overlaid with the world as perceived, represented and managed through visual and other sensory modalities then we have several frames requiring calibration, adjustment, and tuning. Devices and spaces are complicit in the development and interaction between these sensory frames of reference, i.e. metaphors. Metaphor is after all mobile, the carrying of one form across to another. Metaphor, mobility and adjustment coalesce in the tuning of place.[25]

---

24 | Classen, Constance, *Worlds of Sense: Exploring the Senses in History and across Cultures*, London: Routledge, 1993; Connor, Steven, "Edison's teeth: touching hearing," in V. Erlmann (ed.), *Hearing Cultures: Essays on Sound, Listening and Modernity*, Oxford: Berg, 2004, pp. 153-172

25 | Coyne, Richard, *The Tuning of Place: Sociable Spaces and Pervasive Digital Media*, Cambridge, MA: MIT Press, 2010

The Promotion of the Architectural Model

JELLE FERINGA

> "'I understand nothing,' Ivan went on, as though in a delirium. 'I don't want to understand anything now. I want to stick to the facts. I made up my mind long ago not to understand. If I try to understand anything, I shall be false to the facts, and I have determined to stick to the facts.'"
> Dostojevsky, *The brothers Karamazov*, 1880[1]

Introduction
In his article "Finite Nature" physicist E. Fredkin states a radical, provoking idea: "What cannot be programmed cannot be physics. If a process cannot be programmed on a particular universal computer, despite having enough memory and time, then it cannot be programmed on any computer. If we can't program it on an ordinary computer, finite nature implies it can't be a part of physics because physics runs on a kind of computer."[2] Is there an architectural analogy to this statement? However literal the interpretation "what cannot be computed cannot be built" might be, that statement is increasingly gaining in relevance, given that both the conception and manufacturing of architecture increasingly "runs on a kind of computer." The forefront of architecture has become a computational universe.

---

1 | Dostojevsky, *The brothers Karamazov* [1880], New York: W.W. Norton, 1976, p. 224
2 | Fredkin, E., "Finite Nature," in *Proceedings of the XXVIIth Rencontre de Moriond*, 1992 http://64.78.31.152/wp-content/uploads/2012/08/finite_nature.pdf

Therefore it's worthwhile to examine whether Fredkin's theory of computing and physics can be interpreted in an architecturally meaningful manner. However true even this over simplistic appropriation of Fredkin's theory might be, it doesn't do justice to its depth. The statement "what cannot be programmed cannot be physics" constitutes a relation among the laws of physics an object is subjected to and its physical manifestation; the object's programming. This principle underscores a strong coupling between an object's manifestation and signification. If we can accept both architecture's computational turn and Fredkin's statement, the question surfaces whether Fredkin's notion can be subjected to an architectural interpretation? My understanding of Fredkin's idea relates to the advancement of the architectural model.

The promotion of the architectural model
With architecture's computational turn, the model has changed in terms of both modality and denotation. The model has become the *absolute* project reference where it used to be a declaration of architectural intent, a *metaphor* for the project to build. That is to say, the architectural model was promoted; it has evolved beyond an expression of architectural intent, it has moved beyond representation towards a definition. This transgression of the model from a symbolic description to definition is making a dramatic impact on the practice, autonomy and economy of architecture. The digital model has been the catalyst in expanding the scope of architectural form and giving rise to computational architecture's "burlesque" of a quasi-biological form; though little has been said on the radical *epismetic* shift of the model.

The shift from a *representational* to a *referential* model changed what an architectural model embodies. In terms of engineering, the model provides the interface that allows architects and engineers to assess how a building's performance from the model, paving the way for a performance oriented architecture. Legally, the IFC/BIM model will overtake the legal status over a drawing set.[3] The most striking impact the promotion of the model has had, is in the construction process, CAM[4] changed status of the architec-

---

3 | Haynes, Dan, "Reflections on some legal and contractual implications of building information modeling (BIM)," in *Construction Watch*, 2 (9), 1-4
4 | Computer Aided Manufacturing

tural model to an *operative* model. Models and drawing sets have transgressed from a symbolic metaphor and have been promoted to become the project reference. CNC tool paths are a *derivation* of the project's model, an approximation of the original within a given tolerance, an interface between architectural intention and its manifestation. Has the model become a platonic original?

Functional, analogical and figurative discrepancy
Jim Glymph only recently became partner at Frank Gehry when he introduced CATIA to the office, while working on the Fish sculpture at Port Olímpic, Barcelona, a seminal project that both explored the formal register and economical potential that CAM opened up. The Fish scultpure is one of the first projects exploring an organic architecture, while truly achieving this objective would be fishy indeed. The project underscores that while the model has become literal in terms of construction, Gehry's idea is conveyed by means of *connotation* not *denotation*. Nature has no concept of semiotics. Significance is embodied in matter, perhaps this vindicates what is appealing in biomimicry to architect's; matter and meaning in unison at the cellular level.

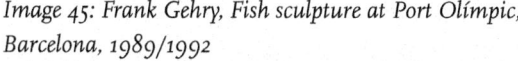
Image 45: Frank Gehry, Fish sculpture at Port Olímpic, Barcelona, 1989/1992

Can a critique of the model offer perspective on the ongoing epismetic shift in architecture? Only two decades later do the ramifications of this shift come within grasp. A remarkable aspect in the work of Gramazio &

Kohler is that the model is dissolved in its architectural *modus operandi* therefore losing its abstraction. The assemblage of the bricks is simultaneously the architectural model *and* its architectural manifestation. A representation of the robotic assembly process would be merely illustrative. Therefore if CNC[5] based building methodologies are to be embraced fully, the promotion of the model also has to be internalized in the conception of architecture. There is a sharp contrast in the architectural application of industrial robots between the work of Gramazio & Kohler and that of R&Sie's "architecture des humeurs." The contrasting positions can be understood through the difference in understanding of the role of the model. In the project of R&Sie, the method of robotic construction is merely suggested;[6] the model of the project is part of an architectural narrative, where in the work of Gramazio & Kohler, the model has become the definitive reference. The fundamental difference is that the architectural model became *operative, literal* in the work of Gramazio & Kohler, fully dissolved in the realization of the architectural artifact, where it remains part of the architectural *narrative, figurative* in the work of R&Sie. When juxtaposed by another, the epismetic dichotomoy becomes apparent. What is evoked when the barrier between the conception and realization is being torn down, when the means of fabrication are innate to the architectural project? What can be articulated when an architect's intent is no longer lost in translation?

Image 46: R&Sie(n), Une Architecture des humeurs, 2010

---

5 | A hypernym for fabrication methods under Computer Numeric Control
6 | It is important to point out that *Viab02* is a model for a robot, not a functional robot

Image 47: Programmed robot building up the brick wall, Gramazio & Kohler, ETH Zürich,

Image 46 & 47: Two opposing epistemic positions

An understanding of the architectural ramifications of CAM in construction cannot be suggested, only demonstrated: "One should be aware that a major difference exists between the precise numeric design and the physical world – geometric and fabrication data do not contain information about physical conditions such as gravity or material properties per se. Conversely, this means anticipating physical requirements at the outset of the parametric design process and using material conditions as well as assembly logics as the basis for coding."[7] It is precisely this *embedding of architectural knowledge within the model* that serves the autonomy of architecture. By altering the architect's deliverable from description to a definition that requires no further interpretation, the architect is placed at the heart of the construction process, consequentially taking up a central role in the realization.

More intricate designs can be realized. A substantial part of the cost involved in CAM is not the materialization itself, but rather the often involved programming the tooling.[8] Deeply integrated design & fabrication process will aid to further explore this potential.

These transitions give rise to a materialistic understanding of the role of the architect. Can architecture be valued as the difference between the market value of the assembly and the cost of raw construction materials plus cost of assembly? Will this realization open up the prospect of Design & Build oriented architectural practices, not unlike Jean Prouve's practice; an architect with the means of production. So far its undeceided whether this prospect is either nostalgic or part of an ongoing effort of architects reclaiming their industrial standing.

The work of *Designtoproduction* has been exemplary regarding the shifting status of the architectural model. *Designtoproduction* is a consultancy firm, focused on the post-rationalization of an architectural model. A capable *enabler*, even though not directly involved in the architectural conception. Has a false schism been brought about? While the model has become literal, it has not necessarily been regarded as such during its architectural conception. An interesting case of an outcome of this position is that of the Centre Pompidou in Metz. What the virtuosity of *Designtoproduction*'s post-rationalization underscores that this roof *is not a straw-hat*, the metaphor on which Shigeru Ban's roof design is based on. Which wouldn't be an issue if it wasn't built like one, and might be a legitimate position, had

---

7 | Gramazio, F., Kohler, M., Oesterle, S., "Encoding Material," in *Architectural Design*, 2010. 80 (4), pp. 108-115

8 | Scheurer, F., Schindler, Christoph, Braach, M., "From Design to Production: Three Complex Structures Materialised in Wood," in *Proceedings of the GA 2005 International Conference on Generative Art 2005*, C. Soddu, Editor, 2005

the architects' design achieved a level of suspension of disbelief. The roof was modeled in an overly simplistic way: a hexagonal pattern is projected from the ground plane and hence bears no relation to how the roof works structurally, which can be observed by the homogeneous thickness of the columns spread under the roof. The radius of the inscribed circle through the hexagon bares no relation to its structural load. As such the roof feels bulky, which sells Ban's initial idea short. Possibly the conceptual model should have been regarded as a declaration of architectural intent, where it mistakenly has been taken as a referential model. What's striking is that the skill and rigor demonstrated in the realization contrasts with the lack of it in terms of its conception. Where the model has become *literal* in fabrication it remains *allegorical* in terms of its architectural conception. The absoluteness of the architectral model as such is brought into view, and raises the question whether *Designtoproduction* should interpreted the CAD model from scratch based on S. Ban's concept, rather than to "post-process" a coarse conceptual model.

Where the Metz Centre Pompidou project struggles with an analogical discrepancy, the recently completed Qatar National Convention Centre by Isozaki[9] deals with a functional discrepancy. The shape of the building, or rather its structure, is the outcome of a topological optimization process, minimizing the volume required to distribute the loads of the roof. The irony here is that there is little load to distribute although the structure suggests the base of a skyscraper. The issue here is not the optimization process per se but rather its naive architectural application. The Centre is a pornographic building; a structure overdosed on Viagra without the hope of ever climaxing.

---

9 | Originally Isozaki's competition entry for a new train station in Florence.

Image 48: Shigeru Ban / designtoproduction – Metz Centre Pompidou, 2010

Image 49: Arata Isozaki, Florence New Station, 2002, Competition model

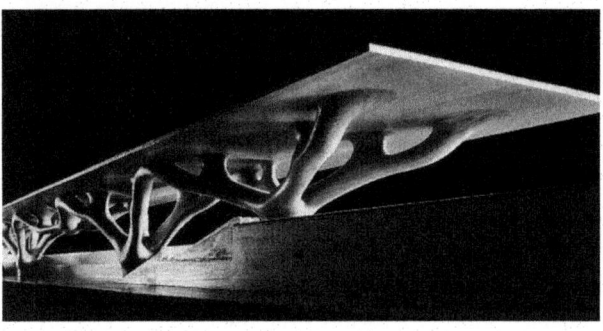

Image 48 & 49: Functional and analogical discrepancy

Why settle for simile?
Architecture's biophile infatuation is worrisome; with the literal turn of the architectural model, the burlesque of biomimicry will rapidly become a backward position. The promotion of the model is a pivotal moment in architecture, one that should not be lost on the callow act of mimises. *Why settle for simile?* Where Haeckel's images were adequate and imaginative in Berlage's era, here they represent a commonplace.

Architecture is situated in a society fueled by genetically modified crops, where genetic material is routinely patented; mimicry as an approach seems an underdeveloped epistemic position, seen in the context of a radically technocratic society. J.J. Tabor's research is a strong reminder that "physics runs on a kind of computer."

To paraphrase Tabor: "We have re-programmed the genomes of living cells to construct massively parallel biological computers capable of processing two-dimensional images at a theoretical resolution of greater than 100 megapixels per square inch. First, we rewired a signal transduction pathway in E-coli to express a pigment-producing enzyme under the control of red light. We then use the engineered bacteria as pixels in biological film."[10]

Image 50 & 51: Bacterial portraiture, J. J. Tabor / Ernst Haeckel, Kunstformen der Natur, 1899

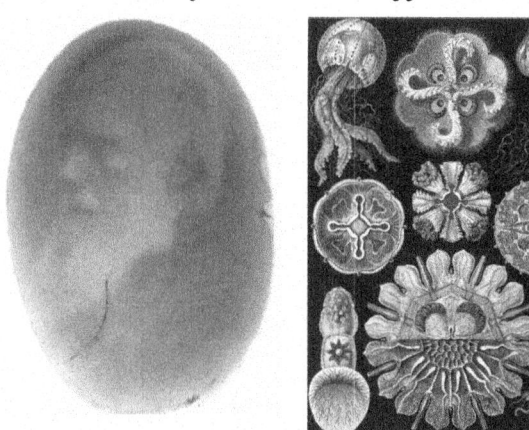

Image 50 & 51: An evolved understanding of the concept of naturein architecture

As nature is sufficiently well understood – we are indeed able to re-program its gene expression –, architecture's superficial emphasis on *simile*

---

10 | Tabor, J.J., "Programming living cells to function as massively parallel computers," in *Proceedings of the 44th annual Design Automation Conference*, 2007, ACM: New York, NY, USA. pp. 638-639

reveals itself as a cold caricature of a retrograde epistemic position. If computing is the runtime of physics, that which precedes nature, than why the self-censorship? Conceptually, a biomimetic approach is one of *representing* an idealized, stylized nature, where GMO's[11] *yet substantiate* this idealized, stylized nature. Tabor continues: "Next, use the 'bacterial photography' technology as tool for the engineering of a massively parallel biological computer which uses cell-cell communication to compute the edges (light-dark boundaries) within images."[12]

Along with the advancement of the architectural model, architectural models should evolve; significance transcribed at the cellular level. What's sure about the explosion-formed anodized titanium cast vase by Greg Lynn is that it will neither rot, stink nor decompose, underscoring that it's not composed of cellulose tissue. Is the resulting artificial/organic hybrid *both, and* or *neither, nor*? Is the gorgeous anodized titanium piece antithetic to its conceptual ambition?

Image 52: Greg Lynn's vase for Alessi

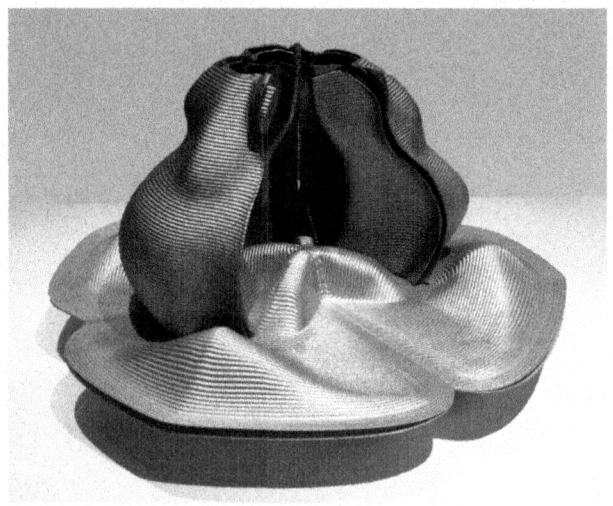

---

11 | Genetically Modified Organism
12 | Tabor 2007, pp. 638-639

Image 53: Hornby's antenna developed for NASA's Space Technology 5 Mission

Image 52 & 53: Complex vs Complexity

How to close the epismetic rift?
The epismetic crisis in architecture is underscored by radical shift in status of the architectural model. How can this rift be brought about? Perhaps Fredkin's notion of *Finite Natures* offers a clue; a close coupling of the laws of physics an object is subjected to and its physical manifestation. The antenna that Greg Hornby evolved for NASA's Space Technology 5 Mission offers perspective. The antenna is one of the components of a satellite that consumes most energy over it's lifespan, therefore it's worthwhile to spend considerable effort optimizing its design. The many non-linear radio-frequencies that an antenna has to be able to deal with make the design task one of great complexity. Different bandwidths interfere with one another, finding a compromise is therefore very difficult. What's stunning about the design is that it has pierced through the ceiling of design complexity of what a traditional designer can achieve. A designer who has limited design resources, limited hours to spend, has finite patience and knowledge of the intricacies involved. While current design approaches in architecture aim for complexification – rendering a straightforward design concept into something that is not –, here we are presented by a design approach that achieves the inverse; an approach of *condensation*. The antenna is so strongly coupled to the phenomena it has to deal with, that it lies beyond

what's considered rational. To the untrained eye, Hornby's antenna looks like someone channeled their anger on a paperclip. While it is straightforward to complexify a design it takes massive computational resources and a great deal of knowledge to *sublimate* a design. Coupling evolutionary computing with simulation forms the toolchain of the design strategy of sublimation. When juxtaposed with Lynn's vase the opposing approaches are underscored; manifestation vs. materialization. What potential does the synthesis of the antithetical design strategies hold? The combined sophistication of Lynn's materialization and Hornby's manifestation offers great architectural promise.

Situated development
John Rieffel developed the concept of *Situated development*: "the evolution of prescriptive representations requires simulating an object's entire assembly, rather than only its final shape, a process which we call 'Situated Development.' In this context, the environment in which evolution occurs is meant to be equivalent to some physical assembly mechanism, such as a rapid prototyping machine."[13] The architectural possibilities of such a design method holds striking potential; not a mere design is evolved, but a holistic building strategy, bridging what Rieffel refers to as the *fabrication gap*. Situated Development creates *motivated complexity*, tapping into the potential of moving beyond *digital craft*. CNC based fabrication methods remain a form of artisanal creation, since translation from a design to CAM code[14] is a highly involved process. The critical difference is that Situated Development gives rise to *implicit fabrication*, where generating a manufacturing code no longer is a post-rationalization of the project. Potentially this approach is a means of unlocking the true potential of CNC fabrication. The involved CAM programming is the reason why a mere fraction of the production potential of CNC fabrication is utilized, with craft, artisanship absolving the relative cumbersomeness of the process.

---

13 | Rieffel, J., *Evolutionary Fabrication: The Co-Evolution of Form and Formation*, Brandeis University, 2006, http://www.demo.cs.brandeis.edu/papers/jrieffel_seeds05.pdf
14 | Computer Aided Manufacturing; g-code, robot code

Image 54: Rieffels' concept of emerging ontogenic scaffolding; a structure is assembled, with the inclusion of gray, temporary scaffolding elements. When these are removed and the structure is subjected to its environment, the structure is altered until it reaches a point of stability

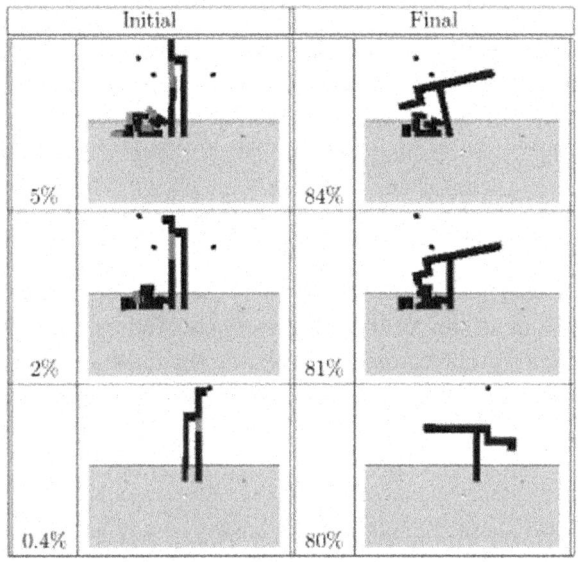

Image 55: Michael Hansmeyer, Sixth Order installation at the Gwangju Design Biennale 2011

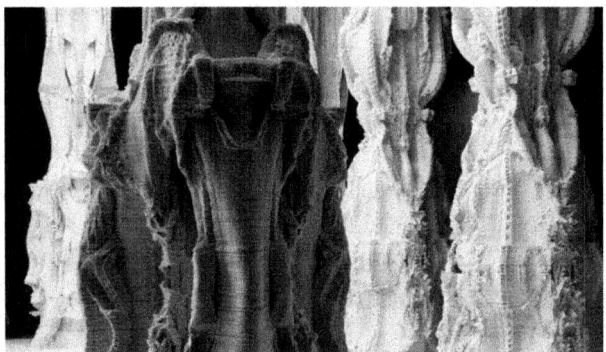

Image 54 & 55: Two opposing forms of complexity

There is a real contradiction in terminology of the artisanship involved in automated manufacturing. While the design resolution is dramatically increased, the threshold to fabrication is taken away. Finally, it's worth pointing out that the design process itself is an important factor in production, of up to 70%.[15]

Such a design approach is diametrically opposed to the formal, biomimetic design approach and raises the question of what can be considered *natural* in architecture. A natural progression towards materialization is exploiting technological propensities. In this light, it's interesting to juxtapose the research of Michael Hansmeyer and John Rieffel. While Hansmeyer achieves a great level of visual complexity, the process of manufacturing the imposing columns involves the patience and endurance of the students involved in manufacturing the project, where Rieffel relies on the effortless collapse of his structures for their final assembly. While the complexity of Rieffel's research is obfuscated by its seeming simplicity so is the elegant algorithmic simplicity of Hansmeyer's project obfuscated by the resulting visual complexity. It is the combined merit of either project which is most promising.

The renewed centrality of fabrication in architecture evokes the idea that architecture perhaps can be considered to be the difference between the cost of the raw building materials and assembling subtracted from the market value of the build project. Even though this point of view is somewhat banal, I find it an optimistic idea. Those architects who will succeed to incorporate knowledge into the architectural model will be able to realize greater architecture quality within similar budget constraints. Design strategies such as *Situated Development* simultaneously embed and evolve knowledge about the architectural model, where materialization is no longer an afterthought, but at the heart of conception. It brings computational architecture towards materialization at a cellular level where advanced architectural conception methodologies are closely entangled with robotic fabrication strategies. If such specialized design methods will emerge, the level of expertise and efficiency involved will advance architecture's autonomy. Even though the visual complexity of the models evolved by both

---

15 | Boothroyd, G., Dewhurst P. and W.A. Knight, *Product Design for Manufacture and Assembly*, New York: Marcel Dekker, 2002

Rieffel's and Hornby's work is lacking, I cannot help but find the approach more radical and stimulating than the featherweight pseudo-complexity all too present in computational architecture. The exploration of condensation, is long overdue.

Soft Monstrosities

Marcelyn Gow

> "When the system of bits and pieces or impulses or whatever is going to replace architecture really starts thinking and acting as additions to our human nerve endings the rules will be scattered. There is only really a rule-for-the-job-at-a-moment-in-time. Architecture is unresponsive."
> Archigram 1968[1]

Currently a strain of *monstrosity*, bred in the context of the electronic paradigm that emerged in the late 1950s, is coming of age, insinuating itself into contemporary notions of materiality and propelling their erosion into less stable forms. This *monstrosity*, a conflation of hard and soft systems, probes beneath the superficies of formal hybridization into the territory of the performative. Monstrosity, in the teratological sense, is characterized by structural or formal deviations from the norm. The combination of various morphological features constitutes a form of monstrosity. The *soft monstrosity* replicates this feature to some extent by intertwining material and electronic systems that respond to human presence. Embedded electronic networks enable materiality to become informed. The coalescence of hardware and software or technological and biological systems was anticipated in the myriad of human-machine dialogues engendered by early information-processing technology. A fundamental correlation between the logics of information-processing technology and the human nervous system was

---

[1] | "Indeterminacy – Relaxed Scene," in *Archigram* 8, London: Archigram, 1968, unpaginated

articulated by Norbert Wiener in his 1948 book *Cybernetics: or, Control and Communication in the Animal and the Machine*. Wiener's analogy was subsequently instantiated in architectural discourse through Kenzo Tange's characterization of urban communication networks in his seminal *Tokyo Plan 1960* and design for the exhibition infrastructure at the 1970 World Expo in Osaka. In the context of media theory Marshall McLuhan reiterated Wiener's analogy throughout the 1960s, citing electronic circuitry as an extension of the human nervous system. In each of these instances the biological is rendered metaphorically through other forms of media.

In 1965 *Time* magazine captured the essence of the *soft monstrosity* in the form of a voracious punch-card consuming super-computer endowed with arms for typing calculations, answering telephones and simultaneously adjusting spools of reel to reel magnetic tape that functioned both as a programming device as well as a pair of gigantic eyes for the machine. In this image the technological euphoria celebrated by Marshall McLuhan as the "electronic extensions of man" is tempered by a profound anxiety surrounding the human-machine dialogue.

The *soft monstrosity* renders in increasingly higher resolution a trajectory that originated in the early years of what sociologist Jaques Ellul dubbed "the technological society" in his 1954 book of the same name.[2] Ellul's emphasis on technologically-regulated procedures and human-machine interfaces (collected under the rubric of "technique"), as opposed to objects, posits the strategic use of technology as a kind of societal *operating system*. Throughout *The Technological Society*, terminology related to recent developments in communications and information-processing technology is deployed metaphorically in order to describe the new environment engendered by *technique*. Discussing the atrophy of human involvement in the process of automation Ellul evokes a communications device. "In this decisive evolution, the human being does not play a part. Technical elements combine among themselves, and they do so more and more spontaneously. In the future, man will apparently be confined to the role of a

---

2 | Although Ellul's book, *The Technological Society*, was originally published as *La Technique ou l'enjeu du siècle* (Paris: Librarie Armand Colin, 1954), it gained widespread recognition in 1964 with its translation into English as: Ellul, Jacques, *The Technological Society*, trans. John W. Wilkinson, New York: Alfred A. Knopf, 1964

recording device; he will note the effects of techniques upon one another and register the results."³

Image 56: "The Cybernated Generation," Time, 2 April 1965

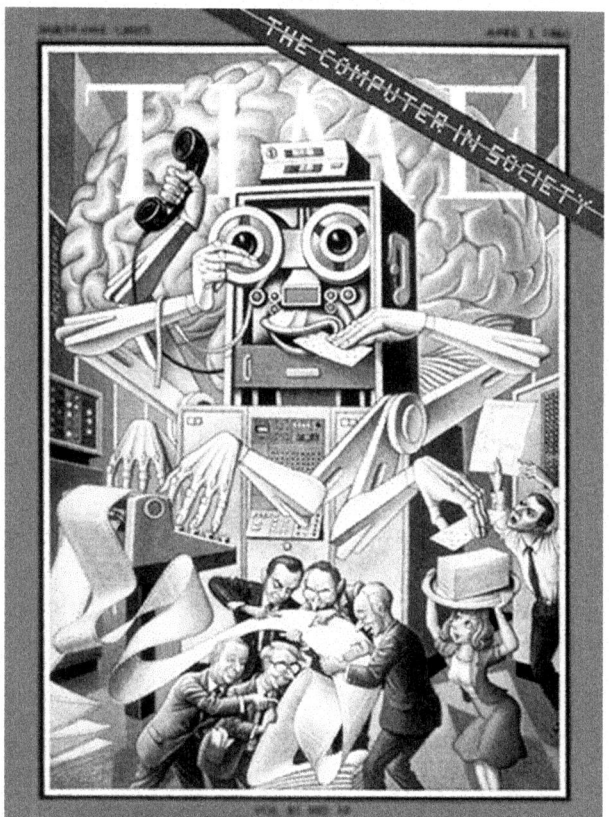

The nature of the metaphors used to describe human interaction with technology changed in tandem with technological innovations. For instance Lewis Mumford, in his 1934 *Technics and Civilization*, evokes an agricultural context and the image of a shepherd when he describes the modern textile

---

3 | Ibid., p. 93; the image of the recording device is reflected in the magnetic tape spools which appear on the cover of the 1967 Random House edition of *The Technological Society*.

worker, "linger[ing] on as a machine-herd."⁴ Ellul's choice of recording devices, seismographs, circuits, and switches to describe human beings and their activities likewise reflects on the electronic paradigm in place at the time he was writing. In some cases communications technology would be posited as a surrogate for human presence altogether. Ellul describes how, "The worker, no longer needed to guide or move the machine to action, will be required merely to watch it and to repair it when it breaks down."⁵ The metaphor of the worker as a monitor would be paralleled by Ellul's description of the artist as "a seismograph that records the fluctuations of man and society."⁶ In both instances the human takes on a passive role, subservient to the technological apparatus and its societal impact.

Kenzo Tange and Arata Isozaki as well as the members of the Metabolist group (Kiyonori Kikutake, Fumihiko Maki, Masato Otaka, and Noriaki „Kisho" Kurokawa, and the architectural critic Noboru Kawazoe; the graphic designer Kiyoshi Awazu, and the industrial designer Kenji Ekuan also became members) addressed the spectrum of possibilities and problems that the new information technology presented. Their work is notable for incorporating principles of systems theory and cybernetics. For the World Design Conference in Tokyo in 1960 the Metabolists published a pamphlet containing several urban projects and a text called, "Metabolism 1960 – The Proposals for New Urbanism." In this text the group elucidated on the significance of the term *metabolism* for architecture operating as a "vital process."⁷

The Metabolists emphasized the idea that society performs as a biological system. Temporal aspects of growth and decay inherent to biological systems played a significant role in their projects. They proposed creating environments comprised of replaceable components in order to approach an architecture that would incorporate indeterminacy. Urban regeneration would occur according to a time based metabolic cycle. This growth princi-

---

4 | Mumford, Lewis, *Technics and Civilization*, New York: Harcourt, Brace and Company, 1934, p. 277
5 | Ellul 1964, p. 135
6 | Ibid., p. 404
7 | "Metabolism 1960 – A Proposal for a New Urbanism," in Kurokawa, Kisho (ed.), *Metabolism in Architecture*, Boulder, Colo.: Westview Press, 1977, p. 27

ple had been taken up earlier on an urban scale by Kenzo Tange who worked together with Sadao Watanabe, Koji Kamiya, Kisho Kurokawa, Arata Isozaki, and Heiki Koh on the seminal *Tokyo Plan 1960*. Tange proposed a decentralized growth of the city into new "cores" and "branches" that would ease congestion on the center of the existing city. The plan, designed to accommodate 10 million inhabitants, called for the construction of a new civic axis that would extend from the mainland into Tokyo Bay. Superhighways and mass transit infrastructure would connect the civic axis to a series of megastructural space frames and floating residential areas.

A text written by Tange on "Tokaido-Megalopolis: The Japanese Archipelago of the Future," elucidates some of the ideas that were manifested in the *Tokyo Plan 1960*. In the section called "The Effect of the Expansion of Communications on the Present Age," dealing with infrastructure and distribution of goods and information, Tange references cybernetics, pointing out that Norbert Wiener had identified two types of connections that hold a society together, "energetic couplings" and "informational couplings."[8] Tange speculates that "informational couplings" will have a significant impact on the urban environment because they are capable of providing feedback and are responsive. Transportation systems like the railway, he argues, have been designed for efficient „energy couplings," essentially the distribution of goods from one place to another. How, he asks, will these mechanical exchanges transform or integrate with the communications channels for transmitting information? Tange uses a cybernetic analogy, positing parallels between the human nervous system and the complex communications networks of the contemporary city. "In large contemporary urban complexes, communications networks twist and intertwine into a complex which must be something like the nervous system of the brain."[9]

In Tange's *Tokyo Plan 1960*, the " informational couplings" were ultimately instantiated as interchanges between traffic loops circulating in opposite directions. These "couplings" are materialized as circulation conduits that are activated at various speeds. An offramp connects from a high-

---

[8] | Tange, Kenzo, "Tokaido-Megalopolis: The Japanese Archipelago of the Future," in Kultermann, Udo (ed.), *Kenzo Tange: Architecture and Urban Design 1946-1969*, New York: Praeger, 1970, p. 153
[9] | Ibid., p. 154

speed circuit to a slower speed circuit instigating a deceleration in the velocity of traffic. Arterial roads are channeled into the circuits of traffic flow. In these loops counter directional circulation allows for exchanges to occur between the various levels – providing access to the civic axis. Connections are thus established between the urban system, the traffic system, and the architectural system. The analogy of the human nervous system and its informational couplings is materialized through these circulation systems.

Image 57: Kenzo Tange, Tokyo Plan 1960, circulation diagram

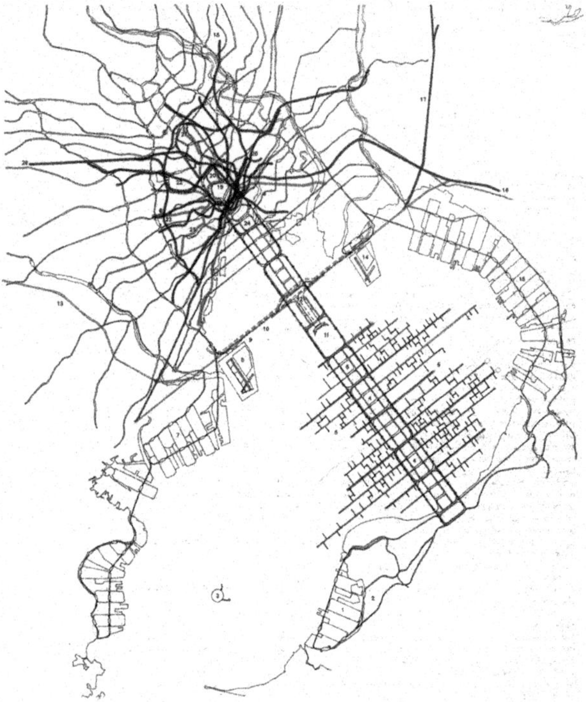

Nine years after the *Tokyo Bay* project, Kisho Kurokawa designed *Metabonate Floating Factory*, a proposal for an offshore extension to a city, which would be comprised primarily of factory buildings for the petrochemical industry, ship building, and fish farms. Hardware, in this case evocative of electronic circuitry, is overt in the project. In the architectural model Kurokawa used a system of channels, conduits, and wires to represent vehicular and pedestrian circulation routes. A circuit, literally a path or route which returns to its starting point like the path which channels electric current, becomes the predominant metaphor for urban growth in the project.

Kurokawa refers to the aggregation of docked circuits as "unit composition," and proposes it to be an efficient organization for the recycling of resources and presumably the recycling of architecture. The cluster of these circuits is almost a direct translation of the electronic components that were featured on the cover of *Fortune's* March 1964 issue on "The Computer Age."

The dilemma that I am sketching out here for architecture, in its attempt to implement the electronic paradigm, is one that negotiates between image and performance. The World Exposition of 1970 (Expo '70) in Osaka acted as a platform where architecture's capacity to integrate the informational nexus was tested on an infrastructural scale. Different ways of responding to the image/performance dilemma began to surface within the context of the master plan for the Expo infrastructure. This was designed by a team of architects directed by Kenzo Tange. In the Expo Theme Pavilion various media were used – the design of the pavilion's structural system, its circulation routes, as well as electronically *programmed* effects – in the interest of producing a flexible, adaptable environment. In this context flexibility should be considered as a multifarious quality encompassing issues of participation as well as the production of architectural affect. In Tange's descriptions of the project we find evidence of the dilemma outlined above, namely to what extent flexibility is engendered through form or through other, less material media. This question continues to resonate in the contemporary architectural discussion.

Tange designed the major infrastructural arteries of the Expo site employing the metaphor of a branching system or tree. The Trunk Facilities, as he called this infrastructure, were intended to give continuity to the entire site. The Symbol Zone was an aggregation of architectural elements that established the major north-south axis of the Expo site. It consisted of the Main Gate (the primary entrance to the site), the Festival Plaza (a vast open plaza with a subterranean exhibition space), and the Space Frame (an enormous roof over the Festival Plaza). The sub-plazas, sub-gate and moving pedestrian walkway acted as "branches" establishing connections to other pavilions and areas of the Expo site. The architectural critic Noboru

Kawazoe, also a member of the Metabolist group, explains the cybernetic analogy that Tange had employed in his *Tokyo Bay* project and that resurfaces a decade later in the design of the facilities for Expo '70. "In your *Tokyo Plan, 1960*," commented Kawazoe, "you said that in terms of information transmission the living body contains two systems – the fluid and the electronic – and that the latter is the more sophisticated. For this reason you proposed an urban axis resembling a tree trunk and branches that would carry out this kind of transmission in a way similar to the operation of the nervous system."[10] Here the image of biological organization is applied as a system of circulation but its performance remains mechanical and does not correspond to the system it emulates.

The aerial theme space at the Festival Plaza was a model "city in the air" containing capsule house prototypes designed by Kurokawa and Koji Kamiya. These full-scale capsule dwellings were suspended directly into the roof structure and reflected the idea of spatial and temporal transformation inherent in a biological system.

The principle was that components could be dismantled, transported, and plugged-in to the nodes of the system thereby forming cellular clusters. Through this technique of „plugging-in" architecture is dematerialized into a series of *transportable units*. It becomes reconfigurable, temporal, and nomadic. The organizational logic of these capsule houses complemented the diffuse structural network of the spaceframe which, in principle, allowed for multidirectional extension.

In his "Capsule Declaration" Kurokawa expands on the ideas of "unit space" and "cell" that he had worked with since 1959.[11] These techniques were used on an organizational level in projects like *Metabonate Floating Factory* and *Floating City*, Kasumigaura. In these projects the cellular organization was used to facilitate circulation. The "capsule" concept, while also cellular in its organization, is described in the more performative terminology of cybernetics, incorporating feedback and information processing. The "Capsule Declaration" begins with the words, „The capsule is cyborg architecture. Man, machine, and space build a new organic body which tran-

---

10 | "Some Thoughts about Expo '70: Dialogue between Kenzo Tange and Noboru Kawazoe," in *The Japan Architect* (JA) 45, no. 5/6-164, May/June 1970, p. 31

11 | Kurokawa, Kisho, "Capsule Declaration," in Kurokawa 1977, p. 84; italics are mine; originally published in *Space Design,* March 1969

scends confrontation. As a human being equipped with a man-made internal organ becomes a new species which is neither machine nor human, so the capsule transcends man and equipment. Architecture from now on will increasingly take on the character of equipment. This new elaborate device is not a ‚facility', like a tool, but is a part to be integrated into a life pattern and has, in itself, an objective existence."[12]

He defined the "cyborg" as "a cybernated organism [...] partly automated, based on feedback and information processes; usually appears in science fiction as half man, half machine."[13]

Kurokawa's contention that architecture will increasingly become more like "equipment" is aligned with Kawazoe's description of the Expo infrastructure. He declared that the Festival Plaza was not a building and the Space Frame was not architecture; instead, together with the moving walkways and trunk facilities, they functioned as "environmental equipment."[14] This equipment included computer-controlled movable seating and stage platforms, and gantries for moving stage gear. An audio system comprised of hundreds of speakers was designed to produce three-dimensional sound matrices. Isozaki considered these electronically-motivated devices to be major constituents in the production of the architectural space.[15]

Undoubtedly the most spectacular pieces of equipment were the "performing robots" designed by Isozaki. Two robots were designed, one called Deme for coordinating performances and one called Deke for controlling effects. The robots, approximately 12 meters in height, were programmable and could perform a series of basic movements including rotating and moving across the floor of the Festival Plaza. Their arms could be used to raise stage sets or performers by bending and extending laterally. Each robot's body housed lighting and audio systems while its dual "head" section contained the control room for this equipment. The robot could be programmed to generate a series of local atmospheric effects – emitting light,

---

12 | Ibid., p. 75
13 | Ibid., p. 75
14 | "Some Thoughts about Expo '70: Dialogue between Kenzo Tange and Noboru Kawazoe," in *The Japan Architect* (JA) 45, no. 5/6-164, May/June 1970, , p. 32
15 | Isozaki, Arata, *Arata Isozaki: Unbuilt*, Tokyo: TOTO Shuppan, 2001, p. 134

sound, and fog. It was also equipped with "information gathering facilities" including microphones and light sensors.

Image 58: Arata Isozaki, RM performing robot, Expo '70

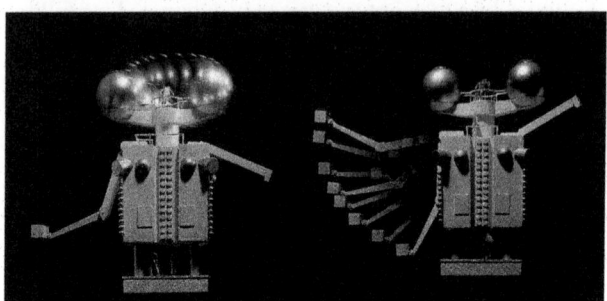

The input of sound or light levels on the plaza could be sent to the control room and used to trigger pre-recorded sounds or to activate the lighting and fog emission systems. The production of these effects was clearly an important consideration for Isozaki in designing the movable elements for Festival Plaza. He described the computer-controlled programs for sound, fog, lighting and image projection as, "employ[ing] flickering media to suggest a vast environment."[16] The practical side of this flickering media was to create temporary attractions on the plaza after the main performances so as to regulate the flow of exiting crowds.

Isozaki used the term *soft architecture* to describe architecture that would become responsive to changing situations and forms of occupation. He acknowledged the fact that form alone would be inadequate to achieve flexibility. "Architecture must now take on multiple meanings," he observed, "its presence can no longer be determined by form; rather it must be flexible and responsive to the flow of time and the needs of a succession of occasions. I call such an architecture 'soft architecture'."[17] It appears that for Isozaki the efficacy of form was challenged by the potency of electronically

---

16 | Isozaki, Arata, "Festival Plaza," in *The Japan Architect* (JA) 45, no. 5/6-164, May/June 1970, p. 59
17 | Isozaki quoted in Pawley, Martin, "Architecture Versus the Movies, or Form Versus Content: Martin Pawley Reports from Osaka," in *Architectural Design* 40, no. 6, June 1970, p. 293; the quote is dated 1969

motivated effects in the production of a responsive environment. The fact that effects could be programmed and time-based implied greater flexibility. The programming of the moving seating platforms and stages to accommodate various performance scenarios and particularly the programming of the performing robots to create a "flickering" distraction, thus ensuring efficient crowd flow, exemplify the predetermined aspects of the technologically driven environment at Festival Plaza. Isozaki's "soft architecture," rather than imaging the human nervous system or cellular growth, instead translated the effectors and receptors of the nervous system as the interaction between humans and electronically programmed machines.

Invisible environment is the terminology chosen by Marshall McLuhan to describe the spatial fallout of the emergent electronic paradigm.[18] In a 1965 lecture called, "The Invisible Environment: The Future of an Erosion," McLuhan anticipated a human environment that would become, to a large extent, dematerialized through advances in telecommunication technology in particular the wireless transmission of electronic signals reflected by the communications satellites. McLuhan envisioned the computer ultimately, "taking over the task of programming the environment itself as a work of art."[19] He suggested that emerging forms of media are so ubiquitous and ambient that they stage an environment which is invisible. They act as a kind of *operating system*, encapsulating their semi-obsolete predecessors and turning them into "art forms."[20]

The rather insidious exchange McLuhan posited between environmental programming or *software* and its *hardware* correlate of the "art form" raises the question of how technology alters the role of the "art form" itself. The "art form" or architecture becomes actively redefined by the very technolo-

---

[18] | McLuhan's talk, "Technology and Environment," was given at the International Center for the Communication Arts and Sciences of the Southern Illinois University in Carbondale, Illinois on 23 October 1965.

[19] | McLuhan's lecture was delivered at the *Vision '65* conference *New Challenges for Human Communication* held at the International Center for the Communication Arts and Sciences of the Southern Illinois University in Carbondale, Illinois on October 23, 1965; the lecture was transcribed in *Perspecta* 11, 1967, pp. 163-67

[20] | Ibid., p. 164; specifically the reference, "[...] every new technology creates an environment that translates the old or preceding technology into an art form, or into something exceedingly noticeable."

gy through which it is usurped. It is the overtly *visible* responses to this phenomenon that play a critical role in the contemporary architectural discussion. A multivalent implementation of the informational paradigm, one that involves a shift from a figural approach, the metaphorical *imaging* of the exchange of information, toward a more operative approach, *performing* the exchange of information, begins to surface in contemporary architectural production. Rather than a biological metaphor being rendered through technological means as in the work of Tange and the Metabolists, technology itself becomes an impulse in the production of sensation. The integration of remote sensing technology, electronics, and micro-computation into material systems alters their performance. The presence of these semi-visible media conflates the material and sensory aspects of architecture to an extent that they become inseparable, a *soft monstrosity*. New architectural *monstrosities* appear in which hardware is partially subsumed by the atmospheric affect of various forms of software, and materiality percolates through responsive networks. Rather than a return to the invisible nature of data projected by McLuhan, these *soft monstrosities* produce invigorated forms of tangible architectural presence and performance.

Servo
These kinds of responsive networks act as parallel processes in the work of *servo*. As contemporary practitioners we inevitably operate in the context of the electronic paradigm, and the extent to which the exchange of data instantiates itself in the material properties of a space, or is sometimes more immaterial in nature, becomes a primary impetus. In several projects we have dealt with the storage and relay of information within a network and how this is reflected both in the form and material organization of the architecture, as well as in more immaterial fallout and the production of secondary effects.

In the *spoorg* project the material capacity of communication, the nexus of interacting channels for the processing, storage, and retrieval of data reflects itself in the architecture. *spoorg* performs as an active and multidirectional material site of feedback. The *spoorg* or 'semi-porous operable organism' takes its name from a primitive, usually unicellular, often environmentally resistant, dormant or reproductive body produced by plants and some microorganisms. These are capable of developing either directly or after fusion with another spore into a new individual which is, in some cases, unlike the parent.

Image 59: Spoorg installation, Los Angeles, 2006

The *spoorg* system is a cellular network that attaches onto the interior and exterior of glass facades and windows. It functions as a shading and speaker system, filtering sunlight and creating an ambient sonic environment through wireless radio communication. Each *spoorg* module is embedded with local intelligence, enabling it to communicate with adjacent *spoorgs*. Reflecting the photosynthetic process whereby plants use sunlight to produce oxygen, *spoorg* uses sunlight to produce sound. Actions and performances are involved as opposed to images. *spoorg* reacts to local as well as environmental changes of light and responds by modulating sound textures based on a series of algorithmic rules, producing larger scale atmospheric effects. Materially it is equal parts architecture, decoration, hardware and software.

Each *spoorg* module is composed of a thin-walled vacuum-cast plastic shell with hollow regions for embedding electronic programming devices including microcontrollers, photo transistors (light sensors), speaker elements and RF modules for wireless radio-communication with adjacent cells. The *spoorg* system revises the conventional notion of modularity as a material aggregate and proposes a composite *information aggregate* where modules of information take on material attributes in the architectural environment. *spoorg* cells can operate individually as well as in dense assemblies – aggregating through stacking and clustering, nesting, cell division or fusion with other cells to create new individuals.

The electronic infrastructure operates with a similar logic. Each unit is responsive to local sensory input and produces sound individually. Instead of one processor that performs one complex task sequentially, *spoorg* is composed of several simple processors operating in parallel to one another and

Image 60: Spoorg installation, Los Angeles, 2006

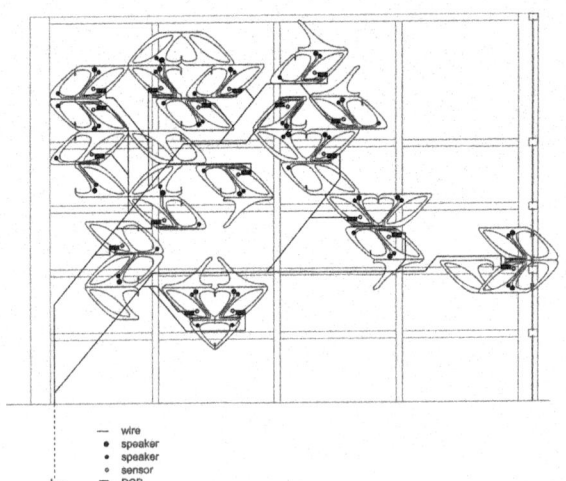

performing simple tasks. Local interactions give rise to global information processing as the individual sound behavioral patterns fuse with input from neighboring cells. This cellular approach allows for the assembly of material, electronic and social networks having different modes and distributions of *connectivity*.

The *spoorg* system was installed in the R.M. Schindler Kings Road house for the exhibition *Gen(H)ome* in 2006. *spoorg's* infiltration of the house occurs in the nursery, which as the nexus of growth and cultivation is an ideal site. By being able to monitor or register atmospheric qualities in the house and exterior environments, the *spoorg* system inverts the convention of monitoring the nursery. *spoorg* communicates through the house envelope, attaching to the interior and exterior of the nursery, creating a porous configuration from the garden to the interior.

Image 61: Spoorg – diagram of inter-cell wireless communication network

The *spoorg* system allows one to *cultivate* and decorate the domestic space by distributing and expanding shading and sound into a modular wall system. Varying states of transparency emerge as the *spoorg* interfaces with natural lighting. Through cultivation (inhabitants' interaction with the spoorg system) sound patterns are generated. Shifts in the density and the pace of ambient sound become apparent through the *spoorgs'* modulations of sound frequencies. Lack of cultivation will result in a decay of the *spoorg*

system's performance. This decay is contingent upon the programming that connects sensor activity to the modulations of sound frequencies – reduced sensor activity will result in reduced sound emission. The difference between decay and growth renders the domestic space with subtle changes of atmospheric moods. The generation of pattern, lighting effects, conditions of acoustic transparency or opacity all begin to re-shape surfaces of the domestic interior.

In the *spoorg* system, the *soft monstrosity* of intertwining material and electronic systems responds to human presence and atmospheric change. It slowly erodes and reconfigures the material envelope of its architectural host. The embedded electronic networks in *spoorg* enable materiality to become informed, momentarily exposing the conflation of the biological and technological. But *spoorg* will also gradually lose the quality of a *soft monstrosity* at the Schindler House. As inhabitants become accustomed to its presence, and the performance of *spoorg* in turn becomes adapted to movements of the inhabitants and the local environmental conditions, *spoorg* becomes increasingly embedded in the architecture upon which it acts.

Video Game Spaces as Architectural Metaphors

STEPHAN GÜNZEL

One way to understand video games is to think of them as "narrative architecture." This term was coined by Henry Jenkins from the media department of the MIT in Boston in 2004.[1] He actually borrowed the idea from Celia Pearce, who already wrote about this aspect in her *Interactive Book* from 1997.[2] The basic idea of Pearce as well as Jenkins is to say that in computer games we experience spaces that were built by game designers with a certain intention. Gamers should recognize these places and spaces due to a former experience. This experience doesn't have to be limited to the experience of a real place, but could also come from films or other media – a simulated place.

Furthermore, these experiences do not have to be explicit; they can be more or less stereotypical, like castles, war fields, dungeons, motorways, etc. But no matter how explicit the reference is, Jenkins points out, that in any case we should think of those places in terms of theme park rides, like "Pirates of the Caribbean," in which the audience is driven through an artificial environment on guided vehicles. Referring to the work of Disney-designer Don Carson, Jenkins calls this an "environmental storytelling."[3]

---

1 | Jenkins, Henry, "Game Design as Narrative Architecture," in Wardrip-Fruin Noah, Harrigan, Pat (eds.), *FirstPerson. New Media as Story, Performance, and Game*, Cambridge/London: MIT Press, 2004, pp. 118-130
2 | Pearce, Celia, "Architecture as a Narrative Art," in C.P.: *The Interactive Book. A Guide to the Interactive Revolution*, Indianapolis: Macmillan, 1997, pp. 25-28
3 | Carson, Don, "Environmental Storytelling. Creating Immersive 3D Worlds Using Lessons Learned from the Theme Park Industry," 2000, http://www.gamasutra.com/view/feature/3186/environmental_storytelling_.php

The "Pirates of the Caribbean" ride in fact is an interesting example as that particular theme park existed prior to the famous films with Johnny Depp: The first version of the ride has been already installed at Disneyland in 1967, which was already a condensation of an existing cliché of the pirate world – fed by films, which again were inspired by literature and fiction in general. The respective medial processes can be understood in terms of transference. The Australian media theorist Angela Ndalianis has written in her influential book *Neo-Baroque Aesthetics and Contemporary Entertainment* from 2004 that we live in a neo-baroque world, because everything has become serial.[4]

It is not just that media went serial, media – as is shown with Ndalianis' main reference, Henri Focillon[5] – have also always been metaphorical in the sense of providing translations, transpositions and transfers. Alongside computer games it can be demonstrated, how such a transfer of urban, architectural- and spatial structures or configurations in general appears in regard to the visual and navigational aspects. This idea has already been raised by the Norwegian game researcher Espen Aarseth, who in 2001 wrote in a key essay of computer game studies that spaces in video games must be understood as allegories,[6] hence as metaphors, that have been made interactive.

Inspired by this idea, Jenkins' term of "narrative architecture" can be revised, as a narration not specific to computer games, which first and foremost are games or interactive items (and not narratives).[7] One must then extend and specify the understanding of metaphors. It might be even more helpful to think of these *metaphors as antecedent metonymies*: in games not only can elements be found that were transferred from a given structure, but also a condensation of that structure or a reduction to the spatial essence.

---

4 | Ndalianis, Angela, *Neo-Baroque Aesthetics and Contemporary Entertainment*, Cambridge/London: MIT Press, 2004

5 | Focillon, Henri, *The Life of Forms in Art* [1934], New Haven: Yale University Press, 1942

6 | Aarseth, Espen, "Allegories of Space. The Question of Spatiality in Computer Games," in Eskelinen Markku, Koskimaa Raine (eds.), *Cybertext Yearbook 2000*, Jyväskylä: University of Jyväskylä, 2001, pp. 152-171

7 | Frasca, Gonzalo, "Simulation versus Narrative. Introduction to Ludology," in Wolf, Mark J.P., Perron, Bernard (eds.), *The Video Game Theory Reader*, New York/London: Routledge, 2003, pp. 221-235

To give an understanding of how computer games function in this regard, I first of all want to show you an example in which not the computer game is the result of a transposition or condensation, but in which the spatial structure of a computer game itself is transposed: the famous Russian game *Tetris* from 1984, whose gaming principle is a purely spatial one, as the task of the game and likewise the problem it poses is: Where is the right place? The falling variety of brick shapes cannot be stopped, but only increased in speed and have to be turned by the player to fit a particular gap.

Image 67: Tetris, 1984

An advertisement for the Honda automobile "Jazz" shows a transfer of the spatial problem of *Tetris* back into "real life"– more precisely into the urban context. This is how the urban landscape would appear when the game is taken as a metaphor. As *Tetris* was said to be in itself a metaphor for capitalism,[8] it seems to be consequent that Tetris could also be used as a metonymy for the lack of free space in megacities.

---

8 | Murray, Janet, *Hamlet on the Holodeck. The Future of Narrative in Cyberspace*, Cambridge/London: MIT Press, pp. 143-144

Image 68: Honda Jazz advertisment

Image 69: Super Mario, 1985

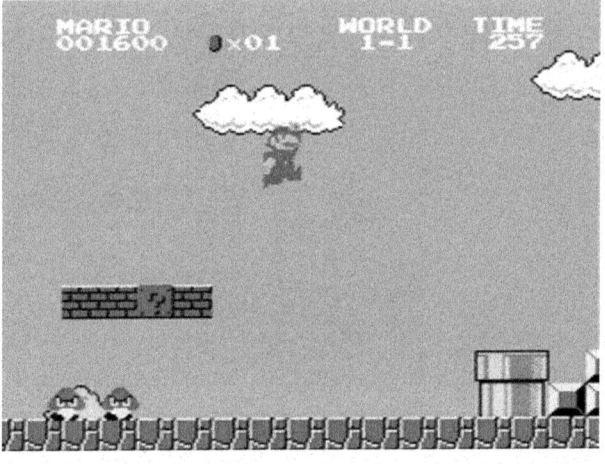

Another example of the way in which games provide metaphors for the city is *Super Mario*: It is one of the ten games that were classified by the Library of Congress to be amongst the ten most culturally valued games in human history.[9] The game is a so-called "platformer" – a game in which the player

---

9 | "Is That Just Some Game? No, It's a Cultural Artifact," in *The New York Times*, March 12, 2007, http://www.nytimes.com/2007/03/12/arts/design/12vide.html

steers the character Mario who has to jump from platform to platform and has to master obstacles. Thus, the game-space functions as a metaphor for a new use of the city.

Image 70: Parkour

Given the influence of Mario it is remarkable, that the sport *Parkour* (or FreeRunning) was not invented earlier. It seems to be a transfer of the game into the urban context. Invented by David Belle, whose father (being a member of the French Army) taught him, how to get from point A to B by the quickest means possible using gymnastic moves between buildings and other elements of the urban environment, the *traceur* transfers the spatial problem or task of the game in the city and its architecture. In terms of theory this "art of movement" represents as a fulfillment of Michael de Certeau's diagnosis that space is constituted by making use of places, especially when the prescribed usage is challenged or contradicted.[10]

The first examples were specific transpositions of game-space-structures into reality. A more common transfer is the way in which games

---

10 | De Certeau, Michel, *The Practice of Everyday Life* [1980], Berkeley: University of California Press, 1984

are metaphors for architecture, urban landscapes or space in general. The most dominant metaphor in this context is that of the container space.[11]

Image 71: Pong, 1972

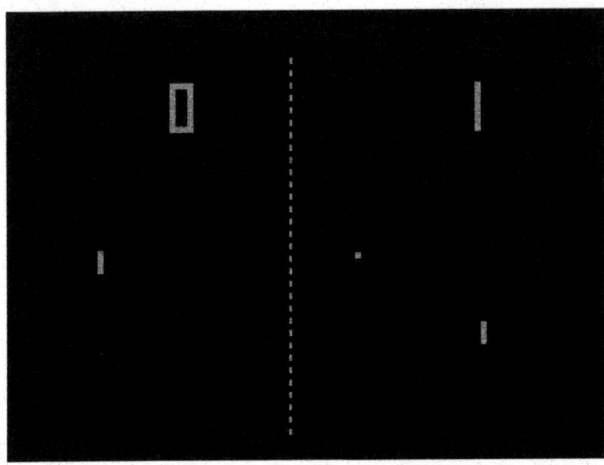

As can be seen in early games like *Pong* from 1972 the space is simply the frame of the screen containing the possible places in which the white spot or ball might move. Still, the "container" is not closed. In fact it is the task of the game to "close" the space by moving the foreshortened lines (representing the ping pong paddle) up and down to function as a blocker. Through this example the container experience is even more direct; contrary to architecture, in which the container needs to be open up (at least with a door and windows) in the game the open sides of the container space need to be closed.

Another metaphor or metonymy (as it is always a condensation of a given space to its very elements) is the labyrinth: It can even be found in combination with the container as is the case in the famous game *Pac Man* from 1980. The labyrinth here appears having a new function and is thus not totally the Cretan labyrinth of antiquity nor the labyrinth of the baroque that

---

11 | Lakoff, George, Johnson, Mark, "Ontological Metaphors," in Lakoff, George, Johnson, Mark, *Metaphors We Live By*, Chicago: University of Chicago Press, 1980, pp. 25-32

took the form of a garden maze.[12] In the case of *Pac Man* the player does not have to cope with the problem of a maze – i.e. not knowing where the exit is – as the aim is not to leave the labyrinth, but to visit all places within it. It is thus a combination of the Cretan and the modern labyrinth where Ariadne's thread has to be eaten up by *Puck Man* (as the figure originally was called in Japan) in the maze, which is monitored by the player.

Image 72: Pac Man, 1980

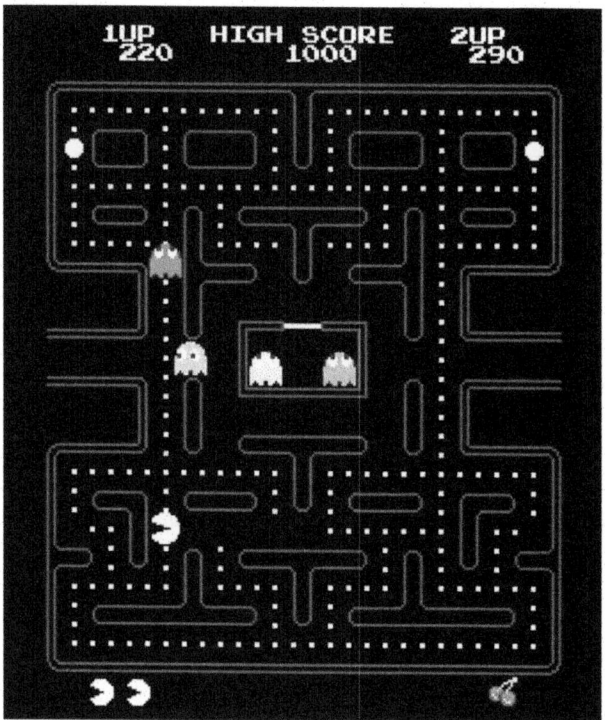

A modification of this situation can be found in *Doom* from 1993, a so-called "first-person-shooter," in which the gamer is thrown into the maze. In those games the point of view of the image coincides with the viewpoint of the character. Still the labyrinth is a pseudo-maze, in which there is ac-

---

12 | Reed Doob, Penelope, *The Idea of the Labyrinth from Classical Antiquity through the Middle Ages*, Ithaca/London: Cornell University Press, 1990

tually only one way to go. The shooter's labyrinth is more or less a folded road, with some detours. Instead of Pac-dots or power pellets that have to be eaten up, in the game obstacles or enemies have to be destroyed.

Image 73: Doom, 1993

Although it is quite common that in first-person games monsters have to be killed, it is not the only subject. The city itself is often the subject of games. And the gaming principle can be that of a *traceur* that has to cope with the architectural structure of a city. This is the case in *Mirror's Edge* from 2008. Thus, this well known game is a condensation of a problem that has transposed from other computer games (*platformer*) into the urban space (*Parkour*) in respect to the architectural conditions and combined with the first person view.

In the final example the city becomes itself a metaphor in games. In addition to action games like shooters, platformers and maze-games, there also exist also strategy games and so-called simulation games. Technically speaking every computer game is a simulation, but what some games do is they provide models for what is called 'reality' or what is offered as a possible reality (as it is the case in flight simulations or war simulations – which have already existed prior to the computer games). For this purpose one can look at a strategic game which is a city simulation or a metonymy of the problems that can appear in a city. *SimCity* from 1989 is also amongst the ten most important games identified by the Library of Congress. In it the growth of a city is simulated and the user is confronted with urban planning problems.

Image 74: Mirror's Edge, 2008

Image 75: Sim City, 1989

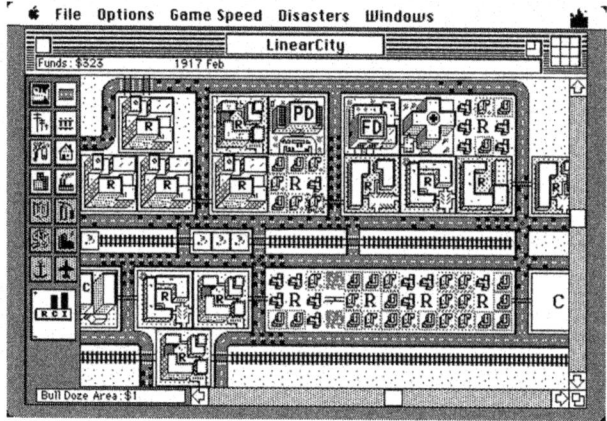

Sometimes these games are said to put the gamer in the position to control a certain territory – this is only partially true as once you made a decision, what to build where, one can only counter-steer the results by developing new grounds. Thus, one does not control the territory as such, but you are only in charge of keeping the urban structures in equilibrium. Here every aspect of the city is reduced to its very function within the urban context: Even people and leisure areas are considered only in their particular value for the system. It is as if Talcott Parsons' view of society had turned into a computer game.[13]

---

13 | Parsons, Talcott, *The Social System*, New York: Free Press, 1951

Diagram, Plan and Metaphor

Holger Schurk

> "When we, as architects, look at the architecture of the past, we all, I believe, try to penetrate its secret. [...] We are concerned with criteria and processes: with the how, before all else. It is this, which is peculiar in our observation: we look in order to learn how it is done. The first thing we learn, often at our own expense, is that this secret does not belong to form in itself."
> Giorgio Grassi 1983[1]

Planning problems in general are declared *wicked problems* by Horst Rittel and Melvin Webber in their essay from 1973, "Dilemmas in a General Theory of Planning." They oppose the *tame problems* predominant in the natural sciences. In a characterization covering several items, Rittel and Webber mainly focus on the lack of systematic and linearity in the solution process of *wicked problems* and outline an open process in its place, in which the beginning and the end are not clearly defined, problem and solution are intertwined, and work phases are changed frequently and erratically.[2] With the help of scientific terminology they attempt to encircle

---

[1] | Grassi, Giorgio, "Form Liberated, Never Sought. On the Problem of Architectural Design," in *Daidalos* Vol.7, 1983, p. 24
[2] | Rittel, Horst W.J., Webber, Melvin M., "Dilemmas in einer allgemeinen Theorie der Planung," in Reuter, Wolf D. (ed.), Horst W.J. Rittel, *Planen, Entwerfen, Design. Ausgewählte Schriften zu Theorie und Methodik*, Stuttgart, Berlin, Köln: Kohlhammer, 1992, pp. 13-35

the specifics of a process, quite simply referred to by practicing architects as *designing*, which is described in new variations time and again. Giorgio Grassi, for instance, refers to a search for form, where "the overcoming of practical difficulties and the definition of form are the same thing."[3] Adolf Krischanitz describes the correlation between form and function as an "implied program"[4] and perceives a tension that arises when the two concepts mutually penetrate each other. Rem Koolhaas emphasizes the contradictions of design and sees them confirmed in the "Paranoid-Critical Method"[5] applied by Salvador Dalí. Applying this method the topics of the unconscious are exploited without having to relinquish logical and systematic assessments.[6] And finally unto Kazuyo Sejima for whom the eminent point in the process of design is the strategic organization of all elements. The examination of technical questions or atmospheric qualities is neglected in the beginning, later to automatically develop in the fairway of the strategy. "Usually, transparency and lightness, in terms of mass, are not the ultimate goals. What we are trying to do is to organize the components in

---

[3] | "This is the peculiar condition of architectural work. It is work where the conditioning factors are really the identification of form; a work where the overcoming of practical difficulties and the definition of form are the same thing. In this work form always comes last. Form, before being defined, has to pass many tests. It overcomes and gets round obstacles, follows unexpected paths, adapts itself, gradually discards anything superfluous about it and gains refinement. Its condition of necessity grows, acquiring weight and experience." Grassi 1983, p. 33
[4] | "Form and function constitute an implicit program. The interpenetration of both areas should build up an inner tension, which evidences certain almost anthropoid characteristics, like for instance pertinence, clarity, openess, order, awareness, frankness and so on. Generating these character traits occurs in the design process not only in the attempt to depict them metaphorically, but also with the layered seeping of the consciousness into the task, which then leads to an expression of this architecture that is both lively and processual." Graff, Uta (ed.), *Adolf Krischanitz: Architecture Is the Difference between Architecture*, Ostfildern: Hatje-Cantz-Verlag, 2010, p. 62
[5] | "Salvador Dali: Die Eroberung des Irrationalen," in Matthes, Axel, Stegman, Tolbert Diego (eds.), *Unabhängigkeitserklärung der Phantasie*, München: Rogner & Bernhard, 1974, p. 272
[6] | Koolhaas, Rem, *Delirious New York*, New York: Rizzoli, 1978

a clear way."⁷ In addition to this complexity, design is characterized as an interdisciplinary process, during which the boundaries of the participating disciplines are not always clearly drawn. According to architecture theorists Robert Somol and Sarah Whiting, the entire discipline of architecture must permanently be redefined during the design process, and can at no stage be pinpointed: "Design is what keeps architecture from slipping into a cloud of heterogeneity. It dilates the fluctuating borders of architecture's disciplinarity and expertise. So when architects engage topics that are seemingly outside of architecture's historically-defined scope – questions of economics or civic politics, for example – they don't engage those topics as experts of economics or civic politics but, rather, as experts on design and how design may affect economics or politics. They engage these other fields as experts on design's relationship to those other disciplines, rather than as critics."[8]

According to this reading design most of all means connecting or short-circuiting unequal or even opposing fields from within and without – question and answer, function and form, analysis and creativity. In a forward movement toward a vague goal, "diverse, so far disconnected systems of experience are suddenly connected by an idea."[9] One could also speak of a continual dialogue; a dialogue, at one stage abstract as a dialogue between the different stages of work, and at another stage concrete, as a dialogue between the participating disciplines and stakeholders. In this connection the question regarding the choice of dialogue tools is of eminent importance. For this reason a brief excursion into the realm of language appears compelling.

In language metaphor is perceived as an instrument for conveying meaning. Similar to the design stakeholder within his discipline, the metaphor does not stand alone, but, according to the theory of linguist Harald Weinrich, is always to be found in the context of a semantic field: "To the same degree as the individual word has no isolated existence in Language, the

---

7 | "SANAA" in Lars, *Cultura y ciudad*, Vol.1, May 2005, p. 18
8 | Somol, Robert, Whiting, Sarah, "Notes around the Doppler Effect and other Moods of Modernism," in *Perspecta* 33, The Yale Architectural Journal, Cambridge: MIT Press, 2002
9 | Lenk, Hans, "Kreativität und Anverwandlung," in *Werk, Bauen + Wohnen* 10/2005, p. 46

individual metaphor also demands a metaphoric field. It is a point in the metaphoric field. [...] In the actual and seemingly punctual metaphor the interconnection of two linguistic semantic regions is realized, as a matter of fact."[10] By suddenly connecting context A with context B, a moment of surprise arises, out of which something new can come into existence. Architect Oswald Mathias Ungers speaks of a "comparison between two events, which are not equal, yet can be compared in an ostensive manner. The comparison is usually found by means of a creative thought connecting different objects and outlining a new image combining the characteristics of both."[11] With regard to this language and architectural design are very close. In an astonishing convergence the metaphor performs what is also expected from the tools applied in the design process: Combination, interaction and multiple coding. Therefore designers apply "metaphor as an instrument of thought serving clearness and vibrancy by avoiding the logical processes it opposes."[12] While their environment is dominated by logical processes, metaphors generate creative, unexpected options lending the design process important and necessary intermediary momentum. In the end a possible solution is favored over others in a global view. As a final consequence design is a selection process, yet the quality level of the selection, however convincing and comprehensive it may be, always depends on the possibilities available for selection. According to Grassi: "The experience we gain by building does not necessarily give us the right answers to other tests. Experience gives us confidence in our judgment, a trust in the means at our disposal, but it never lets us take anything for granted or skip any passage."[13] Hence metaphors are effective at the core of the design process. Sometimes they surface in a concrete manner in the dialogue among the designers or as working titles of concept papers. Much more often, though, they do not actually come into appearance, but obliquely unfold their effect in conventional architectural instruments of design, such as draft, plan or model, which are then frequently applied quite specifically.

---

10 | See: Weinrich, Harald, "Münze und Wort. Untersuchungen an einem Bildfeld," in Weinrich, Harald, *Sprache in Texten*, Stuttgart: Klett-Verlag, 1976

11 | Ungers, O. M., "Entwerfen und Denken in Vorstellungen, Metaphern und Analogien," in Ungers, O. M., *Morphologie: City Metaphors*, Köln: Verlag der Buchhandlung Walter König, 1982, p. 10

12 | Ibid., p. 10

13 | Grassi 1983, p. 35

The manifestation of such an effect within the process can always be observed quite concretely when the observed instruments experience a relatively extreme application or are even over-emphasized. Let us inspect two case studies with regard to this phenomenon: First some designs by the Office for Metropolitan Architecture (OMA), operating since the mid-seventies, and then some designs by Japanese duo SANAA (Sejima Architects and Nishizawa Architects Association). In OMA's work the use of diagrams in central areas is to be observed. As could be expected, OMA's interest exceeds the role of diagrams as a means of communication, mainly concentrating on its effect on the design process. In OMA's work, the diagram functions as a design instrument, in the midst of which metaphor takes effect, activating the previously articulated short-circuits between intuition and reason. "The diagram transforms data into phenomena, combining intellect and imagination and conceptualizing a project [...] The creative momentum lies in the question: What is perceived and represented in which manner?"[4] In SAANA's tool set, on the other side, one is stricken by the drawings, which aim at extreme reduction and clarity, starting from the drafts and reaching all the way to the work drawings. Sejima says: "When you want to judge whether it's a simple idea or a simple scheme, then the concept must be read clearly."[15] Out of the overall range of the drawings the plan holds an eminent position, leading us to the hypothesis that the metaphoric process takes place within the plan as an instrument.

But let us first start with two project groups from the OMA studio. Both the project for the *Les Halles* area in Paris realized in 2003 and the 2005 project for the *Deltametropool* region display small series of diagrams.

In the case of *Les Halles* the horizontal order of a clearly confined rectangle consisting of coloured beams stacked on top of each other is transformed into a substantially more agitated version in the second representation. Here one receives the impression that the beams are drawn upward by an invisible force, which makes them appear as objects invoking associations with curtailed pyramids or oil rigs. The superimposition of the

---

14 | Deen, Wouter, Garritzmann, Udo, "OMA's little helper," in *Archplus* 143, Aachen, 1998

15 | Kazuyo Sejima in "Liquid Playgrounds: Fragments from a conversation between Cristina Diaz Moreno & Efren Garcia Grinda and Kazuyo Sejima & Ryue Nishizawa," in *El Croquis* 121/122, 2005, pp. 22-23

lines makes the coexistence of two worlds perceivable; the "underworld" consisting of the shopping mall and RER station, and the "overworld" consisting of the park and square in midst of the traditional urban morphology of Paris.

Image 62: Rem Koolhaas/OMA, Les Halles, 2003

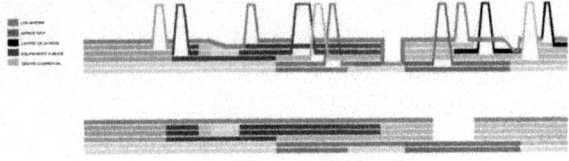

The *Deltametropool* diagram series displays three different systems of reference between the urban agglomeration in the Dutch Randstadt area. In the last one of the three a clear contrast between the Dordrecht/Rotterdam/ Den Haag region and the Amsterdam region is articulated. An orthogonal grid, in contrast to the star like system of Amsterdam, presents the economically stumbling southern wing of the Randstadt as a region with several sub-centers, relinquishing hierarchies and generating homogenous accessibility.

Image 63: Rem Koolhaas/OMA, Les Halles, 2003

The direct transformation of the diagrams into form is remarkable. Both the beam figures of *Les Halles* and the orthogonal grid of *Deltametropool* are refined during the final stages of the design process, yet they remain fundamentally unchanged as spatial systems. In a classically metaphoric manner the semantic fields concept/reality and organisation/form are connected in this design. The specific element of this step most of all lies in the unusually strong confidence afforded to the formal and spatial qualities of the applied diagrams.

Image 64: Rem Koolhaas/OMA, Downsview Park, 2001

An even more progressive application of diagrams is to be registered in the *Yokohama Urban Ring* of 1992 and *Downsview Park Toronto* of 2001. Here the diagram does no longer function as a preparation for the real form; the diagram and physical reality of the project actually start to fusion completely. In the case of the *Yokohama Urban Ring* this is expressed by an unusual equivalence between the information in the plan, the model and the diagram. Behind this stands the intention not only to explain the project itself, but, analogously, to plead for a completely new vision of urban planning, which Koolhaas presented some years later in his text "Whatever

Happened to Urbanism?": "If there is a ‚new urbanism' it will not be based on the twin fantasies of order and omnipotence; it will be the staging of uncertainty; it will no longer be concerned with the arrangement of more or less permanent objects but with the irrigation of territories with potential; it will no longer aim for stable configurations but for the creation of enabling fields that accommodate processes that refuse to be crystallized into definitive form;"[16] The media used in the conception and representation must lend the unconventional and vanguard itself to a face in the Yokohama project. This super ordinate message related in the plan, the model and the diagram stands on one level with the explanations regarding the concrete project for Yokohama. In a self-observation of sorts the metaphor contained in the process is eventually also expressed in language. "[...] A kind of programmatic lava, three layers of public activity manipulated to support the largest possible amount of events with a minimum amount of permanent definition."[17] Similar things happen in the *Downsview Park* project. The work significantly developed in cooperation with Canadian graphic designer Bruce Mau is referred to by Robert Somol as "condensation of the diagram to a logo."[18] On the one hand a field of circular figures generates a physical infrastructure for future developments together with lines crossing the field in a rhizome-like manner, on the other hand a diagram, whose imaginative power reaches so far that it can immediately activate so far not participating stakeholders as a "logo for immediate identity."[19] In analogy to Koolhaas' 1994 text, the performative diagram designed in this manner

---

16 | Koolhaas, Rem, "What ever happened to Urbanism" [1994], in Koolhaas, Rem, Mau, Bruce, *S,M,L,XL*, New York: The Monacelly Press, 1995
17 | See: http://www.oma.eu
18 | "For OMA, however, contingency and imagability are not incompatible. In fact, the image, the condensation of the diagram to a logo, is necessary precisely as an attractor for disparate possible associations and developments. A vague specificity permits future diversity." Somol, Robert E, "All Systems GO! The terminal Nature of Contemporary Urbanism," in Czerniak, Julia, *Case: Downsview Park Toronto*, Harvard University Graduate School of Design, München: Prestel, 2001, p. 131
19 | "With affiliations to an air terminal, OMA's tree-form landscape emerges as a cultivator of megastructure. And this now hybridized megascape is at once an infrastructure (for future development) and a logo (for immediate identity). This linkage of the infrastructural and the graphic at Downsview." Ibid., p. 132

– "ascetic, arid, generic, primitive"[20] – functions as a field for future possibilities by refusing all the determinations of an elaborate plan.

Image 65: Rem Koolhaas/OMA, Downsview Park, 2001

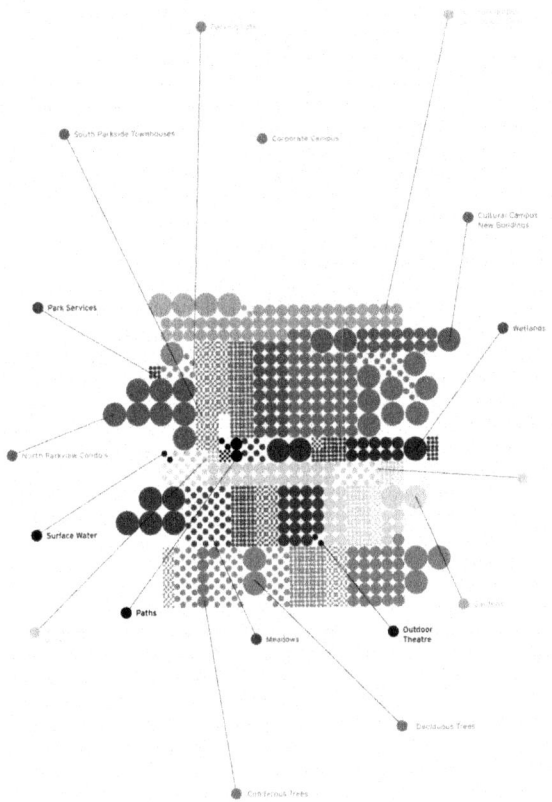

Both in *Yokohama* and in *Downsview* the project seems incorporated in the diagram. A fusion of diagram and project, which consistently also requires that the metaphoric mechanisms not only is effective in the design process,

---

20 | "While the former team deploys a surfeit of notational diagrams – rich, dense, specific and elaborate – the latter stutters the iteration of a single gesture – ascetic, arid, generic, primitive." Ibid., p. 131

but also in the project. The open rules of lava and circle replace rigid master plans as instruments of urban development.

When we now shift our focus to SANAA's works, we simultaneously move from city to building. With "House in a Plum Grove" (2003), "Toledo Glass Pavilion" (2006) and "Novartis Building" (2009) we investigate a single-family house, a museum and an office building.

Image 66: SANAA, House in a Plum Grove, 2003

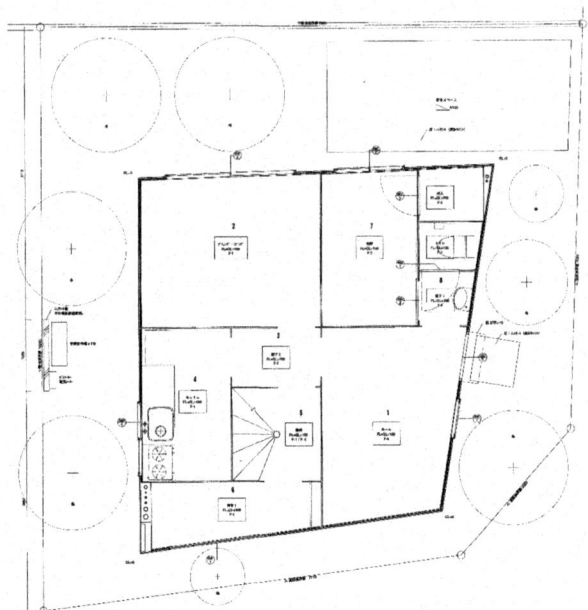

The drawings for "House in a Plum Grove" show work plans with dimension lines and integrated technical notes. The plans seem strangely empty and unfamiliar. The ground floor and the top floor are based on the same ground plan order and are hardly to be discerned. No wall thickness is to be recognized. There is no reference to materials. The entire image appears like the naive drawing of a child, or like a diagram. In the photos of the realized project one can recognize that the wall elements assembled here consist of 16 millimeter thick steel plates and are therefore actually as thin as they appear in the plan. Here again the diagram appears as the determining element within the design process. Drawing and house confirm the thesis Toyo Ito voiced 1996: "You see a building as essentially the equivalent of the kind of spatial diagram used to describe the daily activities for

Image 67: SANAA, House in a Plum Grove, 2003

which the building is intended in abstract form. At least it seems as if your objective is to get as close as possible to its condition."[21] The "Purity of the Diagram"[22] is here not applied as an aesthetic model for the outcome of the process but as a means to an end in the process. SANAA's actual target is to be found in a clarity lying behind the surface to be elaborated in a longsome process, a distillation process of kinds. Or to say it with Sejima's words: "For us it is important to explain the intrinsic relationships of each project quite clearly to show the idea clearly, not through figure, shape or

---

21 | Ito, Toyo, "Diagram Architecture," in *El Croquis* 77, 1996, pp. 18-22
22 | "In propagating the purity of the diagram, SANAA's end game is clarity." Galilee, Beatrice, "Exquisite Diagrams," in *SANAA. Serpentine Gallery Pavilion 2009*, London: Koenig Books Ltd., 2009, p. 71

form but by the most simple and direct way."[23] Here a similar connection between plan and reality appears as in the OMA projects. Yet in contrast SAANA does not replace the plan with the diagram, in fact the plan is conserved in its original form and the regulative and strategic qualities of

Image 68: SANAA, Toledo Glass Museum, 2006

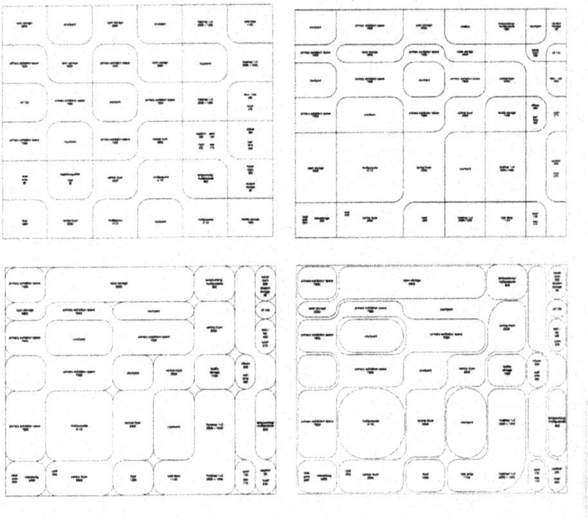

the diagram are integrated into it directly. Here the plan remains the pivot point of the design process. Much information that is added to the plan during the process may graphically not be represented due to simultaneous design decisions, which orients itself along the lines of strategic clarity. Plan and project remain congruent at all times. A principle that is also applied to multi-storey buildings. The Novartis office building in Basel can even be seen as an example for how the principle of clarity is transferred directly to section and facade due to the multi-storey concept of the building.

---

23 | Kazuyo Sejima in "Liquid Playgrounds: Fragments from a conversation between Cristina Diaz Moreno & Efren Garcia Grinda and Kazuyo Sejima & Ryue Nishizawa," in *El Croquis* 121/122, 2005, pp. 22-23

Swiss architect Valerio Olgiati describes the building as a "Rack,"[24] which in a way represents the final condition of simplicity in architecture. One is

Image 69: SANAA, Toledo Glass Museum, 2006

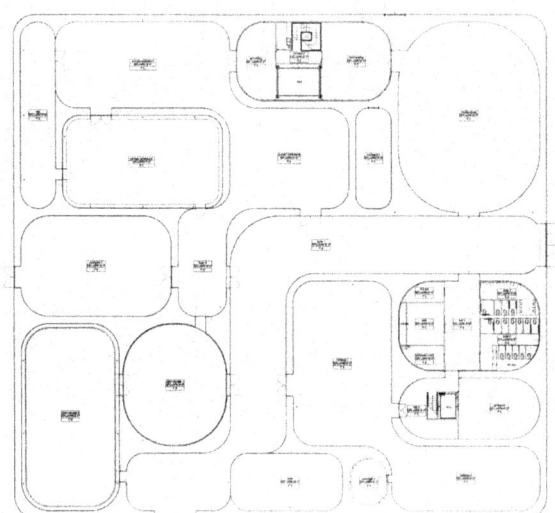

always tempted to explain SANAA's distilled architecture with a minimalist approach, which is, with the words of Moritz Küng, "not in itself incorrect, but it is limited purely to issues of form. After all, in art at least, minimalism rejects narrative and emotional elements and takes an exclusively

---

24 | "I must mention at this point that it seems impossible to me to think a building in a simpler way. Each storey is the same height as the others, including the entrance and attic storeys. There is no show side, all the façades are the same. The unframed window panes are all the same size. All the putty joints between the glass panes in the facades, horizontal or vertical, are of the same with. The floors and roof are all the same thickness. The structure is such that all the distances between the loadbearing dividers are of the same width. And the loadbearing dividers are the same thickness as the floors. The building could be turned vertically through 180 degrees or horizontally through 90 degrees. It would always look the same. Like a rack, in fact." Olgiati, Valerio, "A Rack," in *Novartis Campus – Fabrikstrasse 4*, Basel: Christoph Merian Verlag, 2006, p. 42

rational position."²⁵ In fact the obvious atmospheric density of the zones in SANAA's architecture remains enigmatic at first. Moritz Küng recognizes three principles that can be seen as the basis of all these works and which

Image 70: SANAA, Toledo Glass Museum, 2006

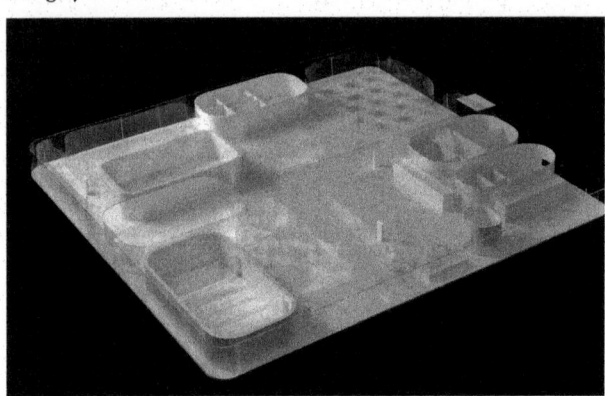

are never separated: "the part is always related to the whole, the whole is always divisible, and each part also incorporates the whole."²⁶ The strategically and conceptually stringent space seems to be more eminent than the physical, visible and tangible space.²⁷ Yet within the processes dominated

---

25 | "A link is often made between SANAA's highly distilled architecture and the minimalist approach. This view is not in itself incorrect, but it is limited purely to issues of form. After all, in art at least, minimalism rejects narrative and emotional elements and takes an exclusively rational position. The well-known pragmatic statement made by the American painter Frank Stella in 1964 – ‚what you see is what you see' – exemplifies the rejection of any form of symbolism or meaning and refers entirely to a reality that existsin ist own right." Küng, Moritz, "Making Space Visible," in Niedermayr, Walter, *Walter Niedermayr, Kazuyo Sejima + Ryue Nishizawa / SANAA*, Hatje Cantz Velag, Ostfildern, Germany, 2007, p. 5

26 | Ibid., p. 6

27 | "However, for SANAA, the atmosphere created is less due to an interest in materials than a by-product of their conceptual rigour. Unlike phenomenologists such as Steven Holl or Peter Zumthor, whose serene, opaquely glazed Kunsthaus in Bregenz, Austria could share a page with many of SANAA's buildings, they

by strategy there could be larger and smaller interspaces for sensual issues. Looking at the plan of the "Toledo Glass Museum" one gains the impression that these interspaces are to be found again directly in the physical spaces between the individual spatial units. In its completeness the interspaces form a continuous structure permanently varying in its proportions, hence generating new spatial and lighting situations. This interspace cannot be entered by visitors to the museum, yet they can sense it at all times, as the consistent use of glass as a spatial boundary make the space and interspace present simultaneously, also generating the specific spatial atmosphere in addition to the specific spatial structure. It is elements like these interspaces that conclude the connection of inside and outside, question and answer, function and form, analysis and creativity described above, and which are left over in SANAA's architecture as a distillate of the design process.

The confinement to only two design processes applied here, i.e. urban projects in the first and architectural projects in the second instance, is an arbitrary selection with the aim of encompassing the widest possible range within the framework of a small study. Theoretically the series could be infinite, as every design process shows the connecting tools capable of producing short-circuits, thus generating the same effects as metaphors do within language. The radicalness of the processes in the works of OMA and SANAA are exemplary in this respect.

---

would always priotise strategic, functional space over the physical – seen and felt – space." Galilee, Beatrice, "Exquisite Diagrams," in *SANAA. Serpentine Gallery Pavilion 2009*, Koenig Books Ltd., London, 2009, p. 71

Crystals
The Entropic Landscape

GEORGES TEYSSOT

> "... [B]y day fantastic birds flew through the petrified forest, and jeweled crocodiles glittered like heraldic salamanders on the banks of a crystalline river."
> J. G. Ballard 1966[1]

In industrialized societies trash heaps are rising, territories are becoming wastelands, and dusty winds blow over cities, howling between giant otherworldly crystals. As already envisioned by Hans Haacke, Ed Ruscha and Gordon Matta-Clarke, huge gashes open up buildings, breakdowns happen periodically in water main pipes, and grass grows through the cracks of asphalt in vacant parking lots. In *The Crystal Land* (1966), Robert Smithson, an enthusiast of J. G. Ballard's novel, described such a landscape: "The highways crisscross through the towns and become man-made geological networks of concrete. In fact, the entire landscape has a mineral presence. From the shiny chrome diners to glass windows of shopping centers, a sense of the crystalline prevails."[2]

For Smithson, ruins, often made of found objects, evoke a state of entropy. Characteristic of our post-industrial societies, they are markers, forms of entropic deterioration which correspond to the experience of increasing

---

1 | Ballard, James Graham, *The Crystal World*, London: Jonathan Cape, 1966,
2 | Smithson, Robert, "The Crystal Land," in *Harper's Bazaar*, May 1966, in Flam, Jack (ed.), *Robert Smithson: the Collected Writings*, Berkeley, CA: University of California Press, 1996, pp. 8-9

Image 71: Johannes Jacobus Scheuchzerus, Crystaux de diverses figures, crystal merveilleux, 1723

disorder in a system. Citing Nabokov's famous line, "the future is but the obsolete in reverse,"[3] Smithson, in his well-known article "Entropy and the New Monuments,"[4] asserted that the artwork of contemporary conceptual artists evoked entropy: "[...] they bring to mind Ice Age rather than the Golden Age. [...] The new monuments are made of artificial materials, plastic, chrome, and electric light. They are not built for the Ages but rather against the ages. [...] Time becomes a place minus motion. [...] A million years is contained in a second."[5]

Further on in the article Smithson noted that "entropy is evolution in reverse."[6] The metaphors used by Smithson are appropriate, inasmuch as, for him, the artist is at home in the desert or in a frozen landscape of ice. And it is an undeniable truth that the desert is the place of maximum en-

---

3 | Nabokov, Vladimir, "Lance", in *Nabokov's Dozen: A Collection of Thirteen Stories*, New York: Doubleday, 1958, p. 202
4 | Smithson, Robert, "Entropy and the New Monument," in *Art forum*, June 1966; in Smithson 1996, pp. 10-23
5 | Ibid., p. 11
6 | Ibid., p. 15

tropy and total crystallization.⁷ Commenting on the work of Donald Judd, Smithson would remark that space is both crystalline and collapsible.⁸

Image 72: Wenzel Hablik, Drei KristallSchlösschen, ca 1920

In *Difference and Repetition* (1968), Deleuze elucidates that the world is dominated by a nomadic condition, characterized by "a completely other distribution which must be called nomadic, a nomad *nomos*, without property, enclosure or measure."⁹ For Deleuze, the question is no longer the distribution of things and the division of persons in sedentary spaces, "but rather a division among those who distribute *themselves* in an open space

---

7 | Ponte, Alessandra, "The House of Light and Entropy: Inhabiting the American Desert," in *Assemblage*, N. 30, 1996, pp. 12-43; Id., "Habiter dans le désert (américain). La Maison de la lumière et de l'entropie," in *Exposé. Revue d'Esthétique et d'Art Contemporain*, n. 3, "La Maison," vol. 1, Orléans, FRAC-Centre, 1997, pp. 68-83
8 | Smithson, Robert, "Donald Judd" (1965), in Smithson 1996, pp. 4-6
9 | Deleuze, Gilles, *Difference and Repetition* [1968], trans. Paul Patton, New York: Columbia University Press, 1994, p. 36

– a space which is unlimited, or at least without precise limits. [...] To fill a space, to be distributed within it, is very different from distributing the space."[10] From sedentary structures of representation to nomadic distribution, a leap has taken place, leading to unsettling difficulties, transcending all limits, deploying errant and delirious distribution.[11] In the same text, Deleuze defined three temporal syntheses which create a line investigating our relation to time. The first, a passive synthesis, Habit (Lat., *Habitus*) was buried in the present. The second, again a passive synthesis, Memory (Gr., *Mnemosyne*) was concerned with the virtual past in an absolute state. The third, this time active synthesis, was geared towards the prospective future, that of the "eternal return," that opened on an unforeseeable new condition. Sedentary distributions, good sense, and common sense, were all based upon one particular, passive synthesis of time, that of habit.[12] Instead, nomadic structures lead to "mad repartitions ... mad distribution – instantaneous, nomadic distribution, crowned anarchy or difference"[13] a state which physics had described in thermodynamics as entropy.[14]

Contemporary information theory begins in the late 1940s with the work of Claude Shannon and Norbert Wiener.[15] Shannon's concept and Wiener's views, which at first sight appear similar, are quite different. Inspired by methods of code breaking and cryptography, Shannon, an electrical engineer, offered an abstract representation of information belonging to the world of symbols exchange. Any other aspect, whether material or energetic, including any meaningful content, was ignored as irrelevant. What remained was the arrangement of symbols, apprehended through a statistical method.[16] The consequence was that information began to take the form of an intangible and immaterial element; a new substance existing alongside matter and energy. Implicit in Shannon's mathematical formula

---

10 | Ibid., p. 36
11 | Ibid., p. 37
12 | Ibid., p. 225
13 | Ibid., p. 224
14 | Ibid., pp. 225 and 229.
15 | Triclot, Mathieu, *Le moment cybernétique: la constitution de la notion d'information*, Seyssel: Champ Vallon, 2008, p. 69
16 | Ibid., p. 70

was the idea of a pure code, a code which in itself has nothing to do with materiality and signification.

According to Wiener, Shannon was concerned with data processing and "coding information," that is, with how best to encode the information a sender wants to transmit.[17] Wiener's cybernetics however, touched a broader field. It aimed to establish a unified theory of forecasting the future by means of a statistical method. Electric filters would be created to reduce the amount of noise in a signal, while information feedback would generate control systems implemented by means of computer control and automation.[18] Shannon and Wiener advanced two different representations of information: as a code for the former and as a signal for the latter. Wiener wanted to apply signal processing to animal, human and machine behavior, and to control their interaction by using processes of a negative feedback. In biology such a process is called homeostasis. Negative feedback describes the act of reversing a discrepancy between a prefigured and actual output.[19] In Shannon, information is better represented by the notion of form. It indicates a form that expresses the singularity of a material layout and refers to a certain quantity of structure and organization present in things.

Following the work of Shannon, Wiener and many others, the determination of the physical status of information was resolved in at least two ways: first as a response to a local issue – how does line noise interfere with telecommunication circuits? Secondly as a global issue: what was the relation between information and entropy?[20] This second approach was inspired by 19th century thermodynamics, for example Sadi Carnot's cycle and principles which described how to produce work from a decrease in heat. After the findings of James P. Joule, Rudolf Clausius developed the classical thermodynamic theory which resolved the puzzle of lost energy. In any thermodynamic system, any irreversible process leads to an incremental dissipation of a small amount of energy: i.e. entropy. Subsequently, Ludwig Boltzmann described the macroscopic diffusion of gas particles

---

17 | Wiener, Norbert, *Cybernetics: or, Control and Communication in the Animal and the Machine*, 2d ed., New York: M.I.T. Press, 1961, p. 10
18 | Triclot 2008, p. 71
19 | Ibid., p. 78
20 | Ibid., p. 217

by a statistical method. Entropy of an isolated system was defined as the natural logarithm of the probability, multiplied by Boltzmann's constant, in an equation that offered the foundation of statistical mechanical entropy. It illustrated how, in an isolated system, entropy evolves in a non-reversible mode towards states that are more and more probable, and less and less ordered, ultimately reaching a final (or more probable) state.[21] From now on, entropy becomes a measure of molecular disorder.

Observing formal similarities between Boltzmann's equation and that of Shannon, Wiener proposed an analogical relation between information and entropy such that information was simply the reverse of entropy.[22] The association between entropy and information was thus based on a definition of entropy derived from the increase of probability: the more a message is probable, the less its quantity of information is elevated. An improbable message is, on the contrary, a highly informative message. The amount of information transmitted over the channels in a message is measured as the negative logarithm of its probability. As a consequence, "the more probable a message is, the less information it gives."[23] By extension, the same can be applied to a system, which is defined as a very probable state: the more its entropy will be elevated, the less its information is relevant or important. Because the equation is a logarithm, it implies that both entropy and information are additive, either in a message or in a system, meaning that the information of many single messages can be added. Wiener remarked that entropy is "a measure of the degree of disorganization of a system."[24] The quantity of information is also interpreted as a measure of the degree of organization of a material ensemble. Here there are no more traces of the intuitive connection between information and knowledge. Information doesn't connect anymore to a cognitive process, but only to the material property of material systems. Information, like entropy, is a physical magnitude that serves as an index of a system's state.

---

21 | Ibid., p. 224
22 | Ibid., p. 224
23 | Wiener, Norbert, *The Human Use of Human Beings: Cybernetics and Society* [1950], 2nd ed. rev., Garden City, N.Y.: Doubleday, 1954, p. 21
24 | Wiener 1961, p. 11

An unintended consequence of this "entropic" understanding of information was that it helped to revive, behind the notion of information, the classical concept of form. Cybernetics raised an important issue: how to connect information to formation, and thus link information to form. Wiener's response was to refer to the idea of pattern: "Messages are themselves a form of *pattern* and organization."[25] The meaning of information therefore has switched toward *in-formation*, in the realm of form-giving. Accordingly, a system in which the quantity of information is elevated, is an ordered system, presenting significant, meaningful forms, as opposed to a state of undifferentiated disorder.[26] What will have an enormous influence on postwar thinking, but also on the artists' sensitivity, is the confirmation of entropy's irreversibility. Once again, the nineteenth century belief in the thermal death of the universe, suggested by Lord Kelvin's second law of thermodynamics, was validated. Such a conviction had since led to the cosmological hypothesis of a world reaching its maximum entropy. In Wiener, one finds two kind of fatigue, or entropy. In the first, information, as opposite to noise, is degraded; it then enters a cycle of exhaustion to the benefit of disorder and homogeneity. In the second, information goes through depletion by the action of time, with an inexorable decrease of its quantity. However, refusing to give in to despair, Wiener suggested that both living organisms and machines appeared as devices whose fate was to temporarily resist the entropic, to bring in some order, induce form and create a difference in a world sinking into chaos: "We are immersed in a life in which the world as a whole obeys the second law of thermodynamics: confusion increases and order decreases. Yet, as we have seen, the second law of thermodynamics, while it may be a valid statement about the whole of a closed system, is definitively not-valid concerning a non-isolated part of it. There are local and temporary islands of decreasing entropy in a world in which the entropy as a whole tends to increase, and the existence of these islands enables some of us to assert the existence of progress."[27] Yet, in Wiener's opinion, nothing suggested optimism because in such a tragic cosmology, entropy would always prevail globally.

---

25 | Wiener 1954, p. 21; Triclot 2008, p. 226
26 | Ibid., pp. 226-27
27 | Wiener 1954, p. 36; Triclot 2008, p. 228

The connection between form and pattern provided Wiener with the basis for a chapter in his book *The Human Use of Human Beings*, published in 1950. Titled the "Organization as the Message," the chapter begins with a reference to metaphors: "Dr [Jacob] Bronowski among others has pointed out that mathematics, which most of us see as the most factual of all sciences, constitutes the most colossal metaphor imaginable, and must be judged aesthetically as well as intellectually, in terms of the success of this metaphor."[28] Interestingly Robert Smithson included this quotation in his four-page article, "Quasi Infinities and the Waning of Space" (1966).[29] Constructed as a kind of montage, the article was illustrated in the margins by the works of architects (the Egyptian pyramids, Claude Nicolas Ledoux and Frank Lloyd Wright), and artists (Ad Reinhardt and Donald Judd), and supplemented by citations from many authors, including George Kubler's *The Shape of Time* (1962).[30]

Smithson's "Quasi Infinities" article reveals a significant connection between Wiener's book and Kubler's *The Shape of Time*, a connection which is crucial in the disclosure of the obsession about the relationship between past, future and technology seen in Smithson's art. Kubler, an art historian, was well aware of information theory, since he uses expressions such as "noise" understood as an interference or impediment in communication.[31] Kubler's book and Smithson's text may therefore be considered through the lens of cybernetics. Just as Wiener had shown how circuitous messages can be, an accumulation of fragmented quotes, references, clips, collages, and marginal citations would share the horizon of identicalness predicted by cybernetics along with the never-ending developments that characterizes entropy.[32] The essay "Quasi Infinities and the Waning of Space" shows that Smithson understood that a space waning under the laws of entropy was also a space exhausted by the weight of history itself, a fatigue generat-

---

28 | Wiener 1954, p. 95
29 | Smithson, Robert, "Quasi infinities and the Waning of Space," in *Arts Magazine*, NY, November 1966, 41, n. 1; in Smithson 1996, pp. 34-37
30 | Kubler, George, *The Shape of Time, Remarks on the History of Things*, New Haven, CT: Yale University Press, 1962
31 | Lee, Pamela M., *Chronophobia: On Time in the Art of the 1960's*, Cambridge, Mass.: MIT Press, 2004, p. 233; Kubler 1962, p. 160
32 | Ibid., p. 252

ed by the infinite accumulation of data, i.e. Quasi-Infinity.[33] Not by chance, in 1963, Ed Ruscha painted an oil painting with a preeminent "Noise" commercial inscription (*Noise, Pencil, Broken Pencil, Cheap Western*), fusing popular imagery, typography, and collage.[34] As mentioned, Wiener believed

Image 73: Edward Ruscha, Noise, Pencil, Broken Pencil, Cheap Western, 1963, oil on canvas

in the metaphor that describes a message as a patterned organization: "It is the pattern maintained by [...] homeostasis which is the touchstone of our

---

33 | Ibid., p. 256

34 | Schwartz, Alexandra, *Ed Ruscha's Los Angeles*, Cambridge, Mass.: MIT Press, 2010, pp. 43-44; see: Schwartz, Alexandra (ed.), *Ruscha, Edward / Leave Any Information at the Signal: Writings, Interviews, Bits, Pages*, Cambridge: MIT Press, 2002, 2004, p. 387; Marshall, Richard D., *Ed Ruscha*, London / New York: Phaidon Press, 2003, p. 41

personal identity. Our tissues change as we live: the food we eat and the air we breathe become flesh of our flesh and bone of our bone ... We are but whirlpools in a river of ever-flowing water. We are not stuff that abides, but patterns that perpetuate themselves."[35]

While Wiener's cybernetics and Shannon's theory of communication were seminal from a telecom and engineering point of view, they were criticized by those trying to discern the relation between information, form, order and probability.[36] The concept of information was caught between two opposite requirements: on one hand, according to information theory, a highly improbable message is a message highly informative; but on the other, information will at the same time be perceived distinctly against the background of noise and pure randomness.[37] During the 1950s, French philosopher Gilbert Simondon addressed this problem by developing an alternative to Wiener's cybernetics. He proposed that we consider information as an intermediary term between form and randomness: "Information is not some form, neither an ensemble of forms; it is the variability of form, the supply of a variation in relation to a form. It is the unpredictability of one variation of form, and not the pure unpredictability of all variation. Thus we would be inclined to make the distinction between three terms: the pure hazard or randomness, form, and information."[38] From then on, contrary to Wiener, information and form have separated, or, at least, the former hasn't be reduced to the latter.[39]

As an attentive reader of Simondon, Deleuze stressed the necessity of recognizing the predominance of multiple forces active upon form. In *Difference and Repetition* (1968), Deleuze determined the link between forces and forms as the two vectors of difference, using Henri Bergson and Simondon

---

35 | Wiener 1954, p. 96
36 | Triclot 2008, p. 232
37 | Ibid., p. 233
38 | Simondon, Gilbert, *Du mode d'existence des objets techniques* [1958], Paris: Aubier, 1989, p. 137
39 | Barthélémy, Jean-Hughes, *Simondon ou l'Encyclopédisme génétique*, Paris: Presses universitaires de France, 2008, pp. 70-71; Triclot 2008, p. 233

as sources.⁴⁰ For Simondon, the crystal's individuation was the formation obtained physically by a difference of potential. Such a difference was the entropic arrow between tension and matter (as in a crystal).⁴¹ Deleuze translated this differentiation in terms of oscillation, a quasi-simultaneous vibration between the actual and the virtual. Actual and virtual are coexistent. Overcoming Bergson's opposition between matter and duration, he transposed the arrow of intensity into the model of a coexistence of the virtual and the actual.⁴² Both statuses are real, but the actual characterizes the completed individual, such as the materialized crystal, while the virtual refers to the problematic field of the pre-individual, when the intensive differentiation is not yet actualized. Deleuze, following Simondon, uses the model of an egg, a paradigm of an intensive body, literally a body without organs, because it is a body going through phases of differentiation.⁴³

By an analysis of the physical-chemical nature of crystals, together with that of the cellular membrane, Simondon had proposed that it was through a peculiar chrono-topology that biological individuation should be considered in its specificity. The singularity of the living consisted in its positioning in such a chrono-topology, a consideration that led to a particular and renewed way of thinking about the categories of time and space. For a crystal in a liquid milieu, the interior is already constituted by the action of a "seed" crystal, and then solidifies. In this case it stands for its past. The limit is the solid state in itself: it represents the present. The exterior, which is what is not yet crystallized, appears to belong to the future.⁴⁴ As Simondon observed: "The rapport between future and past is similar to the one that bonds the amorphous milieu to the crystal [...] The present, a relation between future and past, is like the polarizing, asymmetrical limit

---

40 | Sauvagnargues, Anne, *Deleuze et l'art*, Paris: Presses universitaires de France, 2006, pp. 88-89
41 | Deleuze, Gilles, "On Gilbert Simondon," in Deleuze, Gilles, *Desert Islands and Other Texts, 1953-1974*, New York: Semiotext(e), 2004, pp. 86-9
42 | Deleuze 1994, pp. 208-209
43 | Sauvagnargues 2006, p. 90
44 | Barthélémy, Jean- Hughes (ed.), *Cahiers Simondon*, N. 1, Paris: L'Harmattan, 2009, pp. 56-57; Sauvagnargues, Anne, *Deleuze: l'empirisme transcendantal*, Paris: Presses universitaires de France, 2009, pp. 264-65

between crystal and amorphous milieu. [...] At a physical-chemical level, the individual constituted by a crystal is in becoming, as an individual."[45]

Through Simondon, Deleuze defines interiority as topological in nature, relative and differential. Simondon defines the living as what lives by the polarized membrane, the limit between two different milieus: the interior and the exterior. As expected, there is a difference: while the living lives at the limit, on its borders, inasmuch as membranes repolarize themselves continuously, the crystal polarizes once for all. In a living being interiority and exteriority are everywhere.[46] In the *Logic of Sense* (1969), Deleuze will use Simondon's analysis of crystal formation to redefine time and events: "Events are like crystals, they become and grow out of the edges, or on the edge."[47] Everything happens at the border; and, as in a mirror, everything is reduced to the opposite side of the surface.[48] As in a Möbius strip, the outer surface is continuous with the inner surface. It envelops the entire world, and makes that which is inside be the outside and vice versa.[49] The event's border is a demarcation, line or surface, between the virtual and the actual.

It is interesting to recall how Robert Smithson borrowed a number of motifs from the manuals of crystallography he was collecting, where systems of growth through molecular accretion were described. One of Smithson's favorite books was Charles William Bunn's volume: *Crystals: their Role in Nature and in Science* (1964).[50] Among many, Bunn described two particular modes of growth of crystals: the screw dislocation and the deposition. From crystal symmetry, Smithson borrowed the notion of enantiomorphism, which, for him, gave a precise illustration of the connection between past and future.

---

45 | Simondon, Gilbert, *L'individuation à la lumière des notions de forme et d'information*, Grenoble: Millon, 2005, pp. 90-91; contains "L'individu et sa genèse physico-biologique," (1964) and "L'individuation psychique et collective" (1989); edited text, doctoral thesis (1957)
46 | Sauvagnargues 2009, p. 286
47 | Deleuze, Gilles, *The Logic of Sense* [1969], trans. Mark Lester, Charles Stivale, Constantin V. Boundas, ed., New York: Columbia University Press, 1990, p. 9
48 | Ibid., p. 9
49 | Ibid., p. 11; Sauvagnargues 2009, p. 288
50 | Bunn, Charles William, *Crystals: their Role in Nature and in Science*, New York: Academic Press, 1964, 1966

An enantiomorph is a pair of crystals that are mirror images of each other.[51] Many crystals adopt enantiomorphic forms, in as much as one can find both right-handed and left-handed crystals of the same substance, including quartz, the most common mineral on the earth's surface. Enantiomorphs, although identical in all respects, save their differential "handedness," are totally irreducible to each other. Not by chance, Smithson created an *Enantiomorphic Chamber* (1964), in painted steel and mirrors, as an experiment in mirror relationship, offering a way to think about mirroring that emphasized the irreconcilable difference, as well as the similarity between a form and its reflection.[52]

Image 74: Robert Smithson, Gyrostasis, 1968, painted steel

51 | Roberts, Jennifer L., *Mirror-travels: Robert Smithson and History*, New Haven: Yale University Press, 2004, p. 40
52 | Ibid., p. 45

With *Gyrostasis* (1968), a painted steel installation, going through a diminishing progression to form an angular spiral, Smithson produced a representation of the winding down of time. Everything rotates, and terminates in a state of rigid equilibrium, "as in crystallographic systems."[53] Such a sculpture explores "the crystalline structure of time."[54] The spiral enters in a slow-motion vortex, slows down until it calcifies at "the brittle entropic end of its existence," adopting a "form of crystalline eternity."[55] In Bunns' *Crystals* (1964), Smithson would read another form of dislocation, producing a spiral pattern of growth, named "spiral staircase."[56]

Image 75: Charles William Bunn, Crystals: their Role in Nature and in Science, 1964, 1966

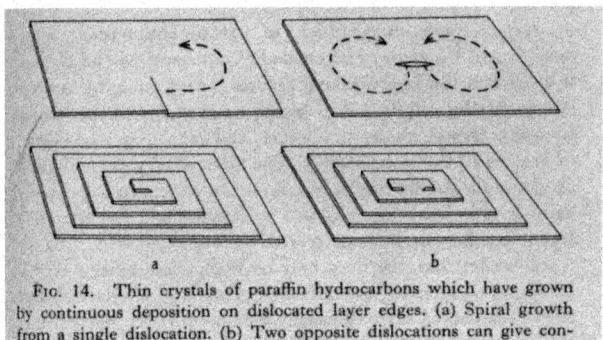

FIG. 14. Thin crystals of paraffin hydrocarbons which have grown by continuous deposition on dislocated layer edges. (a) Spiral growth from a single dislocation. (b) Two opposite dislocations can give concentric layers.

Some pages of his copy of Bunns' volume were excised by a razor blade and pasted in some of his artwork.[57] In a 1972 presentation of the *Spiral Jetty* (1970), Smithson described the installation as "advancing around a dislocation point in the manner of the screw."[58] In *Mirrored Ziggurat* (1966), a pyramid of stacked mirrors, the sculpture reads like a crystal. Here, time is static; it is entropic, as well, an inevitable deposition of time.

---

53 | Quoted in ibid., p. 39
54 | Ibid.; in Smithson 1996, p. 53
55 | J. L. Roberts 2004, p. 39
56 | Ibid., p. 17
57 | Ibid., p. 42
58 | Smithson, "The Spiral Jetty," in Smithson 1996, p. 147

Image 76: Robert Smithson, Mirrored Ziggurat, 1966, stacked mirrors

For Smithson, the key characteristics of entropic systems are their equilibrium, a perfect instance of his "time-crystal."[59] Smithson appealed to the thermodynamic stability of crystal structure to evoke the encompassing terminal equilibrium that he believed subtended all worldly historical conflict.

For many artists and architects of the 1960s, crystallography, symmetry and dissymmetry, and mirror effects, were all devices offering clues about the conditions in which topology operated. For Deleuze, potentialities were active at the surface, at the level of nomadic, pre-individual singularities. They "[...] haunt the surface. Everything happens at the surface in a crystal which develops only on the edges."[60] True, an organism doesn't develop in the same way, "[...] but membranes are no less important, for they carry potentialities and regenerate polarities."[61] Internal and external spaces are placed into contact without regard to distance. Internal and external, depth and height, length and width, have biological value only through this "topo-

---

59 | J. L. Roberts 2004, p. 44
60 | Deleuze 1990, p. 103
61 | Ibid., p. 103

logical surface of contact."⁶² Deleuze used Simondon's distinction between the crystal's superficial pellicle and the organic membrane, remarking that in both cases the surface prevails.⁶³

Image 77: Robert Smithson, Spiral Jetty (1971), panoramic photomontage, August 2007

The virtual is not anterior to the actual; nor is it original, meaning that it shouldn't be positioned as a founding ground, as an origin or a principle. The most significant experience art helps us effectuate is that of coexistence, that perpetual exchange of virtual and actual. Deleuze thought cinema presented time in its purest form, a "crystal of time," combining the central concepts of "crystal-image" and "time-image." The crystal-image is the indivisible unity of the virtual image and the actual image. The virtual image is subjective and in the past, while the actual image is in the present. The crystal-image always positions itself at the limit of an indiscernible actual and virtual image. The crystal-image shapes time as a constant two-way mirror that splits the present in two heterogeneous directions: "one of which is launched towards the future while the other falls into the past. Time consists of this split, and it is [...] time, that we see in the crystal."⁶⁴ Such a crystal is a non-chronological event and is indifferent to the actualization's vital arrow. Actualization, or the passage from the virtual to the actual, so important in biology, is not the most central dimension in time. According to Deleuze, the insistence of the virtual within the actual that he terms crystallization is no less significant. Literally, like an overflowing

---

62 | Ibid., p. 103
63 | Sauvagnargues 2009, pp. 295-296
64 | Deleuze, Gilles, *Cinema 2: The Time-Image* [1985], trans. Hugh Tomlinson, Robert Galeta, Minnesota: University of Minnesota Press, 1989, p. 81; Rodowick, David N., *Gilles Deleuze's Time Machine*, Durham and London: Duke University Press, 1997, pp. 79-118

lake, the virtual "surfaces" in the actual.[65] What one calls "[...] virtual is not something that lacks reality. Rather, the virtual becomes engaged in a process of actualization as it follows the plane, which gives it its proper reality."[66]

In the posthumously published text, "The actual and the virtual", which belongs to the period of *Cinema 2* (1985), Deleuze attempted a further explanation: "[H]ence, there is coalescence and division, or rather oscillation, a perpetual exchange between the actual object and its virtual image: the virtual image never stops becoming actual. The virtual image absorbs all of a character's actuality, at the same time as the actual character is no more than a virtuality. This perpetual exchange between the virtual and the actual is what defines a crystal; and it is on the plane of immanence that crystals appear. The actual and the virtual coexist, and enter into a tight circuit which we are continually retracing from one to the other. This is no longer a singularization, but an individuation as process, the actual and its virtual: no longer an actualization but a crystallization."[67]

In the chapter on "The Plane of Immanence" in *What is Philosophy* (1991), Deleuze warned that concepts (of philosophy) needed also a plane: "it is a table, a plateau, or a slice... it is a plane of consistency, or more accurately, the plane of immanence of concepts: the planomenon" (from the Gr, *planesthai*, to err like the planets).[68] A planomenon instead of a phenomenon. Like a "constructivist" architect, to use Deleuze's term, one needs to lay out a plane, or to cut through a section. For the thickness of the plane and of the map is "a genuine concept": "It is a promotion of the ground,

---

65 | Sauvagnargues 2009, p. 99
66 | Deleuze, Gilles, *Two Regimes of Madness: Texts and Interviews 1975-1995*, David Lapoujade, ed., trans. Ames Hodges, Mike Taormina, Los Angeles, CA: Semiotext(e), Cambridge, Mass.: MIT Press, 2006, p. 392
67 | See Eliot Ross Albert's translation of "The actual and the virtual," in Deleuze, Parnet, Claire, *Dialogues II*, translated by Hugh Tomlinson and Barbara Habberjam, rev. ed., London: Continuum, 2002, pp. 112-5
68 | Deleuze, Gilles, Guattari, Félix, *What is Philosophy?* [1991], translated by Hugh Tomlinson and Graham Burchell, New York: Columbia University Press, 1994, p. 35

and sculpture can become flat since the plane is stratified."[69] The plane of immanence should be thought as the basis of this kind of constructivism.

If the fold is an abstract line (as in Michel Foucault), purely virtual and divergent, it becomes part of the plane. The abstract line is also an "abstract machine" that characterized Foucault's diagram.[70] Two lines created a plane, which can be the transverse for fluxes of desire. The fold is contemporary to the appearance of the plane. Therefore, the plane of immanence is the abstract machine. The plane is created by folds which flux, and fluxes which fold. This is valid also for an artwork: "There is only a single plane in the sense that art includes no other plane than that of aesthetic composition: in fact the technical plane is necessarily covered up or absorbed by the aesthetic plane of composition."[71] While in 1968 Smithson was preparing *A Nonsite (Franklin, New Jersey)*, he drew a provisional theory of the two-dimensional diagram: "By drawing a diagram, a ground plan of a house, a street plan to the location of a site, or a topographic map, one draws a 'logical two dimensional picture.' A 'logical picture' differs from a natural or realistic picture in that it rarely looks like the thing it stands for. It is a two *dimensional analogy or metaphor* – A is Z."[72] A remark by Deleuze about the stratified plane seems to exemplify such a diagrammatic machine: "[i]n art the problem is always that of finding what monument to erect on this plane, or what plane to slide under this monument, and both at the same time."[73]

Moreover, the "constructivist" aspect is reinforced by the fact that the virtuality of planes – both on the qualitative level but also on the intensive side –, is not dissociated from the actual that is being fashioned. For Deleuze, affects and percepts are a compound, creating "blocs of sensations". But percepts are not the perception of those who experience them. They are

---

69 | Deleuze, Guattari 1994, p. 194
70 | Deleuze, Gilles, *Foucault* [1986], trans. Seán Hand, Minneapolis: University of Minnesota Press, 1988, p. 34
71 | Deleuze, Guattari 1994, p. 195
72 | Smithson Robert, "A Provisional Theory of Non-Sites" (1968), in Smithson 1996, p. 364
73 | Deleuze, Guattari 1994, p. 196

not feelings or affections.[74] Because, "[s]ensations, percepts and affects are *beings* whose validity lies in themselves and exceeds any lived."[75] However, the work of art, the compound of affects and percepts, ought to "stand up on its own."[76] It is a monument, but one that may be contained in a few marks or a few lines, or a simple stone. While considering matter and materials, Deleuze went on to say that "all the material becomes expressive. It is the affect that is metallic, crystalline, stony, and so on [...]."[77] And further on: "The landscape *sees*. [...] The percept is the landscape before man, in the absence of man."[78] Thus the landscape is visionary by itself, continues Deleuze, citing Erwin Straus' 1935 volume, *Meaning of Meaning*: "The great landscape has a wholly visionary characteristic. Vision is what of the invisible becomes visible. [...] The landscape is invisible because the more we conquer it, the more we lose ourselves in it. To reach the landscape we must sacrifice as much as we can all temporal, spatial, objective determination; but this abandon does not only attain the objective, it affects us ourselves to the same extent."[79]

Thus for Deleuze, citing Ahab's becoming-whale in Melville's *Moby Dick*, "Affects are precisely these non-human becomings of man, just as percepts – including the town – are the non-human landscape of nature."[80] For Deleuze, we are not in the world, nor in front of the world, we become the world by contemplating it: "Everything is vision, becoming. We become universes. Becoming animal, plant, molecular, becoming zero."[81] Art is indeed the language of sensations, whether it uses words, minerals,

---

74 | Ibid., p. 164
75 | Ibid., p. 164
76 | Ibid., p. 164
77 | Ibid., p.167
78 | Ibid., p. 169
79 | Straus, Erwin, *Du sens des sens: contribution à l'étude des fondements de la psychologie*, trans. G. Thines, J.-P. Legrand, Grenoble: J. Millon, 1989; 2e éd., Grenoble: J. Millon, 2000, p. 519; Straus, Erwin W., *The Primary World of Senses, a Vindication of Sensory Experience*, trans. Jacob Needleman, [*Vom Sinn der Sinne, ein Beitrag zur Grundlegung der Psychologie*, 1935], New York: Free Press of Glencoe, 1963; Deleuze, Guattari 1994, p. 230
80 | Deleuze, Guattari 1994, p. 35
81 | Ibid., p. 169

or plants. Words, crystals, and plants are sediments of the mind; and this is precisely what emerges in Smithson's 1968 text, "A Sedimentation of the Mind: Earth Projects": "Words and rocks contain a language that follows syntax of splits and ruptures. Look at any word long enough and you will see it open up into in a series of faults, into a terrain of particles each containing its own void."[82] What Smithson describes here is the poetical language of corrosion, erosion, decay, and entropic fatigue.[83]

Image 78: Valerio Olgiati, Visitors' Center, Gornergrat, Switzerland, 2004, competition project

Whether it is with crystals, stones, or sand, art erects a monument composed of percepts and affects. However, for Deleuze, the monument is not a memorial: "here the monument is not something commemorating a past,

---

82 | Smithson, Robert, "A Sedimentation of the Mind: Earth Projects," (1968), in Smithson 1996, p. 107

83 | See Tsai, Eugenie, *Robert Smithson Unearthed: Drawings, Collages, Writings*, New York : Columbia University Press, 1991; Jones, Caroline A., *Machine in the Studio: Constructing the Postwar American Artist*, Chicago: University of Chicago Press, 1996; Tsai, Eugenie, Butler, Cornelia (eds.), *Robert Smithson*, [catalog of the exhibition], The Museum of Contemporary Art, sept. – déc. 2004, Los Angeles, Berkeley, CA: University of California Press, 2004

it is a bloc of present sensations that owe their preservation only to themselves and that provide the event with the compound that celebrates it."[84] Art is a language of sensations, "whether through words, colors, sounds, or stone."[85] Art does not have opinions: "Art undoes the triple organization of perceptions, affections, and opinions in order to substitute a monument composed of percepts, affects, and blocs of sensations that take the place of language."[86] And further: "A monument does not commemorate or celebrate something that happened but confides to the ear of the future the persistent sensations that embody the event."[87] Thus, a monument creates aesthetic figures that have nothing to do with rhetoric,[88] figures that arise from a process of translation in becoming the sensations: percepts and affects, landscape and faces, visions and becomings. Hence, "The monument does not actualize the virtual event but incorporates and embodies it: it gives it a body, a life, a universe."[89]

Image 79: Photomontage of the student project "Glänzling" at the ETH Studio Monte Rosa, 2005

---

84 | Deleuze, Guattari 1994, p. 167
85 | Ibid., p. 176
86 | Ibid., p. 176
87 | Ibid., p. 176
88 | Ibid., p. 177
89 | Ibid., p. 177

Paradoxes et ambiguïtés de la métaphore en architecture

Chris Younès

Depuis Aristote, la métaphore est présentée comme un transfert. Il la définit ainsi : « La métaphore est l'application à une chose d'un nom qui lui est étranger par un glissement du genre à l'espèce, de l'espèce au genre, de l'espèce à l'espèce, ou bien selon un rapport d'analogie.[1] » Le grec *metaphora*, qui signifie transport, laisse entendre, comme le souligne Aristote, un double déplacement : celui du mot et celui du sens qui l'accompagne. Ce qui conduit à envisager le type de rapport de relations établies entre les choses et le sens.

Métaphore et langage
Dans son ouvrage « La métaphore vive », Ricœur déploie un vaste questionnement à la fois d'ordre rhétorique et poétique. Il précise qu' « en tant que figure, [la métaphore] consiste dans un déplacement et dans une extension du sens des mots.[2] » Et il ajoute qu'elle est « définie comme trope par ressemblance et que son explication relève d'une théorie de la substitution ». Elle n'est donc pas une comparaison explicitée mais un rapport implicite d'un autre type rendant l'interprétation littérale ambiguë. Trope signifie un mot employé dans un sens différent de son sens habituel.

La métaphore a d'abord été considérée comme une opération du discours par laquelle un nouveau sens est attribué à un mot, selon un critère de ressemblance, de similitude, en substitution à son sens courant[3].

---

1 | Aristote, *Poétique*, XXI, 1457b
2 | Ricœur, Paul, *La métaphore vive*, Paris : Seuil, 1975, p. 7
3 | Ainsi lorsqu'on transporte le mot fleur, qui désigne l'élément végétal connu, sur l'âge d'une personne, on veut signifier qu'il y a une similitude entre ce que

Les rhéteurs parlent d'une comparaison sous-entendue. Elle produit un effet qui consiste à surprendre le lecteur ou l'auditeur en le mettant en face à rapport inattendu. L'intérêt de la métaphore réside dans sa capacité suggestive de rapprochement d'éléments sans qu'il soit énoncé, laissant à chacun le soin de le deviner et de le trouver. Jamais totalement maîtrisable, elle fait du langage une médiation, lui restituant ainsi sa fonction d'œuvre commune entre le locuteur et le récepteur. Ainsi est-elle très prisée dans la poésie et le roman par sa faculté à revitaliser le langage[4]. Certains critiques contemporains vont même jusqu'à dire que la grandeur d'un écrivain tient au fait qu'il invente une nouvelle syntaxe, c'est-à-dire qu'il force la langue à accomplir de nouvelles combinaisons de mots, afin d'inventer de nouveaux

---

représente la fleur pour la plante et ce que représente une période de la vie (la jeunesse) pour un être humain.

4 | De Platon (*Cratyle*, 390d : « Celui-là seul qui, les yeux fixés sur le nom naturel de chaque objet, est capable d'en incorporer la forme dans les lettres et les syllabes. ») à Rousseau (*Essai sur l'origine des langues*, ch.III, Pléiade V, 1964, p. 381 : « Comme les premiers motifs qui firent parler l'homme furent des passions, ses premières expressions furent des tropes. ») et Nietzsche, on a soutenu que les hommes ont d'abord parlé par métaphores et que ce n'est que postérieurement que le sens propre s'est fixé pour chaque mot. Cela revient à dire que les hommes ont inventé le langage en imitant les êtres ou les choses, et en décrivant par les phonèmes les bruits qu'ils font ou les formes qui les distinguent, ou leurs aspects utiles ou nuisibles. Plus tard, les images en seraient venues à se banaliser, à se normaliser et à se faire oublier au profit du sens abstrait. De ce fait, une langue est plus ou moins « avancée », selon qu'elle parle en images ou en concepts, selon qu'elle s'adresse à l'imagination ou à l'entendement. Mais justement dans ce dernier cas, lorsqu'une langue est pour ainsi dire « aplatie » selon les critères de la raison, le besoin se fait sentir de la régénérer par de nouvelles métaphores. Platon qui considérait que le mot était un corps dont le sens était l'âme (*Cratyle*, 386d) a bien pensé ce mouvement historique du langage. Il croit qu'à l'origine, un certain législateur taillait, tel un drapier, les mots à la mesure des choses. Puis, plus les hommes ont parlé, plus l'écart s'est accentué entre le mot et la chose. D'où le besoin de réformer le langage pour réformer la cité. Le nouveau législateur devra refaire les mots et les ajuster à la dimension des choses. Pour lui, le langage, comme toutes les choses de la vie, peut être frappé d'usure et de vétusté. Autrement dit, les images peuvent s'éteindre petit à petit et perdre leur acuité ; d'où la nécessité de les rénover et d'en inventer d'autres plus propres à éveiller l'esprit.

sens en inventant de nouvelles images à même de susciter de nouvelles émotions.

La double face de la métaphore
Deux mouvements caractérisent la métaphore. Ricœur distingue la métaphore morte, qui est pour ainsi dire absorbée par l'usure du langage quotidien, et la métaphore vive, qui au contraire est rebelle en bousculant les habitudes de penser et de s'exprimer. Autrement dit, les images peuvent s'éteindre petit à petit et perdre de leur acuité, d'où la nécessité de les réveiller, de lever l'esprit de plomb en bousculant les habitudes. Et ce d'autant plus que la figure de style et le vouloir signifier littéral abondent dans l'histoire de la métaphore, la transformant souvent en figure morte. Bergson s'est également élevé avec indignation contre le caractère neutralisant et objectivant du langage qui, trop général, est devenu incapable d'exprimer les sentiments et les idées originales. Considérant que les métaphores spatiales ne relèvent pas d'une déchéance de la pensée mais de l'expression du lien qui unit l'espace et la pensée, il en a appelé à une sorte de nécessaire et salutaire régression par le retour à des formes artistiques d'expression imagées qui n'ont pas besoin de passer par la médiation du langage[5]. A l'encontre de Platon, qui voyait la solution dans une réforme du langage, il s'agit pour lui de revenir à des formes d'expression crûment imagées, comme la peinture ou la musique. L'art serait le lieu de naissance des images et de leur usage métaphorique. La peinture, la sculpture ou la musique le sont davantage que la poésie. Car si celle-ci enserre l'image dans les filets du discours, les autres arts l'en libèrent et la présentent dans toute sa splendeur.

Cependant, la métaphore fait fortement polémique. Certains la considèrent comme simple simulacre fallacieux, d'autres pensent qu'elle rapproche du vrai par son pouvoir de condensation et de déplacement. Ainsi, Le Clézio est sans appel. La métaphore détourne de la vérité. « Les métaphores, les paroles sont assez haïssables. Elles encombrent, freinent avec leur air de vouloir signifier quelque chose. Pourquoi tant de détours ? La vérité est immédiate et réelle, elle vient d'un bond, vite comme le regard, précise comme un index qui montre. » Alors que Ricœur, lui, parle de « vérité métaphorique ». En effet, la « métaphore vive » comme « mimesis

---

5 | Bergson, Henri, *Essai sur les données immédiates de la conscience*, Paris : PUF, 1927 (1889), pp. 96, 98, 122-123

créatrice » comporte une puissance de détection de l'expérience humaine et de redescription du réel. La métaphore est vive en ce qu'elle inscrit l'élan de l'imagination productive plus que reproductive. Ainsi, elle n'établit pas un écran contre le réel, mettant au contraire en contact fulgurant avec celui-ci, ménageant son équivoque fondamentale.

De la référence en architecture
L'architecture participe au mouvement de l'extension de la métaphore du langage aux arts et aux sciences. Elle opère également par glissement. N. Goodman, qui a largement contribué à une pensée de la métaphore à la fin du XXe siècle[6], renvoie le questionnement du côté de la référence, considérant que les œuvres architecturales, même s'il y a des exceptions frappantes, ont de multiples manières de signifier, autres que celles de dénoter ou de dépeindre littéralement[7]. Il écrit : « Le vocabulaire de la référence et des termes qui lui sont liés est vaste. En extrayant quelques brefs passages d'un recueil d'articles sur l'architecture, on peut lire que les bâtiments font allusion, expriment, évoquent, invoquent, commentent, citent, qu'ils sont syntaxiques, littéraux, métaphoriques, dialectiques, qu'ils sont ambigus et même contradictoires ! Tous ces termes, et bien d'autres, relèvent d'une façon ou d'une autre de la référence et peuvent nous aider à saisir ce qu'un bâtiment signifie. Je voudrais esquisser quelques distinctions et relations entre de tels termes... Pour commencer, on peut grouper les variétés de la référence sous quatre chefs : 'dénotation', 'exemplification', 'expression' et 'référence médiatisée'.[8] » Par la dénotation, la métaphore décrit, représente voire imite le monde, mais le monde est réinventé par l'exemplification et l'expression.

---

6 | Notamment avec son ouvrage *Languages of Art : An Approach to a Theory of Symbols* [1968], Indianapolis: Hackett Publishing Co, Inc., New edition, 1988

7 | « Les bâtiments ne sont pas des textes ou des images ; le plus souvent ils ne décrivent pas ou ne dépeignent pas... quant aux bâtiments qui eux-mêmes dépeignent, nous pouvons d'abord penser aux magasins qui représentent une noisette, une crème glacée ou un hot-dog. Mais ce n'est pas toujours aussi banal. L'Opéra House de Jorn Utzon à Sidney dépeint un bateau à voiles presque aussi littéralement, même si l'intérêt va plutôt à la forme générale. » Goodman, Nelson, Elgin, Catherine Z., *Reconceptions en philosophie, dans d'autres arts et dans d'autres sciences*, Paris : PUF, 1994, pp. 34-35

8 | Goodman, Elgin 1994, p. 33

La métaphore du vivant
La métaphore en architecture nous confronte donc, comme la métaphore linguistique, aussi bien à la liberté imaginative et expressive qu'à des formes mimétiques. Son ambiguïté entre concept et image, entendement et intuition, imitation et reliance, modèle et poésie, peut être examinée notamment à propos de la métaphore du vivant. Historiquement, celle-ci a été investie d'une charge heuristique et explicative dans les domaines du monde et de la société. Disons synthétiquement que les anciens l'ont employée à propos du cosmos, encore que nous trouvons des cas où elle est utilisée comme modèle de société; il ne s'agit plus alors du vivant mais de l'homme, être raisonnable. C'est Platon qui introduit la conception du monde comme un « animal, véritablement doué d'une âme, d'une intelligence, un animal ayant pour parties tous les autres animaux pris individuellement ou par genre.[9] » Le « modèle » de cet animal est construit par une sorte d'emboîtement ou de réplication, puisqu'il s'agit d'un animal au second degré, un animal qui « contient en lui-même tous les animaux intelligibles, comme ce monde contient et nous-mêmes et tout ce qu'il a produit d'animaux visibles ». Son auteur voulait en faire « un animal entier, parfait et formé de parties parfaites, et en outre qu'il est uni ». Ainsi donc si l'animal donne au monde son image et son « modèle », c'est parce qu'il lui prête son ordre, son unité et sa cohérence ; bref, sa perfection. Ce qui signifie son caractère achevé, actif et autosuffisant. C'est d'ailleurs sur cet aspect que va insister Plotin en reprenant la même métaphore de l'animal. Mais alors que Platon souligne la cohérence et la perfection de la forme extérieure qui assure à l'animal sa subsistance et sa conservation dans l'espace pour penser le monde, Plotin met l'accent sur la constitution interne, sur la concordance des parties et sur la « sympathie » entre elles. A la différence du *cosmos* platonicien qui est un animal en quelque sorte géométrique, celui de Plotin marque fortement son appartenance au monde organique. Si le premier cherche à assurer à son monde une unité et une cohérence dans l'espace, le second tend à garantir au sien une identité dans le temps, une persistance dans la permanence, malgré le changement de ses états. Unité dans l'espace et unité dans le temps, unité externe et unité interne, tout cela se reflète dans une seule « volonté.[10] » « Car un animal unique n'a qu'une volonté » dit encore Plotin, en ajoutant : « Toutes les volontés conte-

---

9 | Platon, *Timée*, 30a, 31a et 32a
10 | Plotin, *Ennéades*, IV, 35, trad. Bréhier, éd. Belles Lettres, 1956, p. 142

nues dans l'univers ont un même but, qui est celui de la volonté unique de l'univers. » Il y a comme une synthèse des parties dans le tout, laquelle synthèse s'effectue à deux niveaux : le physique et le psychique. Et c'est cette synthèse ou « sympathie » qui distingue le vivant de l'inerte. On dira que dans l'inerte les parties se juxtaposent les unes aux autres, tandis que dans le vivant, elles « concourent » ou « conspirent » ensemble.

En revanche, les modernes ont consacré la métaphore organique dans la conception de la société, sous la spécification de « corps ». La métaphore du corps social ou du corps politique, ou de l'organisme, parcourt la philosophie politique de l'âge classique, avant de se faire supplanter, comme dans la conception du monde d'ailleurs, par le modèle de la machine. Leibniz, chez les modernes, est celui qui a réhabilité la double tendance du vitalisme et de l'animisme, non que pour lui le monde soit un animal mais parce qu'il est « plein de vie ». Et ceci en réaction au mécanisme dominant, c'est-à-dire en réaction au cartésianisme. S'opposant à la réduction des corps physiques à de l'étendue et à une inertie passive, il affirme leur activité et leur dynamisme après les avoir doués d'action et de force. Pour lui, les « modernes ont porté la réforme trop loin » en confondant les machines humaines et les machines naturelles, celles de l'art et celles de la création. Or, entre ces deux entités, la différence ne consiste pas seulement dans le degré mais dans le genre même. Une machine artificielle est une machine en elle-même, tandis qu'une machine naturelle « demeure encore machine dans ses moindres parties », entendons qu'elle a « un nombre d'organes véritablement infini », qu'elle est une « machine de machines.[11] »

En somme, bien que le monde lui-même ne soit pas assimilé à un être vivant, il est peuplé de vivants qui sont « les substances simples, les Vies, les Ames, les Esprits ». Leibniz ne refuse pas la métaphore de la machine, il trouve simplement que le mécanisme, acquis essentiel de la science moderne, est insuffisant lorsqu'il s'agit de rendre compte des phénomènes naturels et en particulier ceux qui ont la vie en partage. Une synthèse entre mécanisme, vitalisme et même animisme est nécessaire parce que la nature est ainsi faite qu'elle comporte ces divers aspects. Et c'est en tant que mondes compossibles qu'il a développé sa philosophie.

---

11 | Leibniz, Gottfried Wilhelm, *Système Nouveau de la Nature et de la Communication des Substances* [1695], Paris: éd. Gehrardt, phil. IV, p. 482

S'entre-répondre
La métaphore vive établit des reliances nomades et sauvages qui font évènement, révélant ce qui est sous la conscience. Par sa capacité de déplacer les limites des règles habituelles de liaison, elle est un activateur paradoxal puissant des liens entre là-bas et ici, ceci et cela. Elle porte et transporte au milieu, au-delà de la limite de la substance individuée sise en son topos. Sans abolir toutefois l'écart entre ce qui est rapproché. Ce qui ouvre un vaste champ de possibles interprétations et imaginaires. Aujourd'hui les problématiques de l'écologie existentielle et du développement durable en architecture conduisent à repenser les coexistences et les reliances. Deleuze en appelle à penser en termes de « et – et » plutôt que de « ou – ou ». C'est un monde méta et transfiguré où tout peut se faire écho, qui est à inventer. On le voit bien, la question de la métaphore et de son usage en architecture comme dans tous les arts et les sciences n'est ni neutre, ni stérile. Elle soulève des questions de la plus haute importance impliquant une interrogation sur le destin de l'humanité et le sens de son existence.

The metaphor project

The Hidden Pavilion

DIDIER FAUSTINO

3 into 1
A double pitched roof, a flat roof, a vault, three archetypal shapes fuse into one unit space. The physical body and the mental body meet together in the refuge of mythical architecture, the primitive hut. A pure geometry to recall the principle of architecture as a prolongation of the human body.

Image 94: Hidden pavilion

Locus Amoenus
It grows up from the earth, standing like a belvedere, proud and naturally deeply rooted. But the beauty of the viewpoint is turned towards its inside, meant to be protected from the aggressions of the external world.

A remote place to meet in harmony, away from the turpitudes of life, as Lucrece defines the Locus Amoenus in *De rerum natura*, associating voluptuousness with nature: a nice place where you meet your friends, lying in the sweet grass. The wise man gets together with his friends, in the pleasure of exchange without identification.

Image 95: Origin

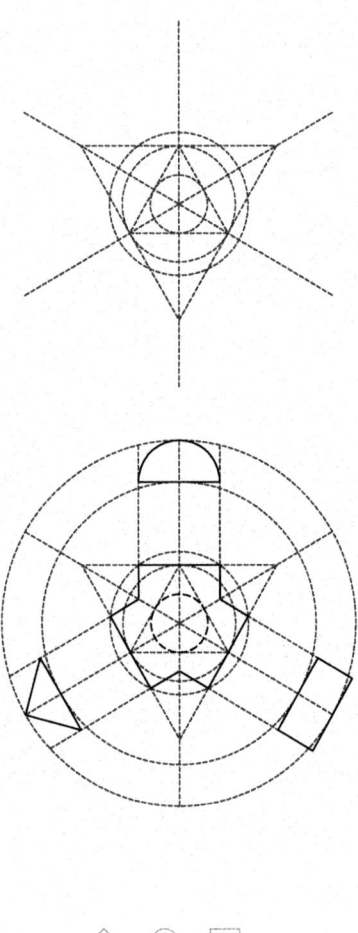

Image 96: Plan

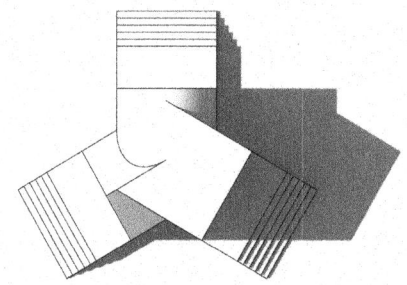

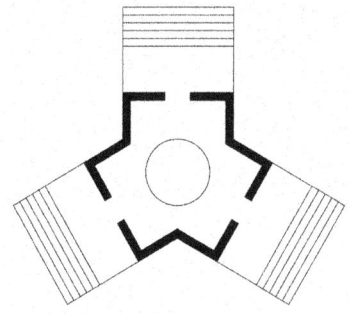

Space of experiences
By experimenting the collision of three entities, confronting but merging smoothly into one, the body is incorporated into the space. The human has to live in the space. *The Hidden Pavilion* reveals the importance of the body, a presence of weight, a chain of lived experiences: flesh / touch / sensation / pleasure.

The space sets us in the presence of ourselves, of our existence.

A sensory, physical and carnal manifestation of existence.

Image 97: Plan

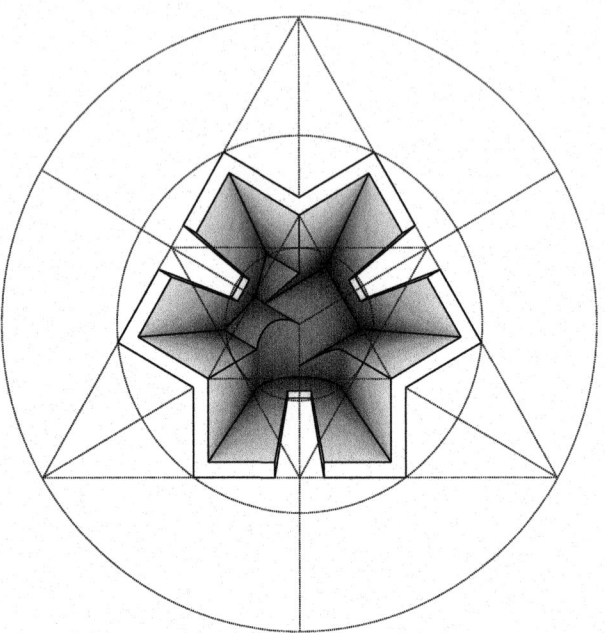

Image 98: Sections

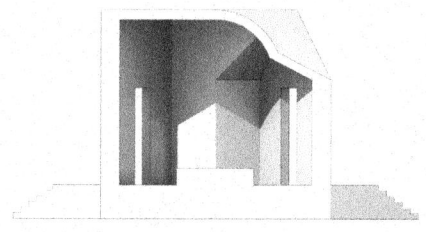

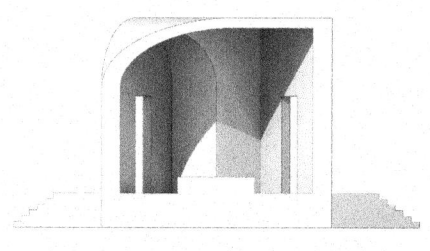

Image 99: Persectives

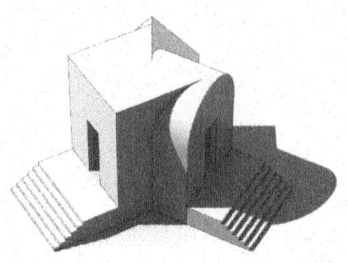

« *Pour que la vérité soit vertigineuse, elle doit choisir d'avoir infiniment tort* »

François Roche

[...] the title was a kind of provocation, it's Jean-Paul Sartre's opinion of Baudelaire, on the obscenity of Baudelaire, to justify how the obscenity cannot work as a vector of transformation... Georges Bataille was reporting and fitting against this straight and ambiguous declaration in the *Literature and Evil* in 1957...

Could we disqualify the monstrosity, the freakiness, as a metaphorical potential to travel somewhere, elsewhere...

It mainly depends on the way the metaphor is considered, as a tooling to reach a point, to turn around a point or to reveal the unreachability of a point...

See the difference between a Reverdy's and Desnos' lines of poetry...

The differences between a kind of childish romantic, gluing and slippery writing (in French) "Dans les ruisseaux, il a une chanson qui coule" or "In the river there is a song which is trimming"

And at the opposite from Robert Desnos, who triggers metaphor as a line of subjectivity, as a line of subjectivation, which forces you to enter a door, similar to the parallel universe of "Alice," a door from where you cannot entirely frame logic and illogic, as a resonance, a stuttering between somewhere and elsewhere...

"Dans le sommeil de Rrose Sélavy il y a un nain sorti d'un puits qui vient manger son pain la nuit"

(Rrose Sélavy the avatar of Marcel Duchamp) translated by: "As Rrose Sélavy sleeps, there is a dwarf, who comes out of a well and eats her bread at night."

Immediately it is bringing something which reaches something else, which is a dynamic moving to a territory where the logic is not appearing as a strata, as an immediate strata, where you cannot so easily unfold the shadow of the relief...which keeps you in suspension, in a suspending time sensation...

Not so innocent: Etymologically "metaphor" and in Latin: *metaphora*, introduces a linguistic strategy to create "a vehicle of transportation" by and through miscorrespondance of understanding.

Image 100: New-Territories (R&Sie),
An architecture „des humeurs," Paris, 2010

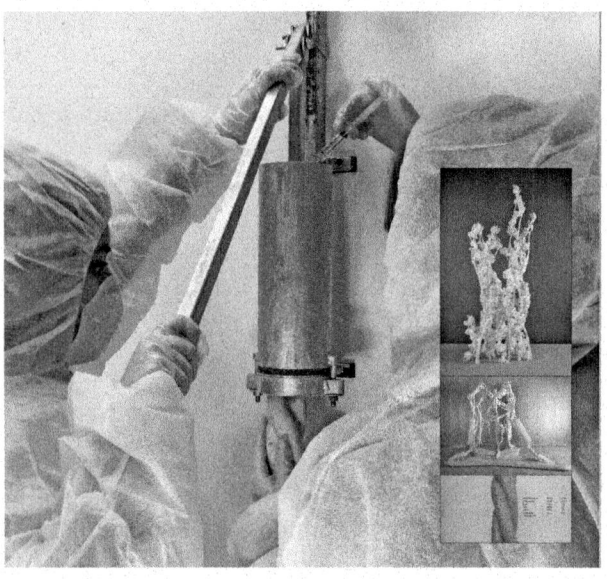

We cannot deny that in the field of architecture, it has been reduced to a kind of notion which manipulates analogy, simulacrum and even mimicry, as a ennobling term to overlap and justify plagiarism ...but if we voluntary avoid to jump and sink in this reductionism approach, we could reintroduce this word as a potential of transportation, as a potential of migration between, yes a "migration between", which never across the bridge and stays in disequilibrium between two territories, as a permanent palpitation between here and elsewhere...schizoid perception to leave the ground, and its physicality, its apparent logic without to reach the next point...floating in your mind, in the *"malentendu"*, both a "fountainhead" of mishearing and misunderstanding...

In a way metaphor is becoming a kind of tool to articulate non-hierarchical, non-linear strategies of knowledge, and simultaneously des-alienate the too predictable appearances embedded in the hypocrisies of games of power, by perturbing, even corrupting its conventional and deterministic "order of discourses."

Image 101: New-Territories (R&Sie) Things which necrose, 2009/2010

Metaphor is carrying both Don Quixote and its vision-illusion and the travellers of Thomas More, back from the Island of Utopia. As a weapon for speculation and narration, articulating knowledge and boundaries of knowledge, line of consciousness and line of subjectivities…as a torture machine, as the torture machine of Kafka's novels "the Penitence Colonies" where the bachelor machine introduces disruption of logic, between pleasure, barbarism, suffering and repulsion,… stuttering between "Eros and Thanatos," to discover a process of translation, of transaction through the travelling to the death…

...I invite you, now, to travel in my own MPD (multiple psycho disorders) through some image material.

The last monograph published with Princeton Press [...] focuses on machinism as a process of transportation, a process of transaction....transactional protocols where the machines are considered non only as a factor of efficiency, etymologically and literally, "the good and slave worker," but also simultaneously as a strategy to develop and unfold narrations, scenario which reciprocally become the "raison d'être" of their own existence. They are pretending to produce "something somewhere," which cannot be reduced to their apparent productivity, going beyond the expertise of their technologies and behaviours of mechanism logic... machines are use in our "practice" or "research as practice" as a line of subjectivity, as a 'pataphysic instable construction. They articulate symmetrically through weird apparatuses different arrow of times, different layers of knowledge, but more efficiently, they are negotiating the endless limit of what we could consider the territory of absurdity, where what seems illogic behaviour is protocolized with an extreme logic of emerging design and geometry, where input and output are described by mathematic rules ...

Neither a satire of the worlds, neither a techno-pessimism or a techno-derision, they are on this limit or they constitute the limit between the territory of conventions, of certainties and stabilities, where it is comfortable to consider everything legitimated by an order, or an intuition of an order, and...and ...the others [territories], all the others...paranoïded, phantasmed, or reported by travellers...

In a casual and basic sense, machines have been always used to elaborate technicism as the extension of the hand, through its replacement, its improving for accelerating the speed and the powers of transformation, of production. But that seems very naïve to reduce machine to this first obvious layer of objective dimension, in a purely functional and mechanical approach, exclusively limited to the Cartesian productive power ship, located in the visible spectrum of appearance and facts. Because in parallel, machines are producing artefacts, assemblages, multiplicity, desires, and are infiltrating *"la raison d'être"* of our own body and mind in the relationship to our own biotopes.[1] Fundamentally everywhere in the nature, they are at the origin of all process of exchanges, of transaction of substances,

---

1 | In reference of the work of Llya Prigogine, where human is considered as a "machinisme" of exchanges, of shared substances IN and OUT and it reverse.

of the entropy and vitalism.² The machines are a paradigm of the body in a sense of its co-extensibility of the nature, through processes, protocols, apparatuses, where transitory and transactional substances³ constitute and affect all the species, their identities, their productions "objectivised and subjectivised" and their relationships...

Image 102: New-Territories (R&Sie), Olzweg, Paris, 2006

The "Olzweg" machine for the FRAC centre, three years ago. A stochastic machine able to smear an existing building, to erase without tabula rasa by smearing (*barbouiller* in French), staggering and stacking the vitrified and recycled glass material coming from collect French alcoholism. It occurs as a graft, as a prosthesis, a freak prosthesis, for the museum of architecture, with an endlessness process of addition and aggregation, without any point of achievement and finitude describing by the way an architecture which lost its totemic appearance, its readable limits and in which people could lose their positioning, their confortable and panoptical way to perceive space as an heterotopia experiment...

---

2 | "Vitalism presumes a monadological rather than atomistic ontology. In Leibniz's 'monadology' all substances are different from one another in opposite Cartesian 'atomism' presumes that matter is comprised of identical parts (atoms)" Lash, Scott, *Critique of Information*, London: SAGE, 2002

3 | "All bodily phenomena can be explained mechanically or by the corpuscular philosophy." Leibniz, *Letters to Arnauld*, 1687

Image 103: New-Territories (R&Sie), Broomwich, Paris, 2008

Image 104: New-Territories (R&Sie), Broomwich, Paris, 2008

The machine of "broomwitch," is a real vehicle of transportation, for travelling from one building to some others, from a conventional fifties design house of André Bloc, to the discovering of his magic freaks constructions in the garden, until an anomaly turns in, on the back of the garden, in the shadows, coming from a parasite invading the abandoned nature. The vehicle is "a beam me up scotty," a time machine, from a predictable "concrete edge" building to the revenge of the nature, post-colonizing its intrinsic logic, and creating on the side, as a collateral effect a building, which is not a building...

Image 105: New-Territories (R&Sie), He shot me down, Korea, 2006-7

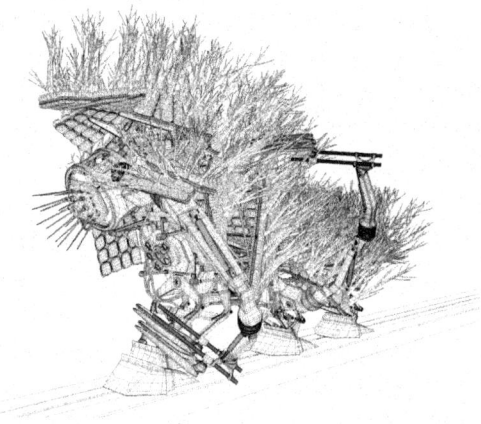

The next one, in South Korea, on the boundaries of nowhere, on the boundaries of the DMZ, which is the zone between south and north, a Stalker zone, if I refer to Tarkovsky's movie, where the war was played, half a century ago, and where all the rusty residue of the battle are still there, even the active anti-personnel landmines, which imprisoned the zone as an eternal cemetery, unreachable, inaccessible. Our project, a museum of contemporary art, is located on this boundary, on this absurd and real situation. We cannot deny where we are – fear and paranoia are vector of life and death, their "situationist" conditions... substances are toxic, dangerous, under military influence...only nonhumans, in this case, could cross the line... to reach the part where nobody goes anymore, where the elves and the witches, the harpies and the ghosts of the forest are back, invading with their whispering noise and ritual dances in the silence of the night... only a robot is going through, a little machine which take risks in this no man's land to bring back on it shoulders the bio-mass of the forest, with a part of the legends, its soil and soul... to become the thermic clothes of a building, using the chemical warmth of the biomass fermentation to insulate it... from the residue of the forest colonized by the traces of the war... which in the same time defined through ballistic impact its own porosity, its own accessibility....

Image 106: New-Territories (R&Sie), He shot me down, Korea, 2006-7

We bought a riffle two years ago, a Chinese rifle sold in Paris to metaphorize the war in Korea... that seems the "world company"...were the AK49 replaced the Winchester. At our studio, the experiments of bullets trajectories inside a volume of clay were the way to trace and cartography the trajectories, implementing by this way simultaneously the impact of violence, aesthetic of violence and design, access, distribution, light, air and views as functionalist metaphors...

Authors

Odile Decq set up her own office just after graduating at La Villette in 1978 while studying at Sciences Politiques Paris where she completed a post-graduate diploma in Urban Planning in 1979. International renown was not long in coming, as early as 1990 actually, with her first major commission: the Banque Populaire de l'Ouest in Rennes. The numerous prizes and publications that distinguished the building underlined the emergence of a new hope directly born from the punk rebellion which turned old conventions upside down. By questioning the commission, the use, the matter, the body, the technique, the taste, the architecture of „Odile Decq Benoît Cornette" offers a paradoxical look, both tender and severe on today's world. They were awarded with a Golden Lion in Venice in 1996. Alone since 1998, Odile Decq has been faithful to her fighting attitude while diversifying and radicalizing her research. She completed the MACRO (Museum for Contemporary Art in Rome) in 2010, the restaurant in Opera Garnier in Paris in 2011 and in 2012, the FRAC (Contemporary Art Museum) in Rennes. GL Events headquarter in Lyon will be completed early 2013.

After having taught since 1992 at Ecole Spéciale d'Architecture in Paris Odile Decq has been directing the school from 2007 to 2012, sharing her time to organize and develop the school to an international level.

Andri Gerber, born 1974 in Bergamo; architectural studies at the ETH in Zürich; from 2000-2002 work for Peter Eisenman in New York; 2008 PhD at the ETH, awarded with ETH medal; 2008-2011 Associate professor at the Ecole Spéciale d'Architecture in Paris, head of the postgraduate programme „Mutations urbaines" with Ghorayeb and Sautereau; 2010-2012 Senior lecturer in theory and history of architecture, University of Liechtenstein; since 2012 Senior lecturer in history of urbanism, Zurich University Of Applied Sciences, Switzerland; since 2012 working on a habilitation project at the gta Institute, ETH Zürich, on the history of the epistemology of urbanism, financed by the Swiss National Science Foundation. Recent publications are *Researching Architecture* (Quart 2010) and *Theorie der Städtebaumetaphern* (Chronos 2012).

Brent Patterson studied philosophy and sociology at the University of Toronto (BA), followed by a masters in Public Health. He worked for a period of 10 years in HIV related ONGs (Toronto, New York, Delhi). He returned to study architecture initially at Parsons in NYC, then the EN-SAPB and Ecole Nationale Supérieure de Paris-LaVillette (ENSAPLV) in Paris where he completed his CEAA. He is currently working on a PhD in philosophy at Paris 8 on „Divided Cities." He teaches history and theory courses at a number of architecture schools in Paris including the Ecole Spéciale d'Architecture (ESA), where he is an associate professor, as well as the Ecole Nationale Supérieure de Paris-LaVillette (ENSAPLV) and the Ecole Nationale Supérieure de Paris-Malaquais (ENSAPM). His interests include: architectural representation, Utopias, ‚radical' architecture from the 60s and 70s, philosophical notions of ‚hospitality' and a questioning of ‚humanism'.

Johannes Binotto, Dr. des., born 1977 is research and teaching assistant at the English Seminar of the Universiyt of Zurich and works as a free author. He has studied german and english literature and philosophy at the University of Zurich while working as a journalist for numerous newspapers and magazines. Since 2005 he has been teaching on „Film and Psychoanalysis" at the Zurich Lacan-Seminar. In his research he is specifically devoted to the intersections of psychoanalytical theory, literature and film, as well as the application of architectural theory in literature studies. Among his most recent publications are essays on subjects such as the Mafioso as male hysteric, the aesthetics of Technicolor or snow in Westerns. Johannes Binotto has written his dissertation on the Freudian uncanny and its spatial representation in art, literature and cinema. The dissertation is about to be published in 2013.

Gernot Böhme studied mathematics, physics, and philosophy at Göttingen and Hamburg, followed by a PhD at Hamburg University in 1965 and a Habilitation at Ludwig-Maximilians-University Munich in 1972. He worked as a research scientist with Carl-Friedrich von Weizsäcker at the Max-Planck-Institute zur Erforschung der Lebensbedingungen der wissenschaftlich-technischen Welt at Starnberg 1970-1977. From 1977 to 2002 he was Professor of Philosophy at Technical University Darmstadt.

In this period he held visiting positions at Harvard, Linköping, Rotterdam, Cambridge, Canberra, Vienna, Madison, Graz and Kyoto. Since 2005 he is director of the Institute for Practical Philosophy at Darmstadt. His background and expertise comprises classical philosophy (in particular Plato and Kant), philosophy of science, theory of time, aesthetics, ethics, and philosophical anthropology.

Philippe Boudon DPLG in architecture, Docteur d'Etat, Professor of schools or architecture (Nancy, Paris-la-Villette) designed and developped the scientific program of Architecturology through the work of LAREA (Laboratory of architecturology and epistemological research in architecture) which he founded. About architecturology cf. Ph. Boudon, Ph. Deshayes, F. Pousin, F. Schatz, *Enseigner la conception architecturale*, Editions de Paris-la-Villette, 2000.

Matteo Burioni studied Art History, Classical Archeology, Classical Philology and Sociology at Johann Wolfgang Goethe-University at Frankfurt am Main and at the Scuola Normale Superiore di Pisa. He was Doctoral Fellow at the Kunsthistorisches Institut in Florenz (Max-Planck-Institut) and Post-Doc at eikones NFS-Bildkritik of the University of Basel. He is Wissenschaftlicher Assistant at the Institute of Art History of Ludwig-Maximilians-Universität in Munich and Research Fellow at the Zentralinstitut für Kunstgeschichte. Publications: *Die Renaissance der Architeken. Profession und Souveränität des Architekten in Giorgio Vasaris Viten*, Berlin 2008; *Das Auge der Architektur. Zur Frage der Bildlichkeit in der Baukunst*, Paderborn 2011 (co-edited with A. Beyer and J. Grave); *Der Grund. Das Feld des Sichtbaren*, Paderborn 2012 (co-edited with Gottfried Boehm).

Rosario Caballero-Rodriguez has a degree in History (U. of Valencia) and in English (U. Jaume I, Castellon) and a Ph.D. in English Linguistics and is currently Associate Professor in the Universidad de Castilla-La Mancha. Her research interests include professional genres, the role of metaphor in genre, and sensory language. She is the author of *Re-Viewing Space. Figurative Language in Architects' Assessment of Built Space* (2006, Mouton), the co-editor of *Sensuous Cognition. Explorations into Human Sentience* (2013, Mouton), and journal papers on metaphor in architectural and wine discourse.

Susanne Hauser is professor of art history and cultural studies at the University of Arts in Berlin. After her Habilitation (cultural studies, Humboldt Universität zu Berlin) in 1999 she taught landscape aesthetics at the Universität Kassel (2000-2003). From 2003-2005 she has been professor at the Faculty of Architecture at the Graz University of Technology and head of the Institute of Art History and Cultural Studies. She held teaching commissions in Innsbruck and Berlin and was visiting scholar in Paris and Washington, D.C. Her fields of interest include the history and theory of architectural design, of cultural landscapes and urban structures. Recent publications include *Kulturtechnik Entwerfen. Praktiken, Konzepte und Medien in Architektur und Design Science* (coed. 2009) and *Architekturwissen. Grundlagentexte aus den Kulturwissenschaften* (coed. 2011 and 2013).

Professor of urbanism at Venice School of Architecture, **Bernardo Secchi** was professor at the Geneva School of Architecture, in Leuven, Paris, Rennes and Zurich and, from 1975 to 1982 Director of the Milan School of architecture; Doctor honoris causa at the University Mendes France, Grenoble, 1994; Grand Prix d'Urbanisme 1994; Mellon Senior fellow at the Canadian Centre for Architecture, Montréal, in 2008.

Bernardo Secchi participated in the study of an inter-municipal plan for Milan (1960-63); worked together with Giuseppe Samonà on the development of the Trento regional plan (1966), and (with Paolo Ceccarelli) on the Aosta Valley plan (1972). Author, with Paola Viganò, of the plan for the Pescara region (1990), and La Spezia (1988-1993), of the plans for Jesi (1987), Siena (1990), Bergamo (1994), Prato (1996), Brescia (1999), Pesaro (2000), Antwerp (2006) and for the historical centre of Ascoli Piceno (1993), of numerous projects on urbanism and architecture: for the rehabilitation of the IP refinery at La Spezia (1989), for the Sécheron district in Geneva (1989), for HLM zones in Vicenza (1992). In 2008-09 is among the ten architect asked by the President Sarkozy to develop ideas and designs for the Grand Paris.

Bernardo Secchi, director of „Urbanistica" from 1984 to 1990, collaborates on „Casabella" and „Archivio di Studi Urbani e Regionali". His books are „Il racconto urbanistico", Einaudi, Torino, 1984, „Un progetto per l'urbanistica", Einaudi, Torino, 1989, „Tre piani", Angeli, Milano, 1995, "La prima lezione di urbanistica",Laterza, Roma, 2001, "La città del ventesimo secolo", Laterza, Roma, 2005.

Caroline van Eck is professor of architectural history at Leiden University, The Netherlands. In 2004, she was the first art historian to be awarded one of the prestigious VICI grants from the Dutch Foundation of Scientific Research (NWO). She has published widely on Renaissance architecture, rhetoric and artistic theory, such as *Classical Rhetoric and the Visual Arts in Early Modern Europe* (2007), edited *British Architectural Theory 1540–1750: An Anthology of Texts* (2003) and co-edited *Dealing with the Visual: Aesthetics, Art History and Visual Culture* (2005), and *The Question of Style in Philosophy and the Arts* (1995).

Benedikte Zitouni is a professor of sociology at the University of Brussels (Saint-Louis). Amongst others, she's been trained at Oxford University, at l'Ecole des Mines and Sciences Po in Paris, and she's been a Visiting Scholar at UC Berkeley. Her books are: *Agglomérer. Une anatomie de l'extension bruxelloise (1828-1915)* (University of Brussels Press & ASP, Brussels, 2010); *Usus/usures, Etat des lieux / How things stand* (Brussels, CFWB Press, 2010, with Rotor and Ariane d'Hoop for the Venice Architecture Biennale). Recently, she's also written articles on Donna Haraway's situated knowledges (reader published by PUF); on the impact of technical professionals in the city (Brussels studies); on the questions of centralization and unification in Brussels; and other. Currently, she's working on an article about the 1980's ecofeminist movement and also on the Leibnizian heritage in French critical sociology.

Elisabeth Bronfen is Professor of English and American Studies at the University of Zurich. She did her PhD at the University of Munich, on literary space in the work of Dorothy M. Richardson's novel Pilgrimage, as well as her habilitation, five years later. A specialist in the 19th and 20th century literature she has also written articles in the area of gender studies, psychoanalysis, film, cultural theory and art. Her book publications are *Over Her Dead Body. Death, Femininity and the Aesthetic* (Manchester University Press) and a collection of essays *Death and Representation*, co-edited with Sarah W. Goodwin (Johns Hopkins University Press). A book version of her dissertation has appeared in English, under the title *Dorothy Richardson's*

Art of Memory. Space, Identity, Text (Manchester University Press). The book *Home in Hollywood. The Imaginary Geography of Cinema* was published by Columbia University Press in fall 2004. The most recent publication are a book on the cultural configurations of the night, published in German: *Tiefer als der Tag Gedacht. Eine Kulturgeschichte der Nacht* and *Specters of War. Hollywood's Engagement with Military Conflict* (Rutgers University Press).

Richard Coyne. The cultural, social and spatial implications of computers and pervasive digital media spark Richard's interest. He enjoys architecture, writing, designing, philosophy, coding, blogging and media mashups. Richard is author of eight books on the implications of information technology and design with MIT Press, Routledge, Addison Wesley and Pitman. He researches and teaches in information technology in practice, computer-aided design in architecture, the philosophy of information technology, digital media, and design theory at the University of Edinburgh. He inaugurated the MSc in Design and Digital Media, in which he also teaches. He is an architect and previously worked at the Universities of Sydney and Melbourne. Richard has served as Head of the Architecture Department and Head of the School of Arts, Culture and Environment at the University of Edinburgh.

Jelle Feringa is currently working on a PhD thesis at the HyperBody Research Group, TU Delft. Jelle has taught and lectured at the ESA, Paris-Malaquias, ETH, TU Delft, IAAC, AA, and Aarhus School of Architecture. He is a founding partner in EZCT Architecture & Design Research, and is co-founder of Odico robotic formworks. The work of EZCT is part of the permanent collection of the Centre Pompidou Center and the FRAC Orléans collection. In 2007 the office won the Seroussi Pavilion. Projects have been exhibited at the Mori Art Museum (Tokyo, 2004), Archilab (Orléans, 2004), Barbican Gallery (London, 2006), Design Miami/Basel (Miami, 2007), Pompidou Center (Paris, 2003, 2007, 2012), Maison Rouge (Paris, 2007), Architectural Association (London, 2007), ScriptedByPurpose (Philadelphia, 2007) International Biennial of Sevilla (Sevilla, 2008), Vivid design gallery (Rotterdam, 2009 / 2011). Jelle's thesis is focused on novel design representations that explore the architectural potential of evolutionary computing. At the Hyperbody group, Jelle has been exploring novel CNC fabrication methods for the production of large volumetric elements, by means of hotwire cutting. In 2011 he set up Hyperbody's robotics lab to further continue this angle of research. For his research work, Jelle relies on Open-Source software. In collaboration with Thomas Paviot, Jelle has been driving the development of an open source CAD framework, PythonOCC a CAD/CAE/PLM development framework for the python programming language and PyRAPID, a robotics framework.

Marcelyn Gow is a partner and founding member of *servo* Los Angeles. Gow received her Architecture degrees from the Architectural Association and Columbia University, as well as a Dr. Sc. from the ETH Zurich. Her doctoral dissertation *Invisible Environment: Art, Architecture and a Systems Aesthetic* explores the relationship between aesthetic research and technological innovation. Gow has lectured internationally and contributed to numerous journals including Perspecta, Via and AD. Gow was the recipient of a 2012 Graham Foundation Grant. She currently teaches graduate design studios and cultural studies seminars at SCIArc – the Southern California Institute of Architecture.

Dr. **Stephan Günzel** is Professor for Media Studies at the Berlin Technical University of Arts. His fields of research cover cultural studies as well as image studies, and theories of space. His publications focus on the debate about a spatial turn und cultural studies and on spatial aspects of media like maps and computer games. He has edited several anthologies and handbooks on space theories and published monographs on Friedrich Nietzsche, Maurice Merleau-Ponty, and Gilles Deleuze.

Holger Schurk, born 1969; 1997 Diploma in Architecture at theUniversity of Stuttgart, Germany; 1998-2001 Collaboration with several architecture firms in Stuttgart, Rotterdam und Amsterdam; since 2001 Partner in dform Architekten Zuerich; Switzerland; 2001-2004 Junior faculty member at the ETH Zurich, Switzerland; 2005-2008 Associate Professor at the Berne University Of Applied Sciences, Switzerland; since 2008 Associate Professor at the Zurich University Of Applied Sciences, Switzerland; EAAE Prize 2011-12 for Writings in architectural education for the essay „Design Or Research in Doing."

Georges Teyssot has taught at the I.U.A.V. (Venice, Italy); at Princeton University's School of Architecture (USA), and at the GTA in the Department of Architecture at Zurich's ETH. Presently, he is Professor at Laval University's School of Architecture (Quebec, QC, CA). He has authored and edited many volumes, including one on *Interior Landscapes* (New York: 1988); and another on: *Die Krankheit des Domizils* [The Disease of the Domicile], (Wiesbaden: 1989). He has directed a collective volume with Monique Mosser, entitled *The Architecture of Western Gardens* (Milan: 1990; Cambridge, MA: 1991; Paris: 1991, 2002; Stuttgart: 1993); republished under a new title, *The History of Garden Design* (New York: 2000). He has written the introduction to the volume of *Diller + Scofidio, Flesh: Architectural Probes* (New York: 1995; reprint, 2011). He was the curator with Diller + Scofidio of an exhibition on *The American Lawn. Surface of Everyday Life*, at the CCA (Montréal, 1998), and the editor of a volume on *The American Lawn* (New York: 1999). Presently, he is publishing a volume entitled *A Topology of Everyday Constellations* (Cambridge, MA: The MIT Press, forthcoming, Spring 2013); and a booklet on: *Walter Benjamin. Les maisons oniriques*, [*Walter Benjamin's Oneiric Houses*], (Paris: 2013).

Chris Younès is a philosopher, professor at school of architecture (Paris la Villette and ESA), in charge of postmaster "Architectures of milieus" and of an international scientific network the "PhilAU" which develops exchanges, researches and experimentations between Philosophy, Architecture and Urban, Head of laboratory Gerphau (Philosophy Architecture Urban)/ UMR CNRS 7218 LAVUE.

Last publications: *Habiter, le propre de l'humain* (dir. Thierry Paquot, Michel Lussault, Chris Younès), La Découverte, 2007; *Le territoire des philosophes* (dir. Thierry Paquot, Chris Younès), La Découverte, 2009; *Philosophie de l'environnement et milieux urbains* (dir. Thierry Paquot, Chris Younès), La Découverte, 2010; *Architecture des Milieux* (dir. Chris Younès, Benoît Goetz), Le Portique, 2010; *Espace et lieu dans la pensée occidentale. De Platon à Nietzsche* (dir. Thierry Paquot, Chris Younès), La Découverte, 2011.

Artist and architect, **Didier Faustino** works on the intimate relationship between body and space. Shortly after graduating from l'Ecole d'Architecture Paris-Villemin in 1995 he created his own architectural agency. His approach is multifaceted, from installation to experimentation, from the creation of subversive visual art to spaces exacerbating the senses. Didier Faustino created the *Bureau des Mésarchitectures* in 2002, received the Académie d'Architecture's Dejean prize for lifetime achievement in 2010 and he was honoured several times in the Chernikhov Prize (Moscow).

Several of his projects entered the collections of major institutions: MoMA, National Centre for Fine Arts, Background national d'Art Contemporain, Beaubourg. They are characterized by their fictional- and their critical dimension, by their freedom of codes and ability to offer new experiences to the individual and collective body, Among his iconic works: the Hermès H Box (2006), a mobile video screening hall to be presented in museums worldwide (Tate Modern in London, Pompidou Centre in Paris, Beyeler Foundation in Bâle, etc.); Body in Transit (2000), a minimal space criticising the transport of illegal immigrants, presented at the Venice Biennale and featured in the collections of the Pompidou Centre; Double Happiness (2009), a set of two swings in the air at the Shenzhen-Hong Kong Biennial, or Sky is the Limit, (2006), a tea room lifted to 20 metres above the ground near the Korean DMZ.

He participated in many personal exhibitions (Cité de l'Architecture et du Patrimoine, CAM de la Fondation Gulbenkian, CCA Kitakyushu, Laxart, Storefront) and he often participated in biennials (Venice, Taipei, Yokohama, Sao Paulo, Istanbul, Beijing, etc.) He created *Evento*, a new artistic and urban event in Bordeaux, in 2009. He his represented by Galerie Michel Rein in Paris and Galerie Filomena Soares in Lisbon.

He dedicates part of his time to teaching and is in charge of the Diploma Unit 2 at the AA School in London since 2011. He frequently gives lectures at major universities and international institutions (MIT, Columbia, Royal Academy of Arts, Bartlett, American University of Beirut ...) and contributes to the Bridge The Gap ?, CCA Lab since 2009.

François Roche is the principal of New-Territories (R&Sie(n) / [eIf/b∧t/c]). He is based mainly in BKK, [eIf/b∧t/c], sometimes in Paris, R&Sie(n), and at fall time NY, Gsapp.

Through these different structures, his architectural works and protocols seek to articulate the real and/or fictional, the geographic situations and narrative structures that can transform them. / Web site: www.new-territories.com.

François Roche architectural designs and processes have been show at, among other places, Columbia University (New York, 1999-2000), UCLA (Los Angeles, 1999-2000), ICA (London, 2001), Mori Art Museum (Tokyo, 2004), Centre Pompidou (Paris, 2003), MAM / Musée d'Art Moderne (Paris, 2005, 2006), the Tate Modern (London 2006) and Orléans/ArchiLab (1999, 2001, 2003). Work by R&Sie(n), New-Territories were selected for exhibition at the French pavilion at the Venice Architecture Biennales of 1990, 1996, 2000 and 2002 (they rejected the invitation that year, and for the international section in 2000, 2004 and 2008, and, in 2010 both International and Austrian Pavilion, and, small multiple buzz in 2012 cession (Dark Side Curating, Slovenian Pavilion, Writing Architecture).

In 2012 François Roche is the guest editor of LOG#25, NY Critical Revue, for the issue released in July 2012: title / reclaim resis(lience)stance.

List of Figures/Copyrights

Odile Decq
Image 1, © Guy Vacheret

Andri Gerber
Image 2, © ESA/Andri Gerber
Image 3, © Guy Vacheret
Image 4, © Guy Vacheret
Image 5, Giovannoni, Gustavo, *Architetture di pensiero, e pensieri sull'architettura*, Roma: Apollon, 1945, p. 157

Johannes Binotto
Image 6, Le Corbusier, *Urbanisme*, Paris: Crès 1925, p. 268
Image 7, © Johannes Binotto
Image 8, © Johannes Binotto
Image 9, © Johannes Binotto
Image 10, filmstill from: Frank Capra, *It's a Wonderful Life*, 1946
Image 11, filmstill from: Frank Capra, *It's a Wonderful Life*, 1946
Image 12, filmstill from: Frank Capra, *It's a Wonderful Life*, 1946

Gernot Böhme
Image 13, © Charles Jencks
Image 14, © MIT Press

Philippe Boudon
Image 15, © Philippe Boudon
Image 16, © Philippe Boudon
Image 17, © Philippe Boudon
Image 18, © Philippe Boudon
Image 19, © Philippe Boudon
Image 20, © Philippe Boudon

Image 21, photography by Philippe Boudon
Image 22, © Philippe Boudon

Matteo Burioni
Image 23, Heinrich von Geymüller, Die Architektur der Renaissance in der Toskana, München 1907, Bd. 3
Image 24, Hypnerotomachia Poliphili, Venedig: Aldo Manutius 1499, f. bIv. Herzog August Bibliothek Wolfenbüttel, Signatur: A: 13.1 Eth. 2°
Image 25, Marco Bussagli, Rom. Kunst & Architektur, Köln 1999, p. 406
Image 26, Huges Sambin, Oeuvre de la diversite de termes, dont on use en Architecture, eduict en ordre, Lyon: Jean Durant 1572, p. 58
Image 27, Joseph Boillot, Nouveaux portraits et figures de termes pour user en l'architecture, Langres 1592
Image 28, Camille, Michael, The gargoyles of Notre-Dame: medievalism and the monsters of modernity, Chicago: The University of Chicago Press 2009

Rosario Caballero-Rodriguez
Image 29, image courtesy of Zwi Hecker
Image 30, image courtesy of Zwi Hecker
Image 31, image courtesy of Peter Hübner
Image 32, image courtesy of Richard Goodwin

Susanne Hauser
Image 33, Lilla LoCurto and Bill Outcault, Kharchenko-Shabanova BS 1sph (8/6) 7_98, 2000, 48" x 57.5", Chromogenic Print. Image courtesy Lilla LoCurto and Bill Outcault
Image 34, © Nicole Tran Ba Vang- From series „Spring/Summer 2001 Collection". Untitled 06, 2001, Color photograph 120cmx120cm
Image 35, Aziz + Cucher, Chimera No. 8, New York (1998), in: Ellen Lupton, Skin: Surface, Substance + Design, London, Laurence King Publishing Ltd, 2002, p. 77
Image 36, Palais des Beaux-Arts de Lille (1997), architectes Jean-Marc Ibos Myrto Vitart. Photographe Georges Fessy, courtesy Jean-Marc Ibos and Myrto Vitart
Image 37, Mike Davies, Polyvalent Wall (1981), in: http://www.hl-technik.de/2/2_01/2_01_06-d.html

Bernardo Secchi

Image 38, Le Corbusier, *Précision sur un état présent de l'architecture et de l'urbanisme*, Paris: Crés, 1930, p.171

Caroline van Eck

Image 39, photo: private collection
Image 40, photography by the author
Image 41, photograph: Leiden University Library
Image 42, photo courtesy of the British Museum, London

Richard Coyne

Image 43, © Richard Coyne
Image 44, © Richard Coyne

Jelle Feringa

Image 45, *Frank O. Gehry. 1987-2003*, Madrid: El Croquis, 2006, p. 26; © Hisao Suzuki
Image 46, courtesy R&Sie(n)
Image 47, © Gramazio & Kohler, Architektur und Digitale Fabrikation, ETH Zürich
Image 48, ©Shigeru Ban Architects
Image 49, Oshima, Ken Tadashi, *Arata Isozaki*, New York: Phaidon Press, 2009, p. 244; ©Yoshio Takase
Image 50, J.J. Tabor, *Bacterial Portraiture*
Image 51, Ernst Haeckel, *Kunstformen der Natur*, 1899
Image 52, Museum für Gestaltung Zürich Grafiksammlung. Umberto Romito © ZHdK
Image 53 image courtesy of Greg Hornby and NASA
Image 54, John Rieffel
Image 55, image courtesy of Michael Hansmeyer. Sixth Order installation at the Gwangju Design Biennale 2011, Photography by Kyungsub Shin.

Marcelyn Gow

Image 56, © Times
Image 57, Kultermann, Udo (ed.), *Kenzo Tange: Architecture and Urban Design 1946-1969*, New York: Praeger, 1970, p .121
Image 58, Yatsuka, Hajime. *Arata Isozaki: Architecture, 1960-1990*, New York: Rizzoli, 1991, p. 42. © Yasuhiro Ishimoto

Image 59, © Servo
Image 60, © Servo
Image 61, © Servo

Holger Schurk
Image 62, El Croquis 131/132, p.392, Courtesy OMA/Rem Koolhaas
Image 63, El Croquis 131/132, p.398, Courtesy OMA/Rem Koolhaas
Image 64, Czerniak, Julia: Case: Downsview Park Toronto, Harvard University Graduate School of Design, Prestel, 2001, p.76, Courtesy OMA/Rem Koolhaas
Image 65, Czerniak, Julia: Case: Downsview Park Toronto, Harvard University Graduate School of Design, Prestel, 2001, p.80, Courtesy OMA/Rem Koolhaas
Image 66, El Croquis 121/122, p.286, Courtesy SANAA
Image 67, El Croquis 121/122, p.290, Courtesy SANAA
Image 68, El Croquis 121/122, p.112, Courtesy SANAA,
Image 69, El Croquis 121/122, p.114, Courtesy SANAA
Image 70, El Croquis 121/122, p.115, Courtesy SANAA

Georges Teyssot
Image 71, Museum für Gestaltung Zürich Grafiksammlung. Umberto Romito © ZHdK
Image 72, photography by Georges Teyssot
Image 73, © Paul Ruscha
Image 74, ©The Metropolitan Museum of Art, New York
Image 75, Charles William Bunn, Crystals: their Role in Nature and in Science, N.Y., Academic Press, 1964, 1966, p. 47; in possession of Robert Smithson
Image 76, ©The Metropolitan Museum of Art, New York
Image 77, courtesy of Gabrielle Nadaud
Image 78, image courtesy of Valerio Olgiati, rendering © Meyer Dudesek Architekten
Image 79, image courtesy of Prof. A.Deplazes / ETH Studio Monte Rosa

All reasonable effort to secure permissions for the visual material reproduced herein has been made. Please contact us in case you are a owner of a copyright we haven't acknowledged.